Agile Java Development with Spring, Hibernate, and Eclipse *is a well-written guide that covers numerous significant technologies, weaving them together using practical and proven methods that will surely provide value to practitioners of every level.*

  —Dan Malks, VP Solutions & Strategic Development,
   JackBe Inc; Author, *Core J2EE Patterns*

Anil's relentless dedication to high quality really shows. This is a very well-written book!

  —Madhu Siddalingaiah, Consultant (madhu.com)

Anil has an uncanny ability to cut to the chase and tell you what you want to know. This book is one of those jewels that appears only infrequently. Instead of voluminous explanations of APIs, Anil provides insightful interpretation in highly visual terms, with a simple example that threads all the way through the book. It is a masterwork of usability, as computer books go.

  —Cliff Berg, founder of Assured by Design, co-founder of Digital Focus,
   author and consultant

Agile Java Development

with Spring, Hibernate and Eclipse

Anil Hemrajani

Sams Publishing, 800 East 96th Street, Indianapolis, Indiana 46240 USA

Agile Java Development with Spring, Hibernate and Eclipse

International Standard Book Number: 0-672-32896-8

Library of Congress Catalog Card Number: 2005937888

Printed in the United States of America

First Printing: May 2006
This product is printed digitally on demand.

Trademarks

All terms mentioned in this book that are known to be trademarks or service marks have been appropriately capitalized. Sams Publishing cannot attest to the accuracy of this information. Use of a term in this book should not be regarded as affecting the validity of any trademark or service mark.

Warning and Disclaimer

Every effort has been made to make this book as complete and as accurate as possible, but no warranty or fitness is implied. The information provided is on an "as is" basis. The author and the publisher shall have neither liability nor responsibility to any person or entity with respect to any loss or damages arising from the information contained in this book.

Bulk Sales

Sams Publishing offers excellent discounts on this book when ordered in quantity for bulk purchases or special sales. For more information, please contact

U.S. Corporate and Government Sales
1-800-382-3419
corpsales@pearsontechgroup.com

For sales outside of the U.S., please contact

International Sales
international@pearsoned.com

Acquisitions Editor
Jenny Watson

Development Editors
Scott Meyers
Songlin Qiu

Managing Editor
Patrick Kanouse

Project Editor
Mandie Frank

Copy Editor
Barbara Hacha

Indexer
Cheryl Lenser

Proofreader
Kathy Bidwell

Technical Editor
Boris Minkin

Publishing Coordinator
Vanessa Evans

Book Designer
Gary Adair

Page Layout
Nonie Ratcliff

Contents at a Glance

Table of Contents

Forewords

The true goal of a foreword is to convince people to purchase the book. So, I guess you have three choices right now. First, you can save yourself some time, stop reading this foreword right now, and simply take my word for it that buying this book is a good way to invest your hard-earned money. Second, you could not trust me, which frankly is a smart thing to do because I'm a consultant, and continue reading this foreword on the chance I might actually say something that resonates with you and thereby motivate you to buy the book. Third, you could decide to not purchase the book, which is likely a really bad idea because the vast majority of Java programmers that I have met could really benefit from this material.

In my opinion, the last thing that the Java community needs is another book describing some "really cool" Java technologies; there are hundreds of books out there already, thousands of magazine articles, and tens of thousands of web pages already covering really cool Java technologies. Luckily, that's not what this book is about. *Agile Java Development* is one of those rare books that teaches skills that you will use throughout your career. Yes, it does cover the fundamentals of Spring, Hibernate, Ant, and a bunch of other stuff that you need to succeed today. But, more importantly, it goes beyond the technology to describe agile techniques, adopted from Extreme Programming (XP) and Agile Modeling (AM), which enable you to succeed at modern software development.

Most Java developers have heard about XP and many have adopted some of its techniques, such as test-driven design (TDD), refactoring, and even pair programming. This is a good start, but it's not enough. In this book, Anil brings his years of experience to the table, describing what actually works in practice. This is different from other books that often share a vision of what the author thinks will work in theory; but as we all know, theory and practice are often two different things.

When Anil first approached me to be a technical reviewer of this book, the thing that most impressed me was his simple, yet effective, approach to modeling on Java projects. In fact, you might want to flip through the book right now and take a quick look at some of the models. I think that you'll notice that his diagrams are very similar to what you develop yourself on actual projects—a refreshing change from the advice presented in many of the modeling books available today. You'll also notice how Anil describes how to move from those simple models to the often-complex code that you write on a daily basis. This I think represents the greatest strength of this book: it presents real-world advice that reflects what top-notch developers actually do in practice.

The book also shows how many of the common tasks that we perform, such as acceptance testing, unit testing, object/relational mapping, system integration, and refactoring, fit into the software development picture. The book starts with the "5,000 foot" process point of view, but dives down to ground level and describes how to use the tools in practice. Most books focus on one view but not the other, but *Agile Java Development* pulls it off nicely and covers both views well. Take a few minutes and browse the rest of this book. I think you'll see what I'm talking about.

—Scott W. Ambler
Practice Leader, Agile Modeling

This book is not easily categorized. Let me explain why it's unusual, and why it deserves your attention.

Easily categorizable books abound in our industry. They are often books about a particular product or API. Some are good; some are bad. You can choose by the cover, the font, the publisher, the credibility of the author—but you have already made a far more important choice: *You know what book you are looking for.* A good such commodity book may make you more efficient in a particular area, but it's unlikely to change the way you work.

Books that are not easily categorizable are much rarer. They relate much more closely to their author, and potentially to you.

The present book shows how valuable such a book can be. Anil Hemrajani has distilled his extensive experience as an architect and developer into a book that abounds in the practical insights of a successful practitioner. Like all the best books, it's an effective communication between author and reader. As with all effective communication, the topic is not limited to the predictable, and it's enjoyable: Anil has a natural writing style that is a pleasure to read.

This book has a remarkably broad scope. It tackles topics that are rarely tackled together, but should be. The process we use to develop software is inextricably linked to the way in which we structure our code and the tools we use to write that code. No effective developer works in a compartmentalized fashion—the many decisions to be made are intertwined—but most books make little attempt to paint the big picture that is essential to getting results.

To develop Java software productively today, you need to understand key concepts such as O/R mapping and Dependency Injection; you need to understand how and why to use techniques such as unit testing and automated builds; and—equally significant—you need to know the best tools for the job, such as frameworks and IDEs. You also need to understand some of the pitfalls to avoid, and how sometimes soft skills are as critical as technology.

Anil has done a remarkable job of bringing these things together into a book that provides clarity in an area that many find confusing. It covers a lot of ground, but never loses sight of its aim—to help readers complete successful projects.

I see this book as a good map. It clearly shows you the path on your journey to successful enterprise Java development. Along the way, you may supplement it with more detailed maps of particular areas. But you will always benefit from the direction it provides.

I recommend this book to anyone setting out to become an enterprise Java practitioner today. It may well change the way you work, for the better.

—Rod Johnson
   CEO, Interface21
   Founder, Spring Framework

About the Author

Anil Hemrajani has been working with Java Technology since late 1995 as a developer, entrepreneur, author, and trainer. He is the founder of Isavix Corporation, a successful IT service company (now Inscope Solutions), and isavix.net (now DeveloperHub.com), an award-winning online developer community that grew to more than 100,000 registered members. He has 20 years of experience in the information technology community working with several Fortune 100 companies and also smaller organizations. He has published numerous articles in well-known trade journals, presented at conferences and seminars around the world, and received the "Outstanding Contribution to the Growth of the Java Community" award from Sun Microsystems, the "Best Java Client" award at JavaOne for BackOnline, a Java-based online backup client/server product, and was nominated for a Computerworld-Smithsonian award for a free online file storage service website. His more recent project is the visualpatterns.com website.

❖

*This is dedicated to my loving and caring wife who has
always patiently supported me (and my odd ways).
Thank you for taking care of everything during the times
I was consumed by projects such as this book. This book
would not be possible without you! And, of course, to
my dearest kids who brighten my every day.*

❖

Acknowledgments

I wrote this book but it wouldn't have been possible without the help of many brilliant people I have the distinct pleasure of knowing. I truly want to thank everyone listed here, from the bottom of my heart!

- Cliff Berg—First and foremost, I want to thank Cliff, a long-time friend and colleague, for inspiring me to write this book and giving me the confidence by validating and supporting my ideas.

- Scott W. Ambler—For agreeing to co-write the foreword for this book and reviewing every single element in it, chapter by chapter. Scott has become one of my idols in this field, given his work on Agile Modeling and Agile Data, so I'm still amazed that he agreed to get involved with this book considering how enormously busy he is. I also want to thank Scott for the www.agilemodeling.com and www.agiledata.org websites; these have been invaluable for me. Scott, thank you.

- Rod Johnson—When I first met Rod, I had no idea I would be writing this book or asking him for a foreword—I just knew we shared similar views and I respected his work a lot. Given the Spring Framework's popularity these days, I'm surprised that Rod even finds time to sleep, so fitting in the foreword for my book was especially meaningful to me (thank you!). I also want to thank Rod for putting together the Spring Framework, something I've enjoyed working with.

- Anil Singh—I cannot even begin to thank (the other) Anil for his help; the long hours, the invaluable feedback, the late nights over the phone discussing the contents of my chapters (3 a.m. at times)—thanks for everything! I particularly appreciate Anil's availability almost any and every time, to discuss my book. Yet, all I can offer in return is a heartwarming *thank you!*

- Dan Shellman—For his *rapid* but detailed and *honest* feedback, which helped make this book so much better. Thanks for tolerating the 100 or so emails I sent over the course of this book. I particularly appreciate your feedback and telephone conversations on weekends and even on family vacations! Dan has been a long-time colleague and friend and I hope this remains the case for a long time to come.

- Haresh Lala—For his constant feedback on anything and everything! Thanks for testing all my code (twice!) and reading my chapters in their earliest, very rough, draft form. Most of all, thank you for helping me during a time when you were super busy with new things in your life.

- Hernando Vera—What would I do without Hernando's astute thinking, clear presentation of ideas, and well-thought-out interpretation of technologies? Hernando has been one of my "go to" guys for almost a decade now. When I'm in doubt, I know I can turn to him for answers from development to design to architecture to process and more. I have yet to meet anyone else that has the full package: brilliant, innovative, current, and most of all one of the nicest people I know.

- Martin Remmelzwaal—Martin and I met relatively recently but I already consider him a close friend. Thanks for reviewing my earlier chapters. However, I particularly want to thank you for responding to my neverending emails about your perspective on various technology, and methodology, related matters. I hope to collaborate with Martin on various projects in the future.

- The Spring Framework team—First of all, you guys are simply awesome! Now, for specific names. I want to thank Alef Arendsen for his review of Chapters 6 and 7 and assistance in general with anything and everything Spring; Alef's review significantly improved Chapters 6 and 7. I also want to thank Juergen Hoeller for his help on declarative transaction management and late discussions about interfaces. Given the spring team's day jobs (helping clients), night jobs (working on the framework), and juggling multiple releases at the same time—well, what can I say but *thanks, guys!*

- Madhu Siddalingaiah—For his guidance in drafting up the outline of this book (and other publishing matters), and also for his valuable feedback on Chapter 8.

- Dave Berman—Dave's in-depth review of Chapter 2 and various discussions about Agile methods helped make the Agile/XP aspects of this book more solid and thorough.

- Jeff Nielsen—For his timely feedback on my diagrams in Chapter 2 and 3 and the XP+AMDD comic series used in this book; I was able to fix some major errors in the nick of time, thanks to Jeff!

- Ramanand Singh—For our initial discussions about Spring and feedback on Chapter 6.

- Pearson staff—I want to thank the staff at Pearson (Songlin, Mandie, Kim, Mark, Barbara, and several others behind the scenes) for producing this book; a special thanks to Jenny for her involvement from beginning to end; her being there helped me during normal and frustrating times. I also want to thank Boris for his in-depth, direct, and valuable review of this book—this book wouldn't be what it is without his help.

- To my friend Peter, thanks for the intellectual stimulus from time to time, which helped me approach the book from unique perspectives. Also, combined with Andy and Missy, thanks for all the laughs, which helped me let loose a bit when I needed it most (particularly during the weeks of continuous 14- to 15- hour days writing this book).

- To the Greenberry's coffee and tea shop staff for providing a comfortable environment, high-speed internet, and great coffee and food; all of these allowed me to work there for hours at a time on this book.

- Last but not least, this book is based on the innovative work of many people in our industry who have become my idols, so to speak. I would like to thank these people, because they helped me indirectly by contributing some invaluable and amazing concepts. Some of these people include Martin Fowler, Kent Beck, Eric Gamma, Ward Cunningham, and others.

We Want to Hear from You!

As the reader of this book, *you* are our most important critic and commentator. We value your opinion and want to know what we're doing right, what we could do better, what areas you'd like to see us publish in, and any other words of wisdom you're willing to pass our way.

You can email or write me directly to let me know what you did or didn't like about this book—as well as what we can do to make our books stronger.

Please note that I cannot help you with technical problems related to the topic of this book, and that due to the high volume of mail I receive, I might not be able to reply to every message.

When you write, please be sure to include this book's title and author as well as your name and phone or email address. I will carefully review your comments and share them with the author and editors who worked on the book.

E-mail: opensource@samspublishing.com

Mail: Mark Taber
            Associate Publisher
            Pearson Education
            800 East 96th Street
            Indianapolis, IN 46240 USA

Reader Services

Visit our website and register this book at www.samspublishing.com/register for convenient access to any updates, downloads, or errata that might be available for this book.

Preface

I BEGAN WORKING WITH JAVA TECHNOLOGY in late 1995, shortly before the Java Development Kit (JDK) 1.0 was formally released. Prior to that, I was programming in C and C++ for many years. I was truly excited about the features that Java offered, such as cross-platform portability, simpler syntax (simpler than C++, for example), object-oriented, secure, rich API, and more.

Over my 20-year career, I have learned a few things. Among these, my favorite is simplicity; anytime I see complexity, I begin doubting whether the solution is correct. This is how I had begun to feel about Java right around 2000, when the Java 2 Enterprise Edition (J2EE) started becoming mainstream. Note that from this point on, I will refer to J2EE as JEE because the "2" was recently dropped from the name by Sun Microsystems.

My growing lack of interest in Java was a result of what I saw as unnecessary complexity in JEE introduced by layers of abstraction. I began to believe that Sun Microsystems (inventor of Java) was focusing Java and JEE on solving the most complex enterprise applications, but somewhat ignoring the relatively less complex, small- to medium-sized applications. Furthermore, I saw the hype take over people's common sense because I ran across projects in which Enterprise JavaBeans (EJB) were used for nondistributed processing, such as local logging. I felt strongly enough about this subject to write a short article for JavaWorld.com in 2000 (http://www.javaworld.com/javaworld/jw-10-2000/jw-1006-soapbox.html) titled, "Do You Really Need Enterprise JavaBeans?" (About five years later, we saw EJB 3.0 specifications being rewritten to become more simplified, to ease the development.) This brings us to this book and the reason I wrote it.

I was recently hired as a consultant for a Fortune 100 company to build an enterprise web application running in a clustered environment. While reviewing alternatives to the standard JEE/EJB model by researching online and having discussions with some smart people, I decided on a solution, which included the Spring MVC web framework, Hibernate object-relational (OR) persistence framework, the Eclipse IDE, JUnit testing framework, Ant build utility, several tag libraries, and a few other products. (All these products are covered in detail later in this book, along with my rationale for choosing these technologies.)

I have enjoyed working with Spring and Hibernate, mainly because they allow me to work with plain-old Java objects (POJOs) and avoid some of the hassles of working with EJBs. Also, working with the Eclipse IDE has been a nice experience. I continue to be amazed at how well this product works, and that is the reason I dedicate a whole chapter in this book to it. In my opinion, products such as the ones mentioned here are breathing new life into Java at a time when Java is at risk of losing its popularity to alternatives such as Microsoft's .NET, LAMP (Linux, Apache, MySQL, and PHP or Python/PERL), and Ruby on Rails.

In this book, although Spring, Hibernate, and Eclipse are highlighted, a key goal for me is to provide you with a complete solution from technical and process perspectives. From a technical perspective, I provide an end-to-end solution (using a variety of tools) for implementing a complete sample web application with transaction management in the backend and suitable for a clustered environment. From a process perspective, I recently switched from using the Rational Unified Process (RUP) to a process composed of guidelines provided by Agile Model Driven Development (AMDD; agilemodeling. com) and Extreme Programming (XP; extremeprogramming.org). As a result, in this book you will find concepts and artifacts such as user stories, release plans, CRC cards, and more. The idea is to provide you with a comprehensive solution for rapidly developing and deploying enterprise Java applications.

One additional note about my background. I have been a developer for almost 20 years, primarily working with core technologies such as C/C++, Java, enterprise relational databases, application servers, Unix, Microsoft Windows, and so on. However, I took a detour for approximately five years around 1998 to build the company I had founded in 1996 (I was doing minimal programming during this time). I later sold this company to get back into development. However, even though I was the CEO of this company and had several people working for me, I got the opportunity to meet and interview literally hundreds of developers over a seven-year period and discuss technology with them. Apart from this company, I also founded an online community for Java developers, grew it to over 100,000 members, and won several awards for this. I hope my experience from these ventures adds a unique perspective to this book.

In summary, I truly hope you will find this book useful and will enjoy reading it!

Who This Book Is For

This book assumes that you have some working knowledge of Java and relational databases (including SQL) as well as experience working on the command line. Aside from prerequisites mentioned here, the following types of people can use it:

- Software Developers/Architects—Developers and architects can gain value from this book because it includes a high-level software development process, application design, and an in-depth and complete inspection of the Java and related files of a fully functional, sample enterprise web application.
- Technical Leads/Managers—Technical leads and managers with a programming background, preferably in Java or similar language, can get an in-depth look at how applications are built using a variety of Java technologies. This knowledge might help during project planning or with staff troubleshooting technical problems

(perhaps just for moral support during frustrating times). Alternatively, technical managers can dive into a specific chapter (for example, Chapter 5, "Using Hibernate for Persistent Objects") to understand how that specific technology works and fits into the big picture.

In addition, as a reader, you might gain some insight from this book on alternatives to JEE that you can use for building a robust enterprise-class application. Furthermore, if you are not familiar with Agile Modeling or Extreme Programming or are looking for a nimble software development process, this book might have just enough to get you going with a complete process for developing software applications iteratively and incrementally.

Goals of This Book

The goals of this book are as follows:

- Agile development—The first and foremost goal of this book is to show you how to do rapid enterprise Java development. This is achieved by combining multiple facets: a nimble/minimal software development process, a simple design (moderate use of design patterns or layers of abstraction), convenience technologies (such as Spring and Hibernate), working with POJOs versus remote objects, and in general, leveraging stable open source technologies whenever possible. In short, the idea is to make Java simpler and faster to work with for developing enterprise-ready applications.

- Complete solution—A close second goal of this book is to provide you with a complete solution, from a technical and process perspective. After reading this book, you should be able to build an entire application, not just technically, but also using the process outlined in this book. In addition, when I cannot cover a given technology in depth, I provide references to resources (websites) for further investigation of the technology. The cool thing about the technologies covered in this book is that you can have a complete system, from the user interface to an embedded database along with the capability to schedule jobs (thanks to the Spring Framework), all self-contained in a single web application archive (.war) file! However, you can always replace the technologies mentioned in here with some other technology of your choice (for example, using an Oracle database instead of HSQLDB). In summary, you will have the complete solution to do this—process and technologies!

- Using an open source only solution is not a goal of this book—Although I have based this book entirely on open source frameworks, tools, and products, preaching an open source only solution isn't a goal of this book. For instance, you can lever-age Java's vendor portability and replace one of the products covered in here with a commercial product. However, open source has come a very long way, and I'm thoroughly impressed by how robust these technologies are and how well documented they are. For example, technologies such as the Eclipse SDK and Hibernate are arguably better than some of their commercial counterparts. You could just as well use all the technologies mention in this book for an enterprise solution and rest assured that they will perform as advertised. In fact, I recently implemented an enterprise solution for a large company using the Spring Framework, Hibernate, Eclipse, JUnit, Ant, and other tools mentioned in this book! However, we also used commercial products such as BEA's WebLogic Server and an Oracle database server. The same company (and several others I know of) are basing their enterprise solutions on the open source technologies I mentioned.

- Quick read—This book is intentionally smaller than the typical 600+ page books you find on Java. This was done to enable you to get through the book quickly and begin using the solutions in the real world. In light of this, I have tried to keep the content in this book streamlined and more to the point. The one downside of not writing an extremely thick book is that I had to make some tough decisions about which material to forego; however, I have tried hard to include all the important process- and technology-related material you will need for agile Java development (as explained in the previous goal of providing a complete solution).

- Simplicity—Whenever possible, I take the simpler approach to accomplishing the same objective over a complex solution. For example, the sample application covered in this book uses minimal layers of abstraction to accomplish our objective. By layers of abstraction, I am referring to the excessive use of design patterns, interfaces, and application partitioning. Each of these makes enormous sense, but using everything in moderation is a good practice and one I like to follow when I am working with a software development process and artifacts produced from such a process. Furthermore, I believe simplicity should also extend to designing, in that I tend to use UML when appropriate, but lean toward simpler, free-form diagrams using tools such as OpenOffice.org, PowerPoint, or Visio versus something heavy like Rational Rose.

- Tips and tricks—As you might already know, when working with tools and technologies, tips and tricks not only make the product work more effectively for you, but also make it more fun to use. I provide tips and tricks for some of the technologies covered in this book. However, the appendixes also contain some goodies such as useful cheat sheets and a list of cool tools.

- Alternatives—Throughout this book (although not in detail), I try to provide alternatives to the solution I am proposing. I realize that one solution does not fit everyone's need. For example, you might be using Sun Microsystems's NetBeans or JetBrains's IntelliJ as your IDE and do not want to switch to Eclipse. This type of scenario is to be expected and is completely understandable. The organization of this book takes this into consideration; you should still be able to gain value from the remainder of the book and replace a technology covered in this book with the technology of your choice (for example, JDO versus Hibernate).

What Is Not Covered

This book assumes that you have working knowledge of Java and a relatively good understanding of JEE. It also largely assumes that you have a reasonable understanding of software development processes, relational databases, n-tier architectures, and so on. Given this assumption, I delve right into the specifics required to build our sample application. Furthermore, I refer you to the respective websites for setup (and advance features) instructions instead of duplicating this information in this book and risk having it become out-of-date.

On the flip side, this book assumes that you have no working knowledge of the key technologies covered here, such as the Spring Framework, Hibernate, Eclipse, and so on. Given this view, this book provides the basics on these technologies to get them to work together; this book also goes one step further to provide you with a brief introduction to some of the advanced features offered by these technologies. Anything beyond what is mentioned here is beyond the scope of this book because there are literally entire books dedicated to many of the technologies mentioned in this book.

What Is Covered (Technologies and Process)

The focus of this book is more on development and less on infrastructure. In other words, I've focused more on the application development technologies such as Spring, Hibernate, and Eclipse than on products such as an application server (for example, JBoss) or database (for example, MySQL). When in doubt, I went with the one easiest to set up. Also, I'm a big believer in getting the functionality implemented in an application first and then optimizing later in the form of refactoring and optimization techniques. What I have presented in this book has been tried in real-world applications that are running successfully in production (some in a clustered application server environment), so I don't want to give you the impression that we are ignoring infrastructure altogether. One of the goals of this book was to keep it short and to the point, so I have chosen to focus almost entirely on a well-designed application that scales well.

Given the operating system (OS) and vendor portability benefits of Java, in theory, when your application is ready to be deployed, you can deploy it to a more robust web application server and database combination. For instance, you could use the low-end products used in this book (Apache's Tomcat and HSQLDB), upgrade to a JBoss Application Server and a MySQL database combination, or further upgrade to a BEA WebLogic Server and Oracle's database server combination, for example. This is the beauty of Java; it is not only OS portable, but also vendor portable.

One more note about the core technologies covered in this book—namely, Spring, Hibernate, and Eclipse. Although these are the technologies I've worked with recently and use in this book, I have provided alternative and competitive technologies in the industry, which I encourage you to look at. For example, if you choose to use JDO rather than Hibernate, you can still gain and apply the knowledge from all chapters, except perhaps the one on Hibernate.

How This Book Is Organized

The chapters in this book are organized so that each chapter builds on the previous one. Furthermore, because the chapters are logically segregated, you could jump into a chapter directly (for example, Chapter 6, "Overview of the Spring Framework") and learn about just that chapter's content. Also, you might want to skip a chapter if you are not interested in using that technology (for example, you might want to use NetBeans instead of Eclipse; therefore, you would skip Chapter 8, "The Eclipse Phenomenon!").

Chapter 1, "Introduction to Agile Java Development," gives you an overview and a preview of the technologies and process we will use in this book. Chapter 2, "The Sample Application: An Online Timesheet System," is primarily dedicated to defining the business requirements for our sample application; however, it also provides a nice overview of AMDD and XP methodologies. Chapter 3, "XP and AMDD-Based Architecture and Design Modeling," covers the design of our sample application. Chapter 4, "Environment Setup: JDK, Ant, and JUnit," covers the environment setup. From here, we enter the world of Java coding at a rapid pace, when we look at programming with Hibernate in Chapter 5. Chapters 6 and 7 are dedicated to the Spring Framework. Chapter 7, "The Spring Web MVC Framework," and Chapter 8 are what I call the "wow!" chapters, because everything converges in these chapters and you will see and appreciate why we went through the earlier chapters in the way we did. You will know what happens underneath the covers and hence have a solid foundation of the technologies such as Spring, Hibernate, Ant, and JUnit. From there, we will cover some advanced concepts and wrap up the book with some goodies in the appendixes.

One other note is in regard to command-line development versus GUI (for example, using the Eclipse SDK). The earlier chapters intentionally use the command line so that you can get some fundamental understanding of how these Java tools work. Then, when you use these tools (for example, Ant and JUnit) in an IDE such as Eclipse, you will know exactly what is going on behind the scenes. This becomes particularly important if the IDE does not meet your needs.

About the Code For This Book

This book is about Java coding and there is a lot of code related to the sample application we will build in this book. This completely functional sample application with all the source code and related files can be downloaded from the publisher's website. Having the code in electronic form versus printed in the book enables you to browse and test-drive the code/application for yourself.

The code itself is referenced and explained throughout the book using notable snippets/excerpts from the complete code. Furthermore, there are two conventions used for this code:

- In certain places, long single line of code (that is, more than 82 characters) have been split into two lines for readability in this book
- The code itself appears in monospace font.

Note

All the book's code is available for download at the publisher's website. For convenient access to this book's example files and source code, as well as any possible updates or corrections, be sure to register your book at www.samspublishing.com/register.

About The Figures For This Book

A picture truly says a thousand words, so you will find many diagrams and screenshots in this book. While I have provided some UML diagrams in this book, I tend to lean towards quick free-form diagrams and instead generate UML diagrams by reverse engineering an application. I don't spend a lot of time on formal diagrams because many of these are throw-away diagrams after they have served their purpose and most projects aren't able to keep these diagrams up-to-date anyways. I'm a big believer that the code and database are the final and most important artifacts.

In summary, I believe diagrams should do the following:

- Be developed only when they will be effective.
- Be self-explanatory (for example, use words versus confusing notations, use legends).
- Be simple, to the point, and really get across the intended message.
- Conform to a standard notation (for example, UML) either if required by your organization, for a handover of a system to another person or group, for code generation, or because you prefer to use a standard notation

One additional note about the figures in this book. In a few chapters, I have repeated/reused figures from previous chapters. This was done for the following reasons:

- To set context for the chapter or section that is about to be discussed
- I did not want to inconvenience you by requiring you to flip back to a previous chapter where the figure was first introduced.

Personal Opinion Sidebars

Throughout this book, you will notice sidebars labeled "Personal Opinion," which is exactly what the content in these sidebar is. I have tried hard to separate this subjective material from the objective material in the book. However, I hope you will find the viewpoints expressed in these sections useful, as they are little nuggets of my experience from various perspectives: as a software engineer, consultant, trainer, author, community builder, and even CEO of an IT services company.

XP and AMDD-Based Comics

You will see an illustration at the top of each chapter that makes up a fictional story throughout the book about an eight-week project using AMDD. The four main characters in this story, also fictional, include a customer (Susan), a Project Manager (Ron), and two programmers (Steve and Raj). The idea behind these illustrations is simple: to add a bit of humor to this book while teaching you about AMDD and XP along the way. Also, the relaxed style of these illustrations is based on my interest in writing books for children (early readers). I must warn you, these get a bit corny, but I hope you will find some humor and knowledge in them.

If you like the style of these illustrations and want to see more of these, please visit visualpatterns.com.

Recommended Resources

This book covers many technologies, and given the nature of this book, it provides just enough information on the technology to complete our sample application. However, each technology warrants a book itself; indeed, there are books dedicated to many of the technologies covered here.

Meanwhile, the following are websites for the key technologies covered in this book. Each provides additional documentation (and in some cases, discussion forums) for their respective technology:

- Agile Modeling   http://www.agilemodeling.com
- Ant   http://ant.apache.org/
- Eclipse SDK   http://eclipse.org
- Extreme Programming   http://extremeprogramming.org
- Hibernate Framework   http://hibernate.org
- HSQLDB database engine   http://hsqldb.org/
- JUnit   http://junit.org
- Spring Framework   http://springframework.org
- Visual Patterns   http://visualpatterns.com

I will provide chapter specific resources at the end of each chapter, so you will have plenty of resources for further reading by the end of this book!

I

Overview

1

Introduction to Agile Java Development

Release 1, Week 1, Iteration 0

Susan: I have approval from upper management to move forward with release 1 of this application.

Ron: Sounds good; I'll have my programmers, Steve and Raj, begin looking at this starting next week; they like programming software, as a pair.

(c) Visual Patterns, Inc.

W HEN JAVA DEVELOPMENT KIT (JDK) v1.0 was released in January 1996, it was a fairly straightforward application programming interface (API). Over the years, Java has matured into a full-blown platform. From JDK 1.0 to JDK 1.5, we have been introduced to many new features, such as the Java Collections Framework, logging API, auto-boxing, generics, and more. Although most of these are useful, Java has also become more complex, especially after the advent of the Java Platform Enterprise Edition (JEE). JEE introduced such concepts as Enterprise JavaBeans (EJB), which sought to simplify vendor-portable, enterprise-level distributed computing, but instead, it introduced unnecessary complexities for 80% of the applications out there. Nowadays, it is not uncommon for many people to think of Java/JEE as being a big and heavy technology. Well, for starters, this couldn't be further from the truth, and second, let's see if we can change this perspective in this book.

In the past few years, many open source frameworks have sprung up to solve some of the problems created by JEE. This book covers some of these open source frameworks (for example, Spring and Hibernate) as well as open source tools (such as Ant and Eclipse), which provide a comprehensive, effective, and elegant solution that can either be viewed as complementary or as a complete alternative to JEE, depending on how you apply these technologies for your specific needs. In addition, nimble software development processes such as Extreme Programming (XP) and Agile Model Driven Development (AMDD) can assist in accelerating the project delivery.

Software development is about people, processes, and technology (and probably in that order of priority). The people are the stakeholders, the customer we build software for. In this book, I will cover the process and technology parts. You will learn how to leverage these tools and technologies to rapidly develop end-to-end applications using Java, from the client tier to the data tier, and more. Along the way, you should see many of the benefits resulting from using these tools and technologies—for example, simplicity and speed of development.

Before we begin, if you have not read the preface, I would recommend at least glancing through it because it provides some foundation for the goals of this book and the way it is organized, and includes some reasons why I wrote this book.

What's Covered in This Chapter

This chapter provides a preview of the key technologies and software development process we will use in this book. In this chapter, you will get an overview of the following:

- The runtime technologies and development tools used in this book to build the sample application
- The software development process used to build the sample application
- How this book is organized

Technologies Used in This Book

This book combines various open source technologies, shown in Table 1.1, which were chosen to provide a comprehensive solution for building enterprise applications based on

Java. I have also provided alternative open source technologies, and in some cases, commercial technologies, in case you don't want to implement an end-to-end system using the technologies covered in this book. As I mentioned in the preface, this book is organized so that you can either read it end to end, go to specific chapters only, or skip a chapter if the technology being covered in it doesn't apply to you (Hibernate, for example).

Although, this book focuses on open source technologies, this isn't because I'm an open source fanatic. In fact, on my consulting engagements, I work extensively with commercial products such as BEA's WebLogic server, Oracle's database server, and other products. However, these technologies can be considered robust enough to deploy an enterprise-ready Java application and they cost you nothing!

Table 1.1 **Technologies Covered in This Book**

Chosen Technology	Category	Free/ Open Source Alternatives	Commercial Alternatives
Spring Framework (springframework.org)	Inversion of Control (IoC) Container, Web Framework	HiveMind and Pico for IoC container; Struts, JavaServer Faces, Tapestry, and others for Web Framework	Not applicable
Hibernate (hibernate.org)	Persistence Framework	EJB, JDO, iBatis	Oracle's TopLink
Eclipse SDK (eclipse.org)	IDE	NetBeans, jEdit, and several others	JetBrain's IntelliJ, IBM's WebSphere Studio Application Developer
Ant (ant.apache.org)	Configuration Management	make, gnumake, nmake, jam, cruise control, maven	Microsoft nmake, MKS make
JUnit (junit.org)	Testing	TestNG, Fit.	Mercury LoadRunner
HSQLDB (hsqldb.org)	100% Java Database	MySQL, PostgreSQL, One$DB	Oracle, Microsoft, Sybase, and more
Apache Tomcat (tomcat.apache.org)	HTTP Server/ Servlet Container	Jetty and several others	BEA WebLogic, IBM Websphere, Caucho Resin, and others
Mozilla Firefox (mozilla.com)	Web Browser	Microsoft Internet Explorer, Opera	Not applicable
OpenOffice.org (openoffice.org)	Office Suite (used for free form diagrams in this book)	Koffice (for Linux KDE)	Microsoft Office, StarOffice, EasyOffice

As I mentioned in the preface, the focus of this book is more on development and less on infrastructure, so I've used the server products that were the easiest to set up and that were, coincidentally, smaller in size. However, as you undoubtedly know, Java is not only operating-system neutral, it is also vendor-product neutral; for example, you could swap out Tomcat with something like IBM WebSphere by deploying our sample application to it. Although this might not be as simple as it sounds, it is certainly possible and something I've done multiple times with JDBC-compliant databases and servlet containers, for example.

End-to-End, Self-Contained Application in a Single WAR File

I would like to emphasize something about the technologies covered in this book and the interesting possibilities they open up. Imagine the capability to have an enterprise-ready application with an embedded database (HSQLDB, in our case), with built-in job scheduling (thanks to the Spring Framework), enterprise-level transaction management, and a few other enterprise services—all within a single, self-contained, readily deployable web archive (.war) file!

The following two sections provide a brief description of each technology or tool, the purpose it serves, and my rationale for selecting it.

Runtime Technologies

This section provides a brief description of the runtime technologies. Runtime technologies are used to run the application after it is deployed, versus development tools, which are used to develop the application. Figure 1.1 provides a visual representation of how these technologies fit together to provide a complete runtime solution.

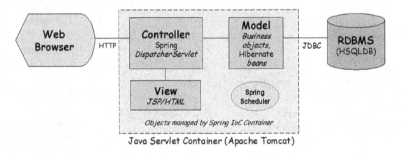

Figure 1.1   How the runtime technologies covered in this book fit together.

Java Platform, Standard Edition (Java SE) Development Kit (JDK)

We will use the latest version of the JDK (for example, 1.5) available from the java.sun.com website. Note that as long as we have JDK 1.4 or later, the technologies covered in this book (Hibernate and Spring, for example) will work just fine.

The Spring Framework (springframework.org)

The Spring Framework contains a large number of classes and packages, but it is designed as a modular framework that can be phased gradually into a project by using only the features needed (for example, web framework). Spring complements Java/JEE by providing an Inversion of Control (IoC) container (explained later in book), a web framework, a transaction management abstraction layer, JDBC helper classes, job scheduling APIs, email capabilities, and more. Spring has been around since 2002 and has gained considerable momentum and support from the community, including commercial vendors such as BEA Systems.

As of the writing of this book, Spring was a frontrunner in the IoC container space; however, its web framework is surprisingly popular, as well. I chose Spring for the web framework because I also needed many of its other features, such as IoC, transaction management, email, scheduling, and more.

The Spring web MVC framework is second to none when it comes to robustness, flexibility, and a well-designed framework. I was pleasantly surprised to find a large number of articles on this framework, a couple of books dedicated to this framework in the making (at the time of this writing), lots of hits on google.com (for the words *spring* and *mvc*), and even a crude online poll indicating Spring MVC was second in use only to Struts (http://www.bejug.org/confluenceBeJUG/display/BeJUG/2005/07/05/Polls+results).

Hibernate (hibernate.org)

Hibernate is an object-to-relational (OR) mapping persistence framework for Java. Hibernate can arguably be credited with bringing OR technology to the forefront for average Java developers and not just specialized OR experts. Hibernate is perhaps the most widely used OR framework currently in the world of Java developers. Hibernate also serves as a good alternative to Entity Beans, which is perhaps one of the reasons EJB 3 has adopted many techniques from Hibernate (and JDO and Toplink). Given these reasons, my decision to go with Hibernate was easier than selecting a web framework.

HSQLDB (hsqldb.org)

HSQLDB is a lightweight but complete relational database management system (RDBMS) written in 100% Java. It supports a subset of the ANSI-92 SQL standard and has a JDBC driver to interface with the database via Java programs. The popularity of HSQLDB has grown steadily over the past few years.

I decided to use HSQLDB because it is lightweight, easy to install, and because the focus of this book is on development, not infrastructure. On a project recently, we used Oracle as our database; however, I used HSQLDB in the initial stages for development while our Oracle database was being set up (slowly, thanks to corporate bureaucracy). If you use 100% ANSI SQL, in theory you could switch back and forth between a local and enterprise database during your development.

Apache Tomcat (tomcat.apache.org)

Tomcat is perhaps the most popular Java-based web server and servlet container. It is a relatively lightweight servlet container that has grown in popularity over the past few years. I chose this product because many developers are already familiar with it, so it seemed like the obvious choice. Similar to HSQLDB, which can be replaced with a more robust database (such as MySQL or Oracle), Tomcat can also be replaced with a more robust web and/or application server, such as BEA's WebLogic.

Development Tools

The following are the development tools we will use to construct our sample application.

Eclipse SDK (eclipse.org)

Eclipse is one of the best things to have happened to Java in recent years. In my opinion, it has given Java a longer life as a dominant technology. In fact, Chapter 8, "The Eclipse Phenomenon!," is dedicated to Eclipse and is loaded with information about the core IDE and the enormous number of plug-ins available for it.

The Eclipse SDK is an open source integrated development environment (IDE) founded by IBM. Eclipse in itself is a platform; however, the capability to develop plug-ins for this platform is what makes Eclipse such a powerful tool—so much so that major product companies are rebuilding or repackaging their products as an Eclipse plug-in. Given that Eclipse is open source, has lots of plug-ins available for it, and has immense and growing industry support behind it, in some ways makes Eclipse a clear winner in the Java IDE space.

Eclipse's basic Java tools include source formatting, building, debugging, and integration with Ant. However, there are literally hundreds of free and commercial plug-ins available for Eclipse. From UML diagramming to database tools, if there is a demand for some functionality, you are likely to find a plug-in for it! Eclipse is covered in detail in later chapters; meanwhile, Figure 1.2 provides a preview screenshot of the Eclipse SDK on Mac OS X, Figure 1.3 shows a screenshot of Eclipse on Windows XP, and Figure 1.4 shows Eclipse on Linux.

Ant (ant.apache.org)

Anyone working with Java these days has almost certainly heard of or worked with Ant. Ant is the most common way to build (and deploy) Java programs today. Although Ant is similar to the Unix make utility, it provides several benefits over the make utility.

Ant is covered in detail in later chapters; meanwhile, the following is a sample Ant `build.xml` file:

```
<?xml version="1.0"?>

<project name="HelloTest" default="printmessage">
 <target name="printmessage">
  <echo message="Hello world!"/>
 </target>
</project>
```

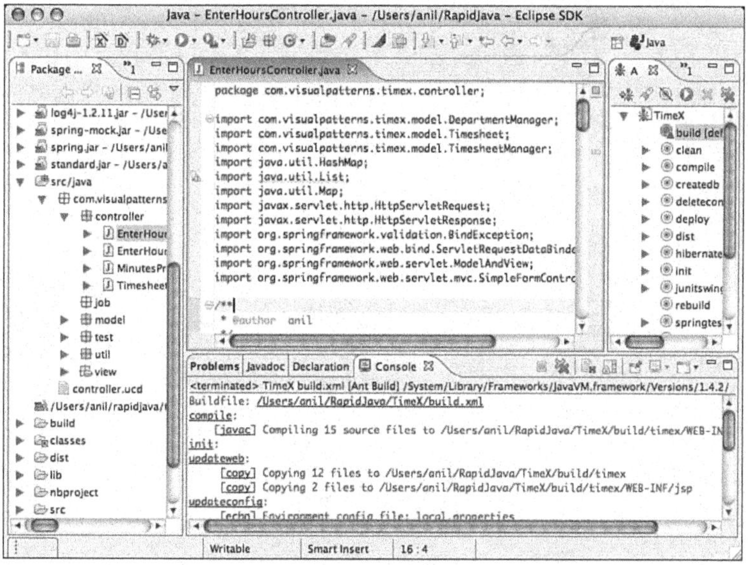

Figure 1.2   The Eclipse SDK 3.1 on Mac OS X.

Figure 1.3   The Eclipse SDK 3.1 on Windows XP.

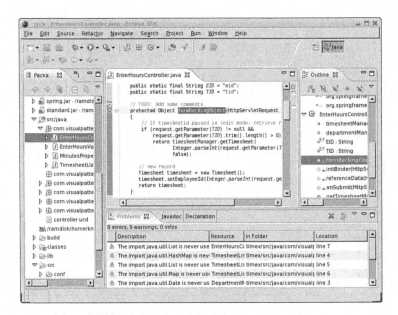

Figure 1.4   The Eclipse SDK 3.1 on Linux.

However, when we discuss Ant in more detail in Chapter 4, "Environment Setup: JDK, Ant, and Junit," you will begin to see how powerful Ant is and why it has become the de facto build tool in the Java community.

JUnit (junit.org)

JUnit is the de facto unit-testing framework used by Java developers today. I wasn't always a fan of writing unit tests first, but recently I have come to appreciate unit tests and the notion of tests first. I'll explain later in this book how to write effective unit tests. Figure 1.5 provides a screenshot of the JUnit GUI tool to give you an idea of how you can unit test your code. However, by the time we are done with Chapter 8, you will appreciate how tightly integrated JUnit is with the Eclipse SDK.

Firefox (mozilla.com)

You might be wondering why a web browser is explicitly listed here. Trust me, it isn't about a browser religion thing. Simply put, Firefox has a lot of features that help in web application development, and we will use a couple of these in Chapter 9, "Logging, Debugging, Monitoring, and Profiling."

What is fascinating about Firefox is the large number of useful plug-ins available for it. At the time of this writing, the https://addons.mozilla.org/ website (also accessible from the Tools, Extensions menu) had 1,091 plug-ins!

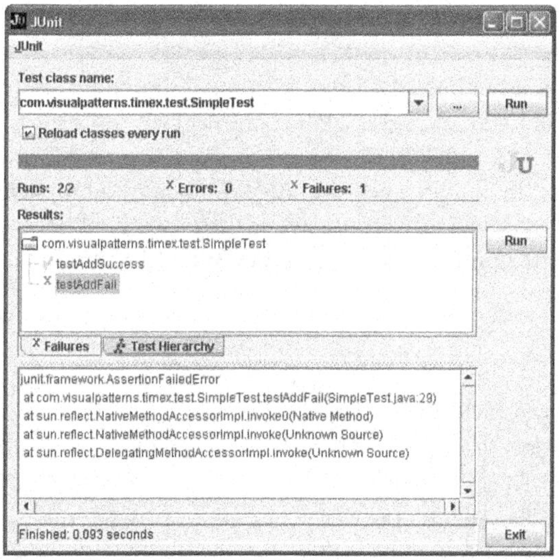

Figure 1.5 JUnit Swing runner on Windows XP.

OpenOffice.org (openoffice.org)

OpenOffice.org is an open source suite of office productivity tools that competes directly with Microsoft Office. At first, I wasn't sure if listing OpenOffice.org explicitly in Table 1.1 was needed, because it isn't a core technology I'm writing about in this chapter. Also, I had checked out OpenOffice.org a couple of years ago when it was still a maturing product, and I wasn't that impressed with it. OpenOffice.org has come a long way and is equivalent to Microsoft Office in almost every respect. In fact, OpenOffice.org can also read and write natively to Microsoft Office files, seamlessly.

I chose OpenOffice.org because I bought a new laptop and wanted to give this new (and of course, free) version of OpenOffice.org a try before investing a couple of hundred bucks on Microsoft Office. I was so impressed with the latest version that I did all my free-form diagrams in this book using the OpenOffice.org suite of office tools.

Software Development Methodology Used in This Book

To make a project successful, I have always believed that active stakeholder involvement, simplicity (design, tools, documentation), common sense, and a basic/minimal software development process does the trick. Furthermore, I do not like to reinvent the wheel, so if someone out there has assembled a good solution that I can use, I will. One such solution I have used in the recent past is the combination of best practices and techniques recommended by the Agile Model Driven Development (http://agilemodeling.com) and

Extreme Programming (http://extremeprogramming.org), or for short, AMDD and XP, respectively.

Prior to the working with AMDD and XP, I was using the Rational Unified Process (RUP) for projects. However, I find RUP a bit heavier on the artifact side. I like the combination of AMDD and XP because both methods are nimble and complement each other; XP focuses on the full life cycle and AMDD focuses on modeling (user-interface model, for example). You will learn more about these two methodologies in the next chapter along with my opinion about why I like Agile Modeling's values, principles, and practices.

Personal Opinion:

A Decade of Java and More to Come

I must admit that this section is more about me than Java, so you can skip this if you don't like personal opinions.

When I reflect back on the years I have spent with Java, I feel old. No, but seriously. I started working with Java in late 1995, when the acronym JDK had not even been established. However, Java's roots actually date back to 1990 (to read more about Java's history, visit wikipedia.org/wiki/Java_programming_language).

In these 10 or so years working with Java, I have met some of the original founders of Java, such as James Gosling, Arthur Van Hoff, Jonathan Payne, and Sami Shaio (you will still find some of these names in the JDK source code). I also had the opportunity to be the fifth person in WebLogic, Inc. (a couple of years before BEA acquired them) but didn't want to relocate (yes, I know, I still kick myself for this once-in-a-lifetime, missed opportunity). I also trained over a thousand students in Java and web technologies for the Learning Tree and later, my own courses. I have published more than 25 articles on Java and even founded (and sold) two companies focused on Java-based solutions. At one of these companies, my staff (and I) provided enterprise Java solutions to many companies. In fact, we introduced Java to several large companies. (I'm particularly proud of personally introducing Java to a fortune 50 company!) In addition, I've attended five JavaOne conferences and received two awards at JavaOne for a pure Java backup software I wrote and an online community I built. Last, I have presented at several user groups and conferences internationally.

Why am I telling you all this? Well, first and foremost, to brag. Second, I hope to bring a unique perspective to this book. But the third reason is that even after a decade, I'm amazed (and pleased) that Java is still considered a dominant technology! In this book, I will introduce you to new technologies that give Java a whole new lifeline, and now I'm convinced that Java will be hot for at least a few more years.

In short, if you are a Java developer, you should be excited about working with an elegant and robust technology that is still very much current and thriving! I hope to prove this to you in this book. Enjoy!

Summary

In this chapter, you got an overview of

- The runtime technologies and development tools used in this book to build the sample application
- The software development process used to build the sample application
- How this book is organized

In short, I gave you an overview of the tools we will use in this book to build our sample application, along with the software development process we will follow. In the coming chapters, we will have some fun with these technologies by putting together a real-world application—a timesheet system.

Recommended Resources

The following websites are relevant to and provide additional information on the topics discussed in this chapter:

- Agile Modeling   http://www.agilemodeling.com
- Ant   http://ant.apache.org/
- Apache Tomcat   http://tomcat.apache.org
- Eclipse SDK   http://eclipse.org/
- Hibernate   http://hibernate.org
- HSQLDB   http://hsqldb.org
- Java open source products   http://java-source.net/
- JUnit   http://junit.org
- OpenOffice.org   http://www.openoffice.org/
- The Spring Framework   http://springframework.org
- Visual Patterns   http://visualpatterns.com

2

The Sample Application: An Online Timesheet System

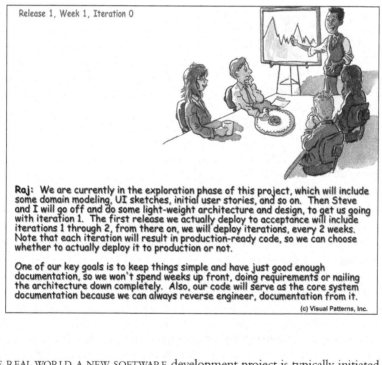

Release 1, Week 1, Iteration 0

Raj: We are currently in the exploration phase of this project, which will include some domain modeling, UI sketches, initial user stories, and so on. Then Steve and I will go off and do some light-weight architecture and design, to get us going with iteration 1. The first release we actually deploy to acceptance will include iterations 1 through 2, from there on, we will deploy iterations, every 2 weeks. Note that each iteration will result in production-ready code, so we can choose whether to actually deploy it to production or not.

One of our key goals is to keep things simple and have just good enough documentation, so we won't spend weeks up front, doing requirements or nailing the architecture down completely. Also, our code will serve as the core system documentation because we can always reverse engineer, documentation from it.

(c) Visual Patterns, Inc.

I N THE REAL WORLD, A NEW SOFTWARE development project is typically initiated because there is some sort of a customer need, problem, or process optimization. This need can be from an internal group or an external party (for example, interfacing with an external partner system or consumer demand for a product). After a problem or need is identified, there is typically some form of a project kickoff meeting to better define the requirements.

As I mentioned in the previous chapter, this book tries to follow a flow similar to how a real-world project might flow. In this book, we will pretend that we have a requirement from an internal group (a fictional customer) and use this requirement to build a sample application named Time Expression.

I considered several types of applications to use as an example in this book; in the end I settled on a rudimentary timesheet system because I believed that it was an application most readers would be able to relate to. For example, you might be an employee or consultant who works by the hour, and you submit your timesheet online (and also get it approved online, and so on).

Our sample application, Time Expression, will have a user interface (UI) as well as some background processing. The UI will be web based and will contain screens that provide the capability to enter hours worked, approve timesheets, run management reports, and more. The background processing will include a weekly (scheduled) batch job that is automatically run to send out a reminder email.

What's Covered in This Chapter

The focus of this book is more on technology and less on process. However, this chapter provides an overview of an *agile* software development process that you can easily apply to your project. I'm a big believer in having a bare-minimum process, even if it is a 1-page checklist of 10 or so items that serves as a memory jogger for things that need to be done as part of the process. (Note: I have included such a checklist in the appendixes.) This minimal process ensures that the project is run efficiently and at the same time is focused on customer satisfaction.

In this chapter, we will accomplish the following:

- Gain an understanding of what our sample application will do by looking at some business requirements.
- Establish a simple software methodology based on Extreme Programming (XP) and Agile Modeling Driven Development (AMDD).
- Develop some high-level artifacts such as a domain model, UI prototypes, high-level architecture, and more.
- Create a simple release plan based on our user stories.

Note

It is important to realize that many of the artifacts shown in this chapter (release and iteration plans, for example) are more for demonstration purposes. However, this chapter is very relevant to the rest of the book because we will implement some of the functionality described in this chapter (for example, the Enter Hours and Timesheet List screens). In general, you can ignore particulars such as dates and estimates.

Also, this chapter assumes that you have a basic understanding of software development process–related concepts (use cases, for example). However, if my brief explanations on the various concepts in this chapter aren't sufficient, I recommend visiting www.agilemodeling.com for detailed explanations. In general, this website is loaded with information relevant to this chapter. Also, visit the extremeprogramming.org website for detailed information on the XP methodology.

Business Requirements

I mentioned earlier that our fictional customer requires a simple online time entry and approval system. Let's go into a bit more detail here.

It is always a good idea to define *what* business problem is being solved, *whom* it is being solved for, and *why* our solution is important to the customer. In addition, it is important to understand what the customer's expectations are: for example, *when* is the solution needed, and what is the project *scope*.

Let's assume that a fictional organization wants to build a timesheet system to manage its hourly staff. To get things started, we can define the problem statement as follows.

Problem Statement

Our employees currently submit their weekly hours worked using a paper-based timesheet system that is manually intensive and error-prone. We require an automated solution for submitting employee hours worked, in the form of an electronic timesheet, approving them, and paying for the time worked. In addition, we would like to have automatic notifications of timesheet status changes and a weekly reminder to submit and approve employee timesheets.

Given our general problem statement, we can break this down into the following feature set or business requirements; this process could be considered a part of *use case analysis*, in the Unified Modeling Language (UML) world:

- Hourly employees should be able to sign in to a web application (once or more each week) and enter their hours for each day of a given week. Along with the hours, the employee must select which department the hours are being billed to.

- Employees will be required to submit their timesheets each week.

- An employee's manager is notified of successfully submitted timesheets. The manager must then approve or disapprove the timesheets.

- After a timesheet is approved or disapproved, a notification is sent back to the employee indicating the updated status of the timesheet. If the timesheet is approved, an email is also sent to the accounting department to process the paycheck for the given employee.

- All users of Time Expression will have one or more relevant reports available to them.

- A weekly reminder email will be sent out to employees who have not submitted their timesheets. Another reminder email is sent to managers who have employee timesheets pending approval.

Now that we have some basic business requirements, we can proceed with our software development process.

Software Development Methodology

Every project, small or large, should have some basic structure or process (methodology) it must follow. This could be a simple one-page checklist or a slightly more formal process. Having no process at all is bad, but too much is equally bad. Finding the right balance depends on the customer's needs and the project size, but in summary, I lean toward having less process with minimal (and "good enough") documentation requirements, rather than having a bloated process that can bog down the customer and developers in paperwork and procedures. In this chapter, I'll provide a basic software development process based on XP and AMDD.

Overview of XP and AMDD

XP and AMDD provide some fundamental guidelines for building software applications effectively and rapidly. XP and AMDD are complementary methods because XP provides a disciplined, full life cycle software development approach that stresses customer satisfaction. AMDD, on the other hand, generally provides effective practices for modeling and documentation, but goes a lot further by providing a wealth of additional best practices that can be tailored to each software development project.

Personal Opinion:

Why Agile Modeling and Extreme Programming?

In recent months, I have become quite fond of the Agile Modeling (AM; agilemodeling.com) values, practices, and principles (see cheat sheets in Appendix J). Similarly I have also grown fond of Extreme Programming (XP; extremeprogramming.org). Furthermore, what makes me even more confident about these methodologies is the plain and simple fact that I have yet to hear anything bad about these methodologies from any developer who has actually worked with them. I'm talking about some very intelligent people who are either working with these two methods or promoting one or both.

AM is about modeling and documentation in an effective manner using simple tools. XP, on the other hand, is a full development life cycle. Both of these align very well with my views on software development—views that are based on experience I have gained over my jam-packed 20 years in IT working for a dozen or more very large, and also some small, companies.

Prior to AM and XP, I had worked with the Rational Unified Process (RUP) and before that some custom home-grown methodologies. Even though I enjoyed using RUP for a while, I began to find RUP a bit on the heavier side when it came to requirements documentation and up front architecture and design; at least this is how I see most organizations using RUP. On the other hand, AM and XP are nimble methods!

It takes a bit of time to get the hang of it; some of this is because of internal resistance to change or misconceptions about XP. However, when you do get it, it does feel good! It feels so natural that you have to sit there and wonder why it took so long. Seriously, these two methods are getting more and more popular by the day because they feel so natural to developers.

Another reason XP and AMDD might take a little getting used to is because these methods don't work in a linear fashion. This is the case because things don't always work in a linear fashion in the real world. Also, this approach facilitates change better than the rigid linear methodologies in which all the requirements must be locked down up front and the customers have their hands slapped if they request too many changes. Change is inevitable, so it is better to deal with it by embracing it. Trust me, it took me a little getting used to because I had been working in the linear/rigid mode for years before discovering XP.

Incidentally, the term *Agile* refers to a wide range of software development methodologies. In 2001, the term *Agile* was collectively agreed upon by representatives of methods such as Extreme Programming, SCRUM, DSDM, Adaptive Software Development, Crystal, Feature-Driven Development, Pragmatic Programming, and others (see manifesto and history at `agilemanifesto.org`). The `agilemodeling.com` website takes this into consideration and serves as a one-stop website for getting a wealth of knowledge on these methods at your fingertips.

AMDD is more specific to development. I chose AMDD for this book because in addition to the fact that the AM viewpoint aligns with my own, I also like that AMDD proposes just good enough modeling artifacts (such as free-form architecture diagrams—my favorite kind). Perhaps these words from the AM website best summarize my feelings about producing artifacts: "Your goal is to build a shared understanding, it isn't to write detailed documentation." Need I say more?

On the XP side, you will find many of concepts used in this chapter and throughout the book; concepts such as user stories, CRC cards, test-first design, release and iteration planning, and more.

I have already stated reasons why these are popular with developers. However, customers love this style of working, too, because both methods are customer focused and require active stakeholder participation. Granted, this does require more of the customer's time, but they are pleased to see constant progress; as a result, fewer things can go wrong with a project because ongoing communication exists between the customer and the developers.

Ongoing communication with the customer also helps the developers stay focused on the end goal and understand the problem domain better and faster. Hence, understanding the customer's problem or need and staying focused on it throughout the software life cycle is essential. By having ongoing communication and easy access to the customer, this task becomes a lot easier.

Let me summarize why this makes so much sense by providing you the end-to-end process using XP. Your team builds and unit tests software daily; the application is integrated often (maybe even continuously as unit tested code is checked in); a production-ready version of the application is deployed every two weeks (iteration); and the customer gets to test drive or fully use the newly added functionality every two weeks (with a full release every two months).

All in all, it is a win-win situation for all project stakeholders.

Although I have some fundamental practices I use on all projects, I typically pick and choose what applies to each project and customize the software development process based on the needs of that project and customer. For example, in our sample project/application in this book, Time Expression, I have used several of the techniques described next and shown in Figure 2.1 (refer to agilemodeling.com/essays/ agileModelingXPLifecycle.htm for details). Note that although I have adopted the XP and AMDD way, there might be a few spots where I customize these methods (Project kick-off, for example) to accommodate what we need for Time Expression.

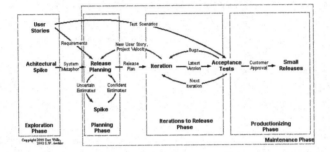

Figure 2.1   The XP project life cycle (source: agilemodeling.com/essays/ agileModelingXPLifecycle.htm); original diagram by Don Wells (http://extremeprogramming.org).

Exploration Phase

The Exploration Phase (Beck, 2000) typically involves a combination of exploratory activities that help you better understand the customer's needs and subsequently how the resulting application will be designed and built. The following are some examples of activities that might take place in this phase of the project.

- Domain model—A domain model helps to define major business concepts (entities) and the relationships among them.

- User interface prototypes and storyboard—These are initial screen mockups to get a feel for how the customer visualizes the application. The storyboard is the flow of the screens.

- User stories—A few user stories get the project started and make up the first release or version of the application. User stories (similar to shall statements in other methods) are written by the customer in a brief sentence or two explaining what the customer wants the application to do. Note that the number of user stories you gather up front will depend on the project, but you should have enough to make a good and useful release.

- Scope definition—It is important to define the scope of the project up front so that you know what needs to be developed and what can be deferred. It also clarifies the customer's expectations.

- Analysis—This can include a combination of whiteboarding, an informal architectural diagram, a glossary, and more.

Planning Phase

Planning can mean different things to different people. For me, it should at least include the following:

- Release plan—This is essentially a plan for the next release (version) of a system and can easily be put together using a spreadsheet program or even a word processing program and/or HTML table. It lists all the user stories that will be included in the next release of the system, grouped together in several iterations. Releases are typically of fixed length, anywhere between one to three months; two months is typically an optimal size.

- Iteration plan—An iteration plan is developed prior to each iteration. It includes the user stories the customer wants implemented in the next iteration. Iterations are typically of fixed length, anywhere between one to three weeks; two weeks is typically an optimal size.

- Define standards (code, database, process)—Before beginning any development, it is a good idea to standardize such things as coding conventions, database naming conventions, processes (build, integrate, deploy), and more.

Active Stakeholder Participation

According to the agilemodeling.com website, "Active Stakeholder Participation is an expansion of eXtreme Programming (XP)'s On-Site Customer that describes the need to have on-site access to people, typically users or their representatives, who have the authority and ability to provide information pertaining to the system being built and to make pertinent and timely decisions regarding the requirements, and prioritization thereof."

Given this, I would recommend to always do release and iteration planning with the customer and developers. Remember, successful projects are typically ones where the customer is actively involved (hence, the phrase *Active Stakeholder Participation*).

For more details on active stakeholder participation, you may want to read the following essay on the AM website: agilemodeling.com/essays/activeStakeholderParticipation.htm.

Iterations to Release Phase (Building Software in Increments)

Iterative development is a term you are probably familiar with. However, understanding of iterative development and what each iteration should include varies from person to person and from methodology to methodology.

For me, iterative development means that each iteration includes design, coding, user acceptance, and deployment of "production ready" code. This code can be deployed to the production environment or, if you are in a large corporation and deploying to production frequently is not practical, perhaps deploying to the acceptance environment will do, so long as it is accepted by the customer, thus allowing you to move on to the next iteration. To summarize, each iteration might include the following activities:

- Development tasks, estimates by developers, and a plan for the next iteration.
- Ad hoc Q & A between developers and the customer.
- Design—CRC cards, UML diagrams, and so on.
- Code—test first, refactor code/database/architecture as required, optimize later.
- User acceptance testing (UAT).
- Deploy iteration to production (or UAT); this step is also referred to as a *small release*.

By delivering iterations in this fashion, you can incrementally build the next release of an application. For example, we might estimate three months for a given project and break it down into two-week iterations, resulting in approximately six iterations.

The bottom line at the end of each iteration is that the project should be deliverable; in other words, the small releases should contain production-ready (stable) code, even it provides only a subset of the complete system.

Scope of Project

The scope of project can be defined in many formats. Sometimes it is as simple as a one-to two-line paragraph described by the customer, or it can be more structured using diagrams. Many organizations go one step further and sign service level agreements (SLAs) with the development team. Also, functional and nonfunctional requirements discussions can also occur to help define the scope.

In the past, I have used a table to show what is included in the scope and what is deferred (or excluded) from scope, as demonstrated in Table 2.1, a sample scope table for Time Expression.

Table 2.1 **Sample Scope Table**

Scope	Functionality
Include	Time Expression will provide the capability to enter, approve, and pay for hours worked by employees.
Defer	Time Expression will not calculate deductions from paychecks, such as federal/state taxes and medical expenses.
Defer	Time Expression will not track vacation or sick leave.

Maintenance

This is where the application enters a maintenance state. This phase might include training for the user, minor enhancements/fixes (in the form of user stories), as needed. Or the customer might want to do another major release, in which case you would start back from the Exploration Phase mentioned earlier in this chapter.

Applying XP and AMDD to Our Sample Application

Now that we have looked at some background on a generic software development process, let's apply parts of this to our sample application.

Domain Model

Let's start our domain model, which essentially has all the data entities and their relationships, but no attributes. This helps to define some initial domain concepts and their relationships to each other. The domain model is typically sketched while working with domain experts and people with business knowledge, such as business users and analysts.

Figure 2.2 shows the domain model for our application, Time Expression. As you can see, our domain model has a simple design because it contains the bare-minimum number of entities to get us going while following a clean design. Again, we just need a simple domain model to start with, something good enough for us to move forward with, which we have now.

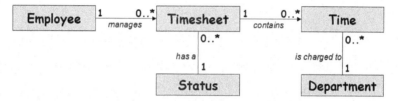

Figure 2.2   Domain model for Time Expression.

User Interface (UI) Prototype

Now that we have a fairly good idea of the features our customer is looking for in Time Expression, we can rapidly mock up some prototype screens to allow the customer to test drive the mocked web application.

By developing prototype screens early on, you put a face to the application, which gets people excited and motivated to get the application built. This is also a good way to eliminate many of the cosmetic changes up front (such as fonts, colors) and come up with an agreed upon consistent look and feel that can be implemented using cascading style sheets (CSS). Furthermore, you can use prototypes to model the business process and subsequently use the same prototypes to define the users' stories (covered later in this chapter).

Figures 2.3 through 2.10 show what the various screens in the Time Expression application will look like. We will begin designing this application in the next chapter;

then, in subsequent chapters, we will get our environment set up and begin developing some code!

At this point, let's keep these screens as simple HTML (versus JSP) files so that we can pull them up locally in a browser instead of having to run them in a Java web server or pull them up in a JSP/HTML editor each time. When working with a customer, it is a good idea to keep technology out of the picture, as much as possible, until you are ready for development—this keeps things simple, so you can avoid any "technical difficulties" and instead focus on the business requirements at hand.

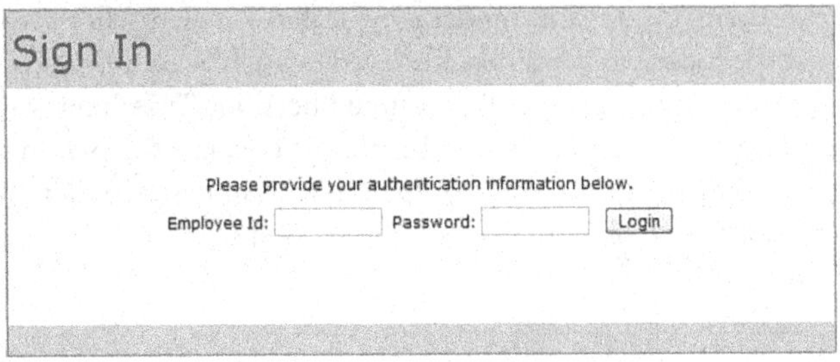

Figure 2.3 Sign-In screen.

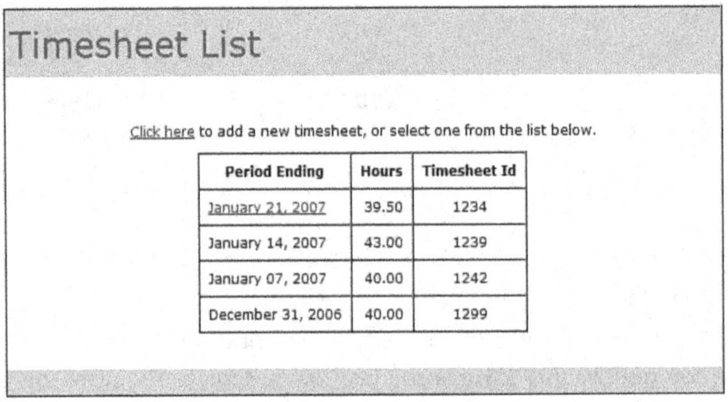

Figure 2.4 Timesheet List screen.

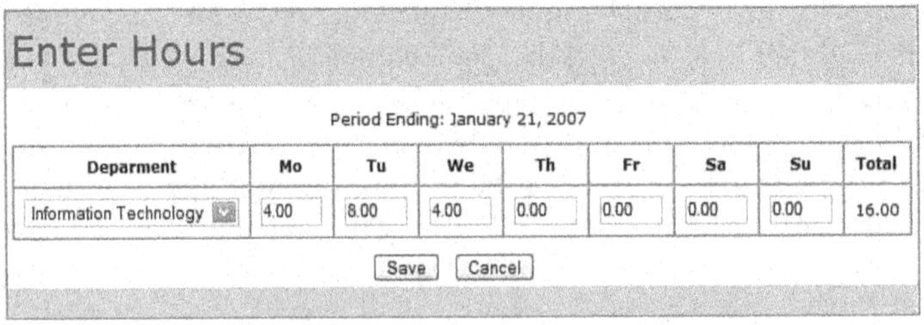

Figure 2.5 Enter Hours screen.

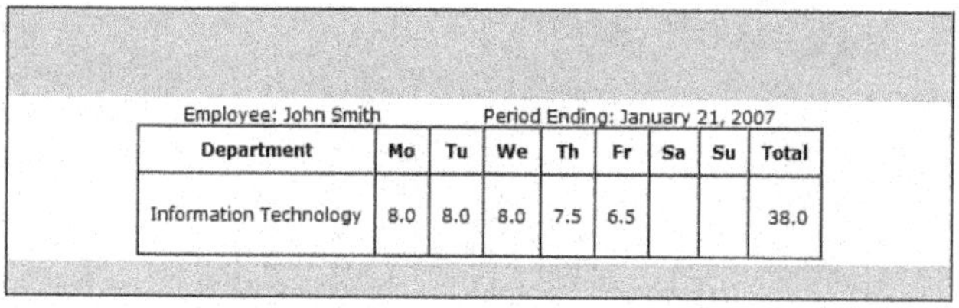

Employee: John Smith			Period Ending: January 21, 2007					
Department	Mo	Tu	We	Th	Fr	Sa	Su	Total
Information Technology	8.0	8.0	8.0	7.5	6.5			38.0

Figure 2.6   Print Hours screen.

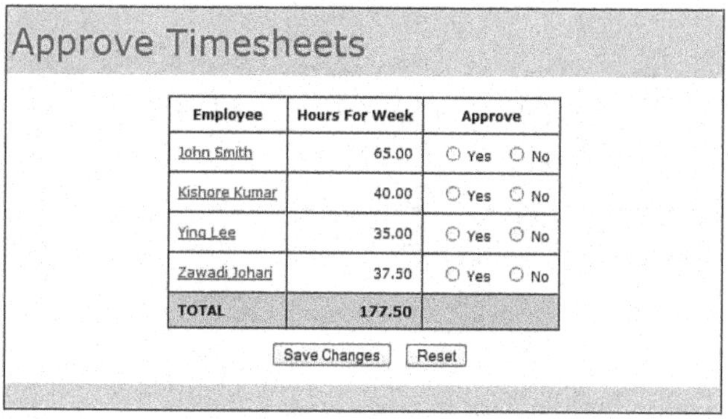

Approve Timesheets

Employee	Hours For Week	Approve
John Smith	65.00	○ Yes ○ No
Kishore Kumar	40.00	○ Yes ○ No
Ying Lee	35.00	○ Yes ○ No
Zawadi Johari	37.50	○ Yes ○ No
TOTAL	177.50	

Save Changes   Reset

Figure 2.7   Approve Timesheets screen.

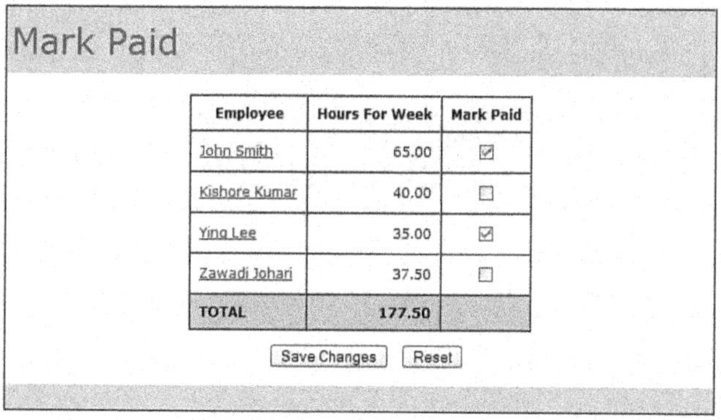

Mark Paid

Employee	Hours For Week	Mark Paid
John Smith	65.00	☑
Kishore Kumar	40.00	☐
Ying Lee	35.00	☑
Zawadi Johari	37.50	☐
TOTAL	177.50	

Save Changes   Reset

Figure 2.8   Mark Paid screen.

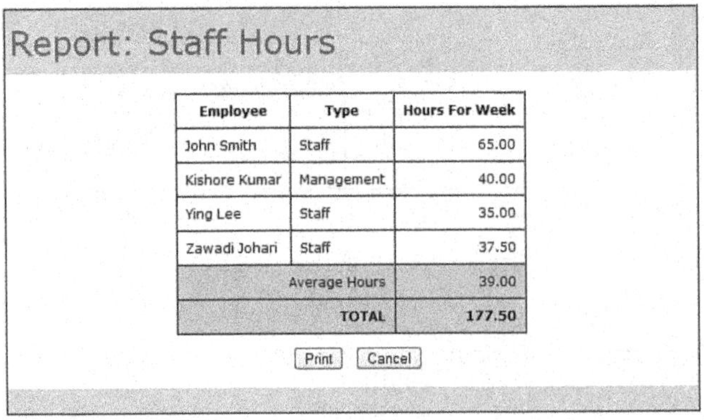

Report: Staff Hours

Employee	Type	Hours For Week
John Smith	Staff	65.00
Kishore Kumar	Management	40.00
Ying Lee	Staff	35.00
Zawadi Johari	Staff	37.50
Average Hours		39.00
TOTAL		177.50

Print   Cancel

Figure 2.9   Report: Staff Hours screen.

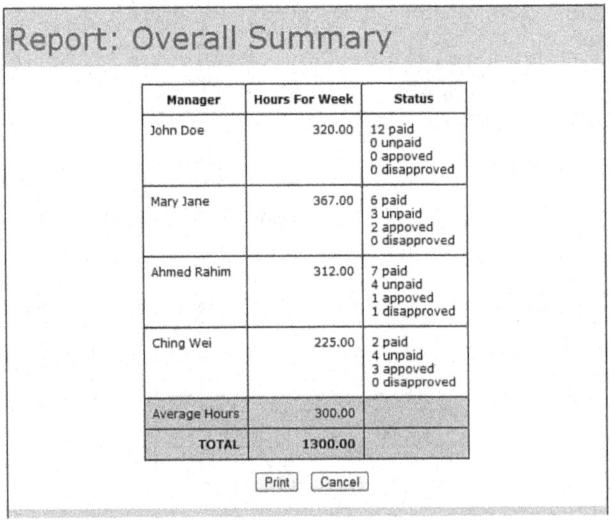

Report: Overall Summary

Manager	Hours For Week	Status
John Doe	320.00	12 paid 0 unpaid 0 appoved 0 disapproved
Mary Jane	367.00	6 paid 3 unpaid 2 appoved 0 disapproved
Ahmed Rahim	312.00	7 paid 4 unpaid 1 appoved 1 disapproved
Ching Wei	225.00	2 paid 4 unpaid 3 appoved 0 disapproved
Average Hours	300.00	
TOTAL	1300.00	

Print   Cancel

Figure 2.10   Report: Overall Summary screen.

Managing Customer Expectations During UI Prototyping

Although UI prototype provides significant benefits, it is important to manage the customer's expectations in this stage, as well. For example, I have run across two problems. First, when customers see prototype screens, they might believe the application is mostly developed and almost ready to be deployed. However, as developers, we know there is a lot more to application development than mocked up screens. Second, user prototyping can get out of hand if the customer is picky about fonts, button placements, and other UI aesthetics. Still, the customer should always come first because they are typically paying for the application, and so you should try to find the right balance when managing a customer's expectations.

Of course, one effective way of getting around this management of expectations is to do hand-drawn UI sketches instead of prototyping. This keeps thing simple because these sketches can be drawn on paper or the whiteboard.

Storyboard

A storyboard, also called a UI flow diagram or website map, is essential to show a navigation map of the various screens. Figure 2.11 shows the storyboard for our sample application. As you can guess from our storyboard, after a user is signed in to the system, the user is directed to an initial screen designated for the user's role type. Users belonging to either the Employee and Manager role have additional functionality that can be accessed from the initial screens.

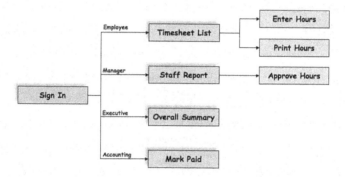

Figure 2.11   Storyboard (also known as a UI flow diagram).

User Stories

Given the business requirements and UI prototypes defined for Time Expression earlier in this chapter, we can now define a set of user stories for our application. As explained earlier in this book, I decided to use XP/AMDD; therefore, you see the use of the term *user story* versus *use case*. Although these serve similar purposes, user stories tend to be shorter than use cases—for example, one to three sentences each. The remaining details can be discussed between the developer and the customer when the developer begins working on a given user story in the planned iteration; hence, the term *active stakeholder participation*.

Use cases come in many formats themselves. The three I'm familiar with are *formal*, *brief*, and *casual*. The casual format is probably closest to a user story because it is short and informal. Formal use cases can entail a page or two of requirements with preconditions, postconditions, success/basic path, failure/alternative path, and other sections for each use case. The reason I have described use case and their formats here is because certain organizations define essential use cases (or even business requirements with "shall" statements) first, and then later break each use case down into one or more (maybe even several) user stories using our guideline of one- to three-day development per user story or development task.

We will use user stories in this book to not only define the requirements, but also to name our Java classes, using the story name/tag, and create acceptance tests. Table 2.2 shows the user stories with the priority and initial estimate to complete. Note that the user stories you might find in the real world might be a bit more detailed than what I have shown in Table 2.2; however, given the simplicity of Time Expression, these work fine for us.

Incidentally, a good book to check out on user stories is Mike Cohn's *User Stories Applied: For Agile Software Development* (Addison-Wesley Signature Series, 2004).

Table 2.2 **User Stories, Priorities, and Estimates for Our Sample Application**

#	Story Name (Tag)	Story Description	Priority	Points (estimate)
1	Enter Hours	User can enter hours worked and save this data.	1	2
2	Timesheet List	Employee can see a list of timesheets previously entered and click the ones that can be modified.	1	1
3	Sign In	User can sign in to system using a valid employee id and password.	2	1
4	Sign Out	Users can sign out of system to end current session.	2	1
5	Reminder Email: Employee	A reminder email is sent every Friday at 2 p.m. to employees who have not submitted their timesheet yet.	2	1
6	Print Timesheet	Employee can print timesheet using best possible formatting in browser and automatic display of print dialog box.	3	1
7	Report: My Hours	Employee can run a report named "My Hours" to view/ print summary of weekly hours.	3	1
8	Submit Timesheet	User can submit timesheet after hours have been entered; submittal email is sent to Manager.	3	1
9	Report: Staff Hours	Manager can run a report named Staff Report to view a summary of a given week's hours for all employees under Manager.	4	1

Table 2.2   **User Stories, Priorities, and Estimates for Our Sample Application**

#	Story Name (Tag)	Story Description	Priority	Points (estimate)
10	Report: Overall Summary	Executive can run a report named Overall Summary to view a summary of a given week's hours for all Managers in company.	4	2
11	Timesheet Approval	Manager can approve/disapprove timesheet;notification email sent to Employee and Accounting department.	5	1
12	Timesheet Payment	Accounting can indicate that Employee has been paid.	5	1
13	Reminder Email: Manager	A reminder email is sent every Friday at 4 p.m. to managers who have timesheets pending approval.	5	1
			Total Points:	15

The estimates shown in Table 2.2 are initial estimates, or *sizing*. The developer provides more accurate estimates at the beginning of the iteration when the user story will be developed, because the user story can be broken down into development tasks to better size the time required to complete the entire user story. Incidentally, I have come across real-world projects where they did not do the breaking down of user stories into tasks, nor did they size the user stories during iteration planning. The reason for this was because sometimes the user story priorities changed or the user story itself changed, so the upfront work was for nothing. Instead, they picked two to three stories on day one of a new iteration and only estimated those.

Points (last column of Table 2.2) are some unit of measure relative to the given project. For example, 1 point could equal 1 regular workday, 1 *ideal* workday, 1 week or another period—whatever the customer and developers agree on. Whatever each point might measure is then used to provide estimates to the customer.

Ideal (development) days are a good way to estimate projects because it factors in planned and unplanned events (for example, meetings, computer problems, sick leave, and so on). The difference between a regular day and an ideal day is referred to as the *load factor*.

A load factor, typically between 2 and 4, is a number you multiply your initial estimate by to come up with an ideal day. For example, I like to use a load factor of 3 for projects where I have a good understanding of the business requirements and technologies. (Note: If you believe there are risks involved, such as a learning curve related to a new technology, you can use a higher number, such as 4 or even 5.) For example, if we know a development task will take me approximately 8 hours of uninterrupted, totally focused, heads-down time, we can multiply that by 3 (that is, 8 * 3) and come up with 24 ideal hours or 3 ideal days (assuming a 8-hour work day).

In this book, we will develop the Enter Hours and Timesheet List (items 1 and 2 in Table 2.2; both with priority 1). So, if we use these two screens as example, it would take 9 actual days to complete these screens (that is, 3 ideal days times the load factor of 3).

Release (and Iteration) Plan

After the customer (end user and/or business analyst) has defined the user stories, the customer and development project manager (and/or developer) can put together a release plan for the next release or version of the application.

A release plan is essentially a project plan listing various system releases and the dates for each release. In this book, we will assume that we have only one release—for example, v1.0.

Releases are typically small, about 1 to 3 months in length. Each release consists of a set of user stories the customer wants implemented in that release. Each release is then further broken down into iterations.

Iterations range between 1 to 3 weeks in length. Each iteration contains a list of user stories chosen from the set of user stories for the given release that the customer wants implemented in that iteration (along with defect fixes from previously failed acceptance tests).

Based on the user stories we defined earlier in this chapter, we can come up with an initial release plan, shown in Table 2.3, to incrementally build release v1.0 of our application.

Table 2.3 **Release Plan**

Iteration	Features	Release Date
0	Environment setup (JDK, Ant, JUnit) and database connectivity demo using Hibernate.	23-Dec-06
1	Small release—All priority 1 user stories.	12-Jan-07
2	Small release—All priority 2 user stories.	26-Jan-07
3	Small release—All priority 3 user stories.	09-Feb-07
4	Small release—All priority 4 user stories.	23-Feb-07

Our release plan does not use priority 5 user stories because these will be pushed off to release 2 of our application. Of course, this is all fictional and many of the examples we have looked at so far, such as the iteration and release plans, are for demonstration purposes only. In the real world, you are bound to see more detailed plans.

After the release plan containing the various iterations is defined for the next release of the software, the developer can begin working on the first iteration.

Prior to each iteration, the customer and development staff get together for an iteration-planning meeting, the outcome of which is an iteration plan for the next iteration. The customer picks the user stories that will be developed in the next iteration. The developers break down each user story into individual development tasks required to implement the user story. This is done so that each development task can be assigned to a developer, but more importantly, the tasks can be used to more accurately estimate the total development effort for the given user story and, in turn, the next iteration.

If the total estimate or points (to implement all chosen user stories for the next iteration) exceeds the total points implemented in the previous iteration (known as the *Project Velocity* in Extreme Programming), the customer must choose which user stories (or defect fixes) to defer to a future iteration or release. If the opposite is true—that is, there is room to get more done in the next iteration, the customer may add additional user stories, defect fixes, or enhancements, if needed.

For our purposes in this book, I have skipped including a sample iteration plan because this book is more about development than process. Also, formats of an iteration (and release) plan can vary, so instead I chose to leverage the release plan (see Table 2.3) and group our user stories by priority in it instead of breaking them down individually in each iteration plan.

Glossary

This is probably a good time for us to define a glossary for Time Expression.

A glossary is essentially a set of common terms, or project vocabulary, that everyone agrees on for the project. This list can include business terms (for example, Timesheet and Approved) or technical terms (for example, Entity, used while discussing the logical data model). The obvious benefit of a glossary is that it gets everyone in agreement with the terminology and definitions of each term to avoid any confusion. (We have enough of that already given the terminology/acronym madness that exists in our industry.)

- Accounting—The accounting department/staff.
- Approved—Status of a timesheet when a Manager approves a previously *submitted* timesheet.
- Employee—A person who works on an hourly basis and reports to a *manager*.
- Executive—An officer of the company, such as CEO, CFO, or COO.
- Hour—A full hour of billable work that can be entered into a timesheet and the *employee* can get paid for.
- Manager—Direct supervisor of an *employee*.
- Paid—Status of a timesheet when the accounting department has issued a check.
- Period Ending Date—This is the last day of each week (Sunday, in our case).
- Pending—Status of a timesheet until the user submits it.
- Submitted—Status of a timesheet when an employee has submitted a timesheet. Timesheet is "locked" from further changes by employee.
- Week—A 40-hour workweek from Monday through Friday.

Whiteboard Architecture

By now, we have enough information to put together an informal architecture diagram. Figure 2.12 shows a high-level architecture diagram for Time Expression (on an indispensable tool of the trade, the whiteboard). By establishing this diagram, the developers and customer can agree on major technologies (for example, Java, database, web/app server) that will be used to build Time Expression.

We will use an electronic and more detailed version of this architecture diagram in the next chapter to help us go one level deeper into the design of the applications. Converting whiteboard diagrams or CRC cards to electronic formats are my personal preference because legibility isn't a real concern with electronic artifacts. However, you could simply digitize artifacts such as whiteboard drawings and CRC cards via tools such as a digital camera and scanner, respectively.

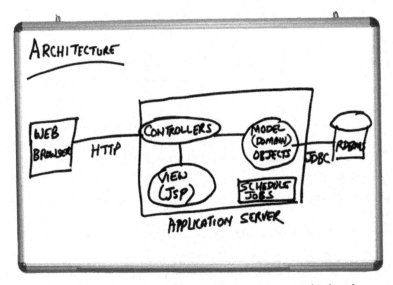

Figure 2.12   An informal, high-level architecture on a whiteboard.

A Note About Wiki Software

When I first heard the term wiki or wikiwiki years ago, I ignored it thinking it wasn't worth my time (possibly because of the way it sounds). However, the use of wiki software has spread like wildfire, and it has become an extremely effective tool to use for collaborating and knowledge management in a project.

According to Ward Cunningham, the inventor of wiki software, wiki is the "simplest online database that could possibly work." Wiki is collaborative software that is essentially installed in a web server and enables you to edit web pages using plain text (with various formatting options). Although this might sound almost too simple, it is a powerful concept.

In a software project, a wiki website serves as a central dumping ground (so to speak) for content, which members of a software team can add or change, collaboratively. This fits very well with the Agile and XP style of working in an iterative fashion. For example, online help documentation for a software being built can be assembled using wiki, iteratively and incrementally, over a period of time (over a two-month release, for example). In fact, most of the personal opinions you see in this book were accumulated using my wiki site over a period of almost a year. It helped to have quick access to editable web pages for a quick brain dump when I had an idea.

There are literally hundreds of wiki engines (software) out there developed in almost every programming language you could think of. There are wiki engines that work with flat-file databases and others that work with relational databases. Some wiki engines provide robust authentication/authorization, whereas others are for personal use. Your biggest problem will likely be deciding on which one to use.

Summary

In this chapter, we accomplished the following:

- Gained an understanding of what our sample application will do by looking at some business requirements.
- Established a simple software methodology based on Extreme Programming (XP) and Agile Modeling Driven Development (AMDD).
- Developed some high-level artifacts such as a domain model, UI prototypes, high-level architecture, and more.
- Created a simple release plan based on our user stories.

Now it is time to begin getting our hands dirty with some design work.

Recommended Resources

The following websites are relevant to and provide additional information on the topics discussed in this chapter:

- Agile Data   http://www.agiledata.org
- Agile Manifesto   http://agilemanifesto.org
- Agile Modeling   http://www.agilemodeling.com
- Extreme Programming   http://extremeprogramming.org/
- Article on PmWiki, a PHP-based wiki engine
  http://visualpatterns.com/resources.jsp
- Wiki site   http://wiki.org/

If XP isn't for you, you might want to check out Agile Unified Process (a lighter version of RUP) at http://www.ambysoft.com/unifiedprocess/agileUP.html.

II

Building the Sample Application

3

XP and AMDD-Based Architecture and Design Modeling

Release 1, Week 2, Iteration 1

Raj: Steve, between our UI prototypes, domain model, CRC cards, and so on, I believe we have done enough design for iteration 1; what do you think?

Steve: Yeah, let's not over-engineer this application. We need to get coding, so we can shake-out our initial design work. By the way, we need to define some quick coding and integration standards first, so we are on the same page.

I N THIS CHAPTER, WE FINALLY BEGIN to get into the technology side of things, so now begins the fun part.

In a truly iterative development environment, all the architecture and design issues would not necessarily be finalized up front. Refactoring (improving code without impacting its functionality) plays a big role in constant improvement to the initially established design because invariably you will find better ways to do something when you are actually coding. Furthermore, while the scope of the project can be defined up front, the user requirements can continue to evolve from iteration to iteration versus having everything locked-down up front. With requirements, the idea is to have a lot of interaction with the stakeholder and be able to ask ad hoc questions.

Although some work can be done up front, such as the user stories, high-level architecture, user interface prototypes, domain model, standards and so on, other design issues can be resolved in the iteration they are applicable to. Furthermore, as we will see in Chapter 5, "Using Hibernate for Persistent Objects," and Chapter 7, "The Spring Web MVC Framework," writing tests first can also help with the design of your classes, so you don't have to have all the fine details of your classes figured out up front; in other words, you can take a just-in-time approach to design, so to speak.

However, some upfront design is bound to happen, perhaps in iteration 0 (perhaps when you are trying to demonstrate a proof-of-concept, which shows that the chosen technologies can work end-to-end, from the user interface to the database, for example).

> **Note**
> Also, in iterations 1 and 2, perhaps fewer user stories get coded because of the extra time required for design and environment setup work; this can include a domain model (explained later), definition of business objects, Java naming conventions, build/integration process/scripts for the team, and so on.

In this chapter, I hope to provide you with an end-to-end approach using modeling and process guidelines provided by Agile Model Driven Development (AMDD; agilemodeling.com) and Extreme Programming (XP; extremeprogramming.org).

What's Covered in This Chapter

In this chapter, we will accomplish the following architecture and design objectives for our sample application, Time Expression:

- Develop a free-form architecture diagram
- Explore objects using CRC cards
- Assemble an artifact I like to call an application flow map
- Develop class and package diagrams for Time Expression
- Establish our development directory structure and look at some sample file names (we will create in later chapter)
- Look at the steps we will follow in the upcoming chapters for end-to-end development of our screens
- List advanced concepts we will need to consider as our sample application evolves: exception handling, scheduling jobs, transaction management, logging, and more

Design Approach and Artifact Choices

In the previous chapter, we looked at an XP-based approach to defining business requirements and working with the customer. In this chapter, we will drill down into some minimal architecture and design to help us get going with building Time Expression, using popular technologies such as Hibernate, the Spring Framework, the Eclipse SDK, and many other related tools such as Ant, JUnit, and more.

If you have come across the myth that XP programmers don't design or document, I hope this misconception will be cleared up by the end of this chapter, because it couldn't be further from the truth. Let me give you a preview of what I'm talking about.

Take a look at Figure 3.1, which shows some possible artifacts you can produce at the release or iteration level. Release-level artifacts are ones you produce prior to a new release; iteration-level artifacts are ones you produce prior to each iteration. These aren't all mandatory for every project, so we can pick and choose the ones we need. However, between Chapter 2, "The Sample Application: An Online Timesheet System," and this chapter, I have chosen to demonstrate as many of these as possible, and practical, for Time Expression. At the end of this chapter, I will show you another diagram that will tie together all the artifacts produced as a result of our efforts between the previous and this chapter (but don't cheat by looking now, because it is a detailed diagram and I don't want to overwhelm you at this point).

At the very least, what you will see in this chapter will give you one perspective. This process might or might not work for you. However, there must be some things good about these methodologies, because developers love them, and I have seen many successful projects as a result of these methods. Also, in our case, the artifacts we will produce in this chapter are essential to the rest of this book, and this process will help get us there.

As you can see from Figure 3.1, we have a few artifacts to produce in this chapter, so let's move forward. However, before we do, I want to provide two perspectives from real-world users of XP.

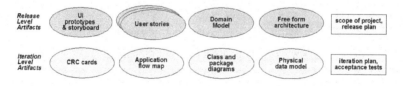

Figure 3.1   XP/AMDD style choices for artifacts to produce at
release and iteration levels.

A project director working at a Fortune 50 company told me recently, "When we kick off an iteration, the first day of the iteration is usually spent reviewing stories and breaking them into tasks. The exercise of breaking them into tasks is truly a design session. What we ended up observing is that something like 20% of the developer's time, during an iteration, was spent in design. If you add all that time for all developers, across all iterations, it was a large number—which truly debunked the 'no design' comments."

To give you another perspective on the XP style of working, consider this statement from a senior architect at a well-established IT solutions company that has deployed more than a dozen successful projects using XP and AMDD techniques: "There is also another level of design that happens on an XP project which is at the daily level. Refactoring is a design activity. Although the iteration-kickoff design is an important step, it is the design work after the code is written that makes the difference between an OK design and a truly elegant one."

The difference with the XP approach, is that the architecture and design happens throughout the application's release cycle, not just up front. In other words, the application continues to evolve through the various iterations. The benefit of this approach is that the design is actually applicable to what you are building, not three to six months into development when the requirements could have changed—something that is certainly possible in our fast-paced and ever-changing world today.

Free-Form Architecture Diagram

Figure 3.2 shows the high-level architecture for our sample application. Note that this has been converted to an electronic version from the whiteboard version we saw at the end of the previous chapter. Converting it to an electronic format is a personal preference; you could just as easily take a digital picture of the whiteboard version, but I personally like clean and readable diagrams.

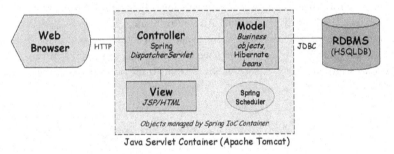

Figure 3.2   High-level architecture for Time Expression.

The architecture is fairly straightforward. We have our standard three-tier web architecture with the client tier (web browser), middle tier (application server), and our data tier (database).

Also standard is the use of the model-view-controller (MVC) design pattern, as you find in most Java-based web frameworks these days. The controller is the point of entry of the HTTP/web request; it controls the model and the view. The *model* deals with data, which is obtained by the controller and passed to the *view* for rendering in a presentable way. In our case, the view will be written using JavaServer Pages (JSP).

What makes our architecture interesting isn't that it uses a MVC pattern, but rather what's in the middle tier, namely the Spring Framework and Hibernate, two technologies we will cover in detail later in the book. Hibernate, as you will see later, makes database persistence very easy because you can reference database tables and records as plain old Java objects (POJOs). The Spring Framework (springframework.org) provides many benefits, as well, especially when you're working with POJOs. For example, we will use the Spring MVC for our web framework because it makes for cleaner code (when compared to something like Struts). Another notable feature of the Spring Framework is the support for scheduling jobs rather than depending on an external scheduling service such as CRON or the Windows Scheduler. Of course, the core feature provided by the Spring Framework is the inversion of control (IoC) functionality, which we will learn about in later chapters.

From User Stories to Design

We covered a variety of user stories in Chapter 2. For the sake of brevity, we will not develop every single user story in this book. However, the user stories I have chosen will given you complete end-to-end working examples of a form and a no-form screen. In addition, we will look at advanced topics, such as implementing application security using interceptors, sending emails, and scheduling jobs, which take care of a couple more user stories covered in Chapter 2.

In the rest of this chapter, I will provide examples based on at least the first two user stories, tag named *Enter Hours* and *Timesheet List*, in Chapter 2.

Exploring Classes Using CRC Cards

Figure 3.3 shows the domain model we established in Chapter 2. The domain model enables us to explore domain or business objects. The user stories will enable us to discover the web-based user interface controller classes. So, let's look at coming up with objects for the Timesheet List user story next, to see exactly how CRC cards work.

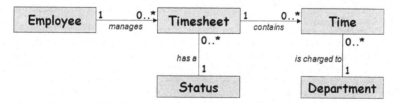

Figure 3.3 Domain model for Time Expression.

Figure 3.4 shows the Timesheet List UI prototype from Chapter 2. As I mentioned, we already know our user interface will be web based and will use the MVC paradigm. So, let's approach the discovery of our initial classes from the MVC perspective.

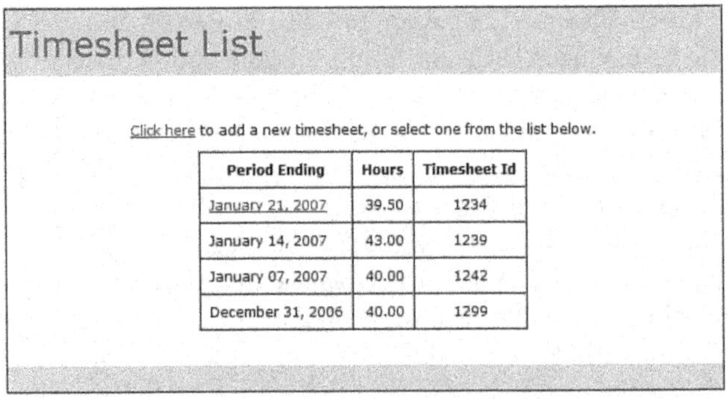

Figure 3.4   Timesheet List screen.

On the model part of the MVC, we already know some entity names for Time Expression from our domain model. For the controller part, we know the user story tag (*Timesheet List*, in this example) from Chapter 2. Given these, we can now proceed with our initial class design using CRC cards.

In case you have been wondering, CRC stands for class, responsibilities, and collaborators. Table 3.1 shows the layout of a sample CRC card along with some explanations for the three components you see there. Note that although I have shown an electronic version, CRC cards can actually be done on basic 3" x 5" index cards and later translated into a class diagram (if needed).

CRC cards provide an informal object-oriented technique for discovering interactions between classes. I like CRC cards because they can be used in an informal session with developers or users to discover objects without the need for a computer. Furthermore, CRC cards can be used to develop a formal class diagram, if needed (something we will do later in this chapter).

Tables 3.2 through 3.4 show some sample CRC cards for the actual classes we will develop later in this book, to meet the requirements for the Timesheet List screen.

Table 3.1   **A Simple CRC Card Layout**

Class Name (Noun)	
Responsibilities (obligations of this class, such as business methods, exception handling, security methods, attributes/variables)	**Collaborators** (other classes required to provide a complete solution to a high-level requirement)

Table 3.2   **Sample CRC Card for Timesheet Class**

Timesheet	
Knows of period ending date Knows of time Knows of department code	

Table 3.3   **Sample CRC Card for TimesheetManager Class**

TimesheetManager	
Fetches timesheet(s) from database Saves timesheet to database	Timesheet

Table 3.4   **Sample CRC Card for TimesheetListController Class**

TimesheetListController	
Controller (in MVC) for displaying a list of timesheets	TimesheetManager

We just covered some basics about CRC cards. For now, we have a good enough idea of what we need to move forward with the next step.

Application Flow Map (Homegrown Artifact)

In past projects, I have used a table similar to Table 3.5. This format is homegrown, in that it is something I came up with. I call it an *application flow map* because it shows me how a user interface will function (or flow) end to end. This technique also nicely maps the user stories to the *view* (the "V" in MVC), which maps to the *controller* and, finally, to the *model* objects.

Table 3.5   **Sample Application Flow Map**

Story Tag	View	Controller Class	Collaborators	Tables Impacted
Timesheet List	timesheetlist	TimeSheetListController	TimesheetManager	Timesheet
Enter Hours	enterhours	EnterHoursController	TimesheetManager	Timesheet Department

A Complementary Technique

In comparing this application flow map to techniques such as class diagrams or CRC cards, you will find that this map complements CRC cards and class diagrams. CRC cards list, among other things, responsibilities of each class, which is lacking in the application flow map. Class diagrams on the other hand, show relationships, cardinality, behavior (methods), attributes, and possibly more, which are more details than I like to have in this map.

By putting together classes in a textual and table format, we could also search for class names (in a large system, for example) and also sort these easily using a spreadsheet program or command-line utilities.

Extending the Application Flow Map with CRUD Columns

This table can also be altered for use with non-UI stories such as the Reminder Email: Employee user story. For example, the view and controller class columns can be replaced with a single column named Job, for instance.

Furthermore, you can extend this table by splitting the Tables Impacted column into four separate CRUD (create, read, update, delete) columns. This not only shows which tables are impacted, but *how* they are impacted, by the various collaborator classes. By adding CRUD columns, you essentially provide end-to-end flow of a user story (from the view to the database and back) in one row of our table.

UML Class Diagram

Next, we will look at a rudimentary class diagram. This is an optional step in my opinion (see sidebar on UML diagrams) because our CRC cards and application flow map provide us with enough information to move forward with coding. However, class diagrams can be a good thing when used appropriately.

Figure 3.5 shows a sample and minimal class diagram for the classes we have defined so far.

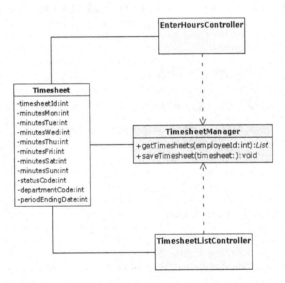

Figure 3.5 Sample class diagram for Time Expression.

Personal Opinion:

UML Diagrams

Over the years, I have used several types of UML diagrams, including the essential class diagram, package diagrams (my favorite), and the less-often seen deployment diagram.

Then there are ones that I am not a fan of, such as the popular sequence diagram. I don't like this diagram because I find it gets complex and cumbersome quickly. However, I'll be the first to tell you that I do not have better and alternative ways to do what some of these diagrams do (at least not yet anyway, but eventually I hope to because I'm currently conducting some research in better ways to model/ diagram—check the visualpatterns.com website for updates periodically, if you are interested).

Meanwhile, I use UML diagrams when appropriate because I think they add value when used in the right place and at the right time. In fact, I think UML diagrams are most useful when generated using reverse-engineering tools to document the system already built (perhaps during a system handover).

I hope I don't come across as being dismissive about UML, because this isn't quite my intention, especially since it took a lot of work over a number of years from some intelligent people to make a standard such as UML even possible. (In fact, this is precisely why I'm basing all my research on work that has already been done instead of simply trying to reinvent the wheel.)

My main complaint about UML diagrams is that they get complex very quickly, specially for larger projects. Another issue I have with UML is that it requires special tools, which, because of software licensing costs, can be expensive for an organization. In addition, some of these tools can have a steep learning curve and hence require training for the people using these tools (one common example being Rational Rose), resulting in additional cost to the organization.

Furthermore, simpler tools such as OpenOffice.org, Microsoft PowerPoint, Microsoft Visio, and other similar tools provide the capability to connect a variety of shapes (rectangles, for example) using connectors, which are essentially straight or curved lines that connect two objects and stay tied to those objects when you move them around. This is a powerful feature because it enables you to create flowchart-like diagrams. I use connectors extensively, as you will see in many free-form diagrams in this book; in fact, almost all diagrams in this book were developed using OpenOffice.org!

Also, I tend to follow practices recommended by Agile Modeling, such as modeling with a purpose and producing good enough artifacts. Furthermore, I update these only when it hurts, because many artifacts can be thrown away after they have served their purpose. After implementing a design in code, you already have your documentation—yes, the code. (As I mentioned earlier, code can be reverse engineered to produce pretty class and other diagrams.)

What makes the idea of heavy documentation seem like sheer madness is the fact that I cannot recall one software development project where the documentation was maintained until the very end and matched the end product. This is the case because we live in a fast-paced world with sometimes unrealistic software delivery deadlines, and it becomes a difficult task to keep the documentation up-to-date.

In summary, use UML diagrams when appropriate, but don't be shy or hesitant about using simple, yet effective, free-form diagrams. Let me end by providing the same blurb from the agilemodeling.com website I provided in Chapter 2: "Your goal is to build a shared understanding, it isn't to write detailed documentation."

UML Package Diagram

For our sample application, Time Expression, we will use the prefix `com.`
`visualpatterns.timex` for our package name.

If you have worked with Java already, you probably know that the first part of the
package name is typically tied to an organization's domain name, just used backwards.
For example, `com.visualpatterns` is the reverse for `visualpatterns.com`, which happens to be my website. The `timex` portion of our package name is derived from the
name of our sample application. The remainder, the suffixes, for our package names are
shown in Figure 3.6, a rudimentary UML package diagram.

> **Note**
>
> I have chosen very basic Java packages names to match our MVC pattern-based design. For example, we
> could have called our model package something like `domain`, but I prefer to match things up—for example,
> matching the package names with the architecture or application flow map. That way, someone new taking
> over my code can easily follow its organization. So, a fully qualified package name for the model package
> would be `com.visualpatterns.timex.model`.

As you might guess, the controller package will have controller-related classes in it. The
job package will contain our email reminder job. The util package contains common
and/or utility code.

Last but not least, the test package will contain our unit test code. Although I have
chosen to place our test classes in a separate package, many developers prefer keeping the
test classes in the same directory as the implementation code they are testing. This is a
matter of preference, but in my opinion, having a separate package/directory for the test
classes keeps things nice and clean in the actual implementation package directories.

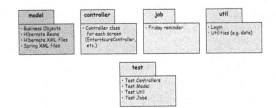

Figure 3.6   UML package diagram for Time Expression.

Directory Structure

Figure 3.7 shows the directory structure we will use for our sample application. This
should look pretty straightforward and familiar; the most notable subdirectories here are
src, build, lib, and dist. This figure will be referenced in later chapters (Chapters 4, 5, and
7, for example) and the directories relevant to each chapter will be discussed in a bit

more detail, when needed. Meanwhile, Figure 3.7 provides a brief description for all the key directories.

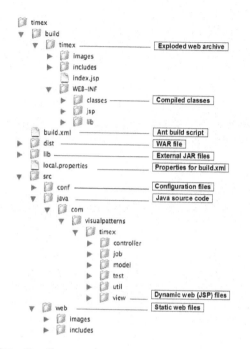

Figure 3.7   Development directory structure for Time Expression.

Sample File Names

Given our directory structure shown in Figure 3.7, we can now come up with some sample filenames for the classes we discussed in this chapter. For example, for the Timesheet List screen we discussed earlier in this chapter, we will most likely end up with the following files under the `timex/src/java/com/visualpatterns/timex/` directory:

- `controller/TimesheetListController.java`
- `model/Timesheet.java`
- `model/TimesheetManager.java`
- `test/TimesheetListControllerTest.java`
- `test/TimesheetManagerTest.java`
- `view/timesheetlist.jsp`

End-to-End Development Steps

Given what we have learned in this chapter so far, we can put together the steps that will be required to develop (code) for our first user story, from the web UI to the database, and back. Here are tasks that will most likely be required to complete the first user story:

- Set up our environment including the JDK, Ant, and JUnit (in Chapter 4)
- Write test and implementation classes for model package (using Hibernate in Chapter 5)
- Write test and implementation classes for controller package (using Spring Framework in Chapter 7)

Acceptance Tests

Acceptance tests can serve as our detailed requirements as they do in many Agile style projects. One example is a list of valid operations a user can perform on a given screen. The idea of using acceptance tests as requirements is feasible because these tests are something our customer expects our application to conform to. For our purposes, we will use them only for our unit tests; however, it is becoming more and more common in the real world to use acceptance tests as detailed requirements.

The following sections are our list of acceptance tests and something we will implement for the user stories we will develop. In the real world, these types of acceptance tests would be provided by the customer.

Sign In

- The employee id can be up to 6 characters. The password must be between 8 and 10 characters.
- Only valid users can sign in.

Timesheet List

- Only a user's personal timesheets can be accessed.

Enter Hours

- Hours must contain numeric data.
- Daily hours cannot exceed 16 hours. Weekly hours cannot exceed 96 hours.
- Hours must be billed to a department.
- Hours can be entered as two decimal places.
- Employees can view and edit only their own timesheets.

Other Considerations

As I mentioned earlier, we need to do just enough architecture and design to get us going. Although we did a reasonable amount of architecture and design in this chapter, there are a lot of things we haven't discussed yet but will in later chapters, such as the following:

- Application security—This will be covered in Chapters 7, "The Spring Web MVC Framework" and 10, "Beyond the Basics."

- Transaction management—This will be covered in Chapter 5. We will see how to programmatically implement transaction management using Hibernate.

- Exception handling—In Chapter 10 we will look at handled and unhandled exceptions and provide some guidance on when to use one versus the other.

- Other features—Features required for Time Expression such as scheduling jobs and sending emails will be covered in Chapter 10. Other topics also discussed in later chapters include logging, tag libraries, and more.

Big Design Up Front Versus Refactoring

According to Martin Fowler (refactoring.com), refactoring "is a disciplined technique for restructuring an existing body of code, altering its internal structure without changing its external behavior." Many developers have been refactoring code for years, but Martin Fowler gave it a formal name (and I'm glad he did).

As you begin to code an application, you will invariably find better ways to do things than you might have originally thought of (before coding began). For example, this could include removal of redundant code or cleaning up of code. Hence, I am a big believer that refactoring should always be an open option, not just for code but also for database design, architecture, documentation, build/integration scripts, and more. It also alleviates the burden of figuring out the entire design and process of an application up front.

For example, I recently came across a portion in an essay on the agiledata.org website, which helps summarize how I feel about this subject; this portion states that "Agile developers iterate back and forth between tasks such as data modeling, object modeling, refactoring, mapping, implementing, and performance tuning."

Take this book, for example. This is essentially a project for me as I'm developing a sample application from scratch and a book alongside it. Although I have done some upfront planning, I don't have 100% of the answers figured out, but I am not worried because I can refactor the architecture, design, code, or process used for Time Expression in later chapters because I want to make progress now instead of spending too much time trying to think of every possible scenario that could go wrong.

In short, you should definitely do some initial architecture and design, but keep in mind that if there is a way to improve something that adds value, such as simpler or cleaner code, and if it is not too late in the process (for example, the day of acceptance tests or deployment), you should go ahead and refactor!

Summary

In this chapter, we covered a lot of material and accomplished the following objectives we established at the beginning of the chapter:

- Develop a free-form architecture diagram
- Explore objects using CRC cards
- Assemble an artifact I like to call an application flow map
- Develop class and package diagrams for Time Expression
- Establish our development directory structure and look at some sample filenames (we will create these in later chapters)
- Look at the steps we will follow in the upcoming chapters for end-to-end development of our screens
- Review a list of advanced concepts we will need to consider as our sample application evolves

At the beginning of the chapter, I promised you a diagram to show you how we got here and some of the artifacts we produced along the way. (Did you cheat and take a peak already?) Figure 3.8 shows this diagram. Of course, this also clearly shows that XP has artifacts at various levels—conceptual, physical, and even in implementation. Note that the lines shown in Figure 3.8 are unidirectional because this is how we developed these artifacts in the previous and in this chapter. However, in the real world, these would be bidirectional because there is input coming from one direction and feedback going back in the opposite direction.

One parting thought on the subject of artifacts and documentation. Remember, that the database and code are the most important artifacts of all! I cannot emphasize this enough. The other artifacts we discussed in this book are merely ones you pick and choose, depending on your needs (these are not required). Furthermore, many of these optional artifacts could potentially be discarded after they have served their purpose, because most people don't update these anyway. However, code is always current because that is what the application for the customer is built with; the database can outlive all software programs written around it, so that should be considered the most important component of a system.

Speaking of database and code—now it is time to get our hands dirty and begin setting up our development environment using tools such as Ant and JUnit in the next chapters, so we can actually begin coding!

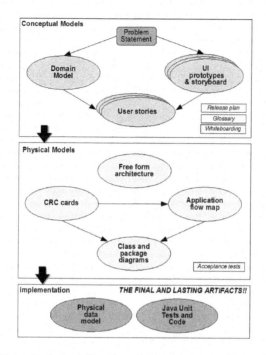

Figure 3.8   Conceptual, physical, and implementation artifacts for Time Expression.

Recommended Resources

The following websites are relevant to or provide additional information on the topics discussed in this chapter:

- Agile Model Driven Development   http://www.agilemodeling.com
- Agile Data   http://www.agiledata.org/
- Extreme Programming   http://extremeprogramming.org
- CRC Cards   http://c2.com/doc/oopsla89/paper.html

4

Environment Setup: JDK, Ant, and JUnit

Release 1, Week 4, Iteration 2

Steve: Hi, Ron. Things are on track. We are trying to deploy the application to production since it passed the acceptance tests. Raj is checking some minor network problems that are preventing us from connecting to the server. Anyway, we should be on target for our upcoming iteration meeting a week from Monday.   (c) Visual Patterns, Inc.

IN THIS CHAPTER, WE WILL get the bare-bones set of tools installed so we can begin to develop, build, test, and deploy our Java code.

One of the goals of this book is to be a quick read and not to provide you with redundant, or even out-of-date, information. Hence, I'm not going to provide setup instructions for the various tools covered in this chapter (for example, Ant). Instead, I will refer you to their respective websites because all the tools covered in our book provide you with ample, up-to-date setup instructions.

What's Covered in This Chapter

In this chapter, we begin the setup of our development environment with the following core tools required for our Java development through the remainder of this book:

- Java Platform Standard Edition (JSE) Development Kit (JDK) setup—Because this book is about Java technologies, this is the first software we need to have working before we can do anything else.

- Ant—This is the de facto utility for building and deploying Java-based applications.

- JUnit—This is a simple unit-testing framework and standard way of unit testing Java code these days.

- Make It All Work Together—Finally, we will put together all three technologies and try out a simple unit test.

> **Note**
> The complete code for the examples used in this chapter can be found within this book's code zip file (available on the book's website).

In later chapters, we will add to this environment by installing products such as a database, a web server, an IDE, tag libraries, and more.

Java Platform Standard Edition Development Kit (JDK)

Because we are doing Java development, it would make sense to have the necessary Java tools (for example, compiler) set up. If you do not already have the JDK installed on your machine, or if you have an older version than ones required by JUnit and Ant, you should get the latest version from the java.sun.com website and have it set up on your machine so that commands such as `java` are in your path.

After downloading and installing Java, you should be able to type the command `java -version` to test your setup and ensure you have the correct version of the JDK, as shown next:

```
C:\anil\rapidjava\timex>java -version
java version "1.5.0_06"
Java(TM) 2 Runtime Environment, Standard Edition (build 1.5.0_06-b05)
Java HotSpot(TM) Client VM (build 1.5.0_06-b05, mixed mode, sharing)
```

Directory Structure

Let's revisit the directory structure we covered in the previous chapter. Figure 4.1 shows the directory structure. It is important to see this again now before we jump into the Ant discussion. Let's review some of the more notable subdirectories here:

- src directory will contain all the Java, HTML/Javascript, XML, and all other input/source files that we will develop ourselves.

- build will contain the output of our builds (for example, compilation, copying of web and library files, and so on).

- lib will contain all external JAR files required to run our application.

- dist will contain our web archive (.war) file, which contains all the web-related files, compiled .class files, .jar library files, and more.

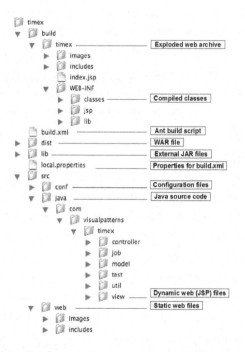

Figure 4.1 Development directory structure for Time Expression.

Ant

I would not be exaggerating by claiming that Ant (ant.apache.org) is perhaps the single most important and widely used tool in the world of Java today! Therefore, mastering this tool is the key to rapid Java development. So, it is no surprise that I'm covering this tool directly after the JDK section, because I consider Ant the most vital tool to install after you are done with the basic Java setup.

By now you probably realize the important role Ant plays in Java development. We will use Ant extensively in this book! For example, we will use it to build our application, deploy it, run various Java programs, create our database, run our tests, and more.

Ant was originally developed by James Duncan Davidson, from the Open Source Program Office at Sun Microsystems. Ant is a cross-platform build tool that eliminates a lot of complexities and quirks that can be found in tools such as Unix make. Instead of using shell commands proprietary to the operating system, Ant uses XML files to specify various tasks. Ant is a highly extensible tool, mainly because of the huge market of built-in and external (open source and commercial) tasks available for Ant, which makes it so powerful. In addition, you can easily write your own custom extensions.

Given that Ant itself is developed in Java, it is portable, and according to the Ant website, it has been tested on various Unix systems, Microsoft Windows, Mac OS X, and others. The ant.apache.org website provides ample (and up-to-date) information on how to get Ant set up on your system; if you do not already have Ant installed on your system, you should go ahead and do so at this point.

When you do have Ant set up successfully, you should be able to run the ant command without specifying the full path. That is, the ant command should be in your path because the remainder of our book will reference ant without the full path. For example, if you typed **ant -version** on the command line, you would see something similar to what is shown in Figure 4.2.

A Simple Ant Build File

Ant, by default, expects a `build.xml` file in the current directory, if you do not provide the ant command with any arguments. Let's try out a sample build.xml file; you might recall the following tiny Ant script from earlier in this book. It provides a target that executes the echo task:

```xml
<?xml version="1.0"?>
<project name="HelloTest" default="printmessage">
<target name="printmessage">
<echo message="Hello world!"/>
</target>
</project>
```

For example, if we saved this minimal XML code in a file named `build.xml` and in the same directory type **ant**, the command and its output would look as follows:

```
> ant
Buildfile: build.xml
printmessage:
[echo] Hello world!
BUILD SUCCESSFUL
Total time: 0 seconds
```

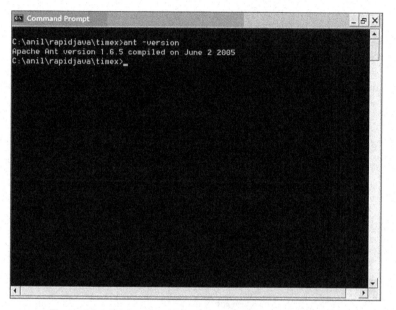

Figure 4.2 Testing the ant setup by running `ant -version`.

A Comprehensive Ant Build File

"Hello world" examples are good, but let's move toward building a comprehensive Ant build script for our sample application.

Note

This book's downloadable code shows the complete build script for our sample application, `build.xml`, along with `local.properties`, a file used by `build.xml` to load some external properties. Both of these files will be placed in the top-level directory, `timex/`.

Note that the use of `local.properties` here demonstrates a handy way of having different property files for different configuration management environments such as development, test, staging, and production.

Ant Concepts

Before we inspect our `build.xml` file step-by-step, let's review some basic concepts about Ant.

The key concepts in Ant include a project, properties, targets, tasks, and elements. *Properties* are variables you can set for the ant session. *Targets* contain blocks of XML code that get executed in the form of tasks. *Tasks* are the actual executables, such as the built-in javac task. Tasks in turn can contain *elements* (for example, *dirset* or *fileset*).

Step-by-Step Walkthrough

Now, we will review the key targets in our `build.xml` file, but first, let's look at a graphical representation of this file, shown in Figure 4.3. You may also want to review Figure 4.1 one more time before we begin this walkthrough, because our Ant build script is closely tied to this development directory structure.

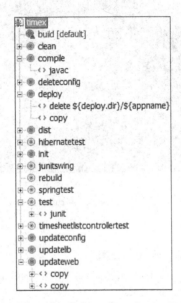

Figure 4.3   Hierarchical view of our Ant `build.xml` file.

The first XML element that must appear in an Ant file is `project`, as shown here:

```
<project name="timex" basedir="." default="build">
```

The next few lines essentially set internal variables (properties) for our script. Most of these properties are related to the various source and destination directories we will use, as shown in this excerpt (notice how we can use internal variables, surrounded by a dollar sign and braces; for example, `${dist.dir}`):

```
<property name="appname" value="timex" />
<property name="lib.dir" value="lib" />
<property name="war.dir" value="build/timex" />
<property name="war.file" value="${dist.dir}/${appname}.war" />
<property name="webinf.dir" value="${war.dir}/WEB-INF" />
```

After the properties are set up, the script sets up the classpath, which is used by various other tasks in the file. The classpath essentially includes two sets of files: all the .jar files in our lib/ directory and the compiled class files under build/timex/WEB-INF/classes/, as shown next:

```
<path id="master-classpath"
    description="Master CLASSPATH for this script">
  <fileset dir="${lib.dir}">
    <include name="*.jar" />
  </fileset>
  <pathelement location="build/timex/WEB-INF/classes/" />
</path>
```

The next target in our build script, init, ensures that certain output directories (under build/) are created in order for other tasks in our build script to be successful (note, this is accomplished using the depends attribute in other targets):

```
<target name="init" description="Setup for build script">
  <mkdir dir="${class.dir}" />
  <mkdir dir="${libs.dir}" />
  <mkdir dir="${jsp.dir}" />
</target>
```

Our *updateweb*, *updatelib*, *deleteconfig*, and *updateconfig* targets basically copy or delete web and library-related files to the destination directory.

The next interesting target is compile, which compiles .java files in src/java/ to .class files under build/timex/WEB-INF/classes/, as demonstrated here:

```
<target name="compile" description="Compiles .java files to WAR directory">
  <javac srcdir="${src.dir}" destdir="${class.dir}" debug="true"
      failonerror="true" classpathref="master-classpath" />
</target>
```

Our dist target creates a WAR file and deploys it to the pathname the internal variable ${war.file} points to (that is, dist/timex.war). An interesting thing to note about this target is the use of the war task and fileset element (known as an Ant type). The war task creates a .war file; the fileset type can be used to specify an individual file or a group of files (using include and exclude pattern sets). Examples of both the war task and the fileset element are shown here:

```
<war destfile="${war.file}" webxml="${src.dir}/conf/web.xml">
  <fileset dir="${war.dir}">
    <include name="**/*.*" />
```

```
            <exclude name="**/web.xml" />
            <exclude name="**/test/*.class" />
            <exclude name="**/*mock*.jar" />
    </fileset>
</war>
```

The other notable targets include deploy, clean, and test. The deploy target copies the .war file to a destination directory (we will use it to deploy to an Apache Tomcat webapps directory). The clean target deletes files from the destination directory. We will use the test target later in the chapter.

Ant Task Categories

The following are some of the tasks we used in our build.xml file:

- Archive tasks such as war
- Compile tasks (that is, javac)
- File tasks such as copy, delete, move, and others
- Miscellaneous tasks such as echo
- Property tasks for setting internal variables

Other built-in tasks worth exploring include the following categories:

- Audit/coverage tasks
- Deployment tasks
- Documentation tasks
- Execution tasks
- Mail tasks
- Preprocess tasks
- Property tasks
- Remote tasks

As I mentioned earlier, we will use Ant to build and deploy our web archive (.war) file. In the next chapters, we will continue to use the command line for working with Ant. However, when we look at Eclipse in Chapter 8, "The Eclipse Phenomenon!," we will switch to using Ant within Eclipse (shown in Figure 4.4), which makes editing and running the (same) Ant build.xml much easier!

We will also look at a few more handy tasks in Chapter 10, "Beyond the Basics." Again, entire books are dedicated to Ant, so as you might guess, I have merely scratched the surface here. However, the idea in this book is to get you going rapidly. If you have the need or interest to explore further, you can find ample information online and in print for all the technologies I have covered in this book.

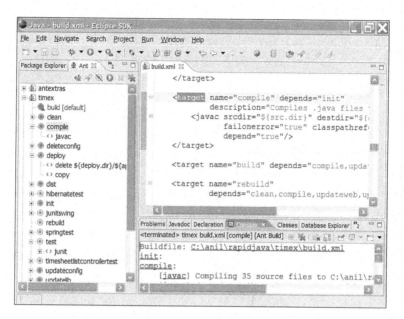

Figure 4.4   The Ant view in Eclipse.

JUnit

JUnit, originally written by Erich Gamma (Gang of Four, Design Patterns book) and
Kent Beck (also author of Extreme Programming), is an open source Java testing framework commonly used for unit testing of Java code. It can be downloaded from the
junit.org website; this website provides not only setup instructions, but also articles on
unit testing and many benefits to writing tests first.

Test-driven development (TDD), a term coined by Kent Beck, can enable better code
design, cleaner code (fewer print/debug statements and test scripts), and more efficient
code. Because we will follow this approach by writing tests first in this book, it makes
sense to cover JUnit directly after JDK and Ant sections.

JUnit Standalone Runners

For setting up JUnit, again I will refer you to the installation instructions found on the
product's website, junit.org. The JUnit test runner (Java main class) comes in two flavors:
a textual version and a graphical version. The graphical version is available in two variations, a Java Swing-based one (recommended) and an older, AWT-based one.

After you have JUnit set up correctly, you should be able to type the following command (from the JUnit install directory; for example, `C:\junit3.8.1`) and be able to run the Swing version of JUnit's user interface, shown in Figure 4.5:

```
java -cp junit.jar junit.swingui.TestRunner
```

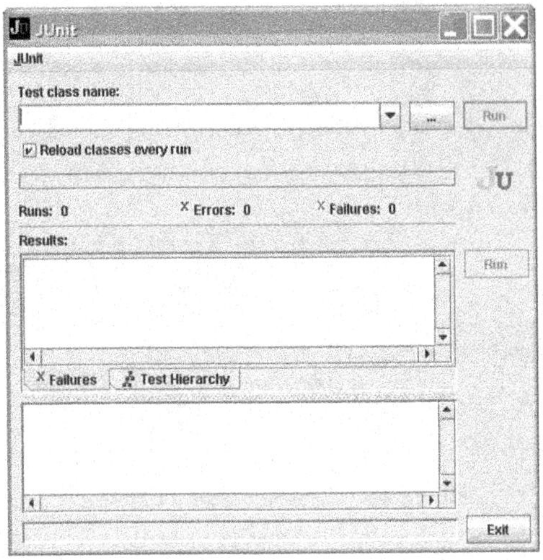

Figure 4.5   The JUnit Swing-based test runner.

JUnit in Eclipse SDK

In the next chapters, we will continue to use the standalone JUnit test runners for working with JUnit, described here. However, when I introduce Eclipse later in the book, we will switch to using JUnit within Eclipse (shown in Figure 4.6), which makes running and debugging JUnit tests much more convenient. However, there might be times when you want to run batch tests using the Ant junit task on a server or even test a single class outside of the IDE, using one of the JUnit built-in runners.

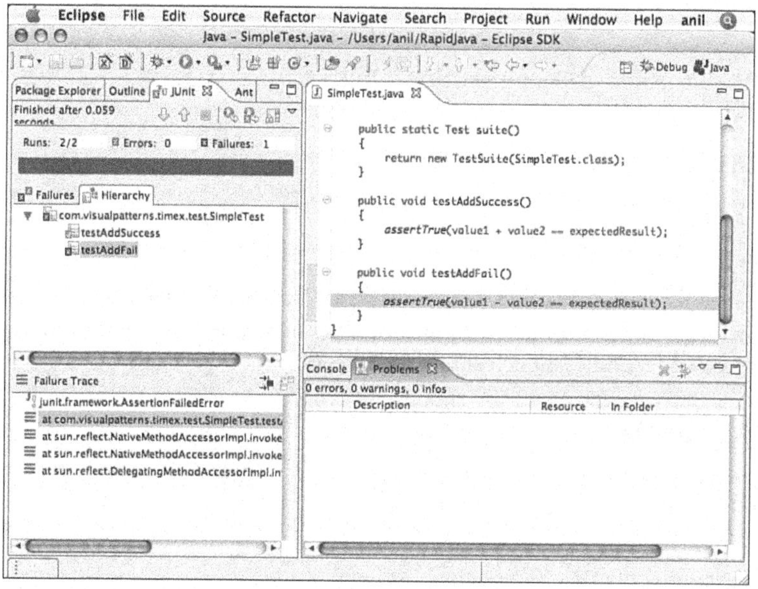

Figure 4.6   The JUnit view in Eclipse.

SimpleTest: Making the Tools Work Together

Assuming we have the JDK, Ant, and JUnit set up correctly, we should be able to now write a sample JUnit Test and try it out.

Regardless of which flavor of JUnit we use, we can either pass it our test class name or type it into the UI runner. For example, if we wanted to write a very simple test case to test the fact that $2 + 3 = 5$, we would do the following:

- Develop a JUnit test class—for example, SimpleTest.java.
- Run the JUnit class using one of the JUnit runners.

SimpleTest.java

This book's code file (available on the book's website) shows the complete code for SimpleTest.java. The code should be fairly straightforward to follow. There are two test methods: testAddSuccess and testAddFail, as shown here:

```
public void testAddSuccess()
{
    assertTrue(value1 + value2 == expectedResult);
}

public void testAddFail()
{
    assertTrue(value1 - value2 == expectedResult);
}
```

The `testAddSuccess` method will be successful, whereas the `testAddFail` method will fail (because 2 minus 3 does not equal 5). The success or failure is determined by the JUnit `assert` methods, which throw an exception if the test failed.

JUnit Assert Methods

We saw an example of JUnit's `assertTrue` method in our example previously; JUnit also provides several other flavors of assert methods, as shown next:

- `assertEquals`
- `assertFalse`
- `assertNotNull`
- `assertNotSame`
- `assertNull`
- `assertSame`
- `assertTrue`

Running SimpleTest (a Single JUnit TestCase)

To try out the code we saw for SimpleTest, we need to create the `SimpleTest.java` file, compile it, and try running it. So, let's create the `SimpleTest.java` file under our `src/java/com/visualpatterns/timex/test/` directory. Then we can simply type the **ant** command from the `timex/` directory to compile our unit test source code.

Now, let's try running our SimpleTest test case (from the top-level `timex/` directory) using the JUnit test runner, as demonstrated here:

```
C:\anil\rapidjava\timex>java
➥-cp \junit3.8.1\junit.jar;build/timex/WEB-INF/classes
➥junit.textui.TestRunner com.visualpatterns.timex.test.SimpleTest
```

We should see something similar to what is shown in Figure 4.7.

We could also run `SimpleTest.class` in the JUnit swing runner, as shown next (Figure 4.8 shows the result of this command):

```
java -cp \junit3.8.1\junit.jar;build/timex/WEB-INF/classes
➥junit.swingui.TestRunner
com.visualpatterns.timex.test.SimpleTest
```

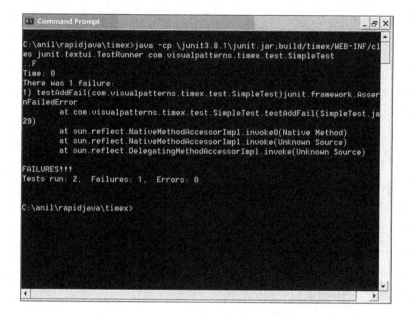

Figure 4.7   Running SimpleTest in the text runner.

The `junit.framework.AssertionFailedError` related messages you see in both the test runners is actually a good thing; these are valid JUnit errors because our testAddFail method failed.

Running JUnit Tests in a Batch

There is one more way we can run JUnit—that is, as an Ant task. Next we'll take a look at how we do that.

First, let's copy the `junit.jar` file from the JUnit install directory to the `<ant-home>/lib` directory; for example, on Microsoft Windows you would type something like **copy \junit3.8.1\junit.jar \apache-ant-1.6.5\lib**. This enables us to use the junit Ant task.

Second, we need to copy the same `junit.jar` to our `timex/lib` directory; this also will assist with our builds using Ant.

Now let's revisit our `build.xml` file. This file contains a target named `test`, which uses the *junit* task, as shown in the following excerpt:

```
<target name="test" depends="compile">
    <junit printsummary="true" showoutput="yes" filtertrace="false">
        <classpath refid="master-classpath"/>
      <batchtest fork="yes">
              <formatter type="plain"/>
        <fileset dir="${class.dir}">
```

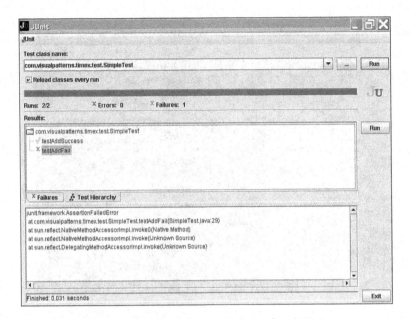

Figure 4.8   Running SimpleTest in the Swing-based JUnit runner.

If we run the command **ant test**, the results of the batch test would appear in a file named `TEST-com.visualpatterns.timex.test.SimpleTest.txt` in the current directory, an excerpt of which is shown here:

```
Testsuite: com.visualpatterns.timex.test.SimpleTest
Tests run: 2, Failures: 1, Errors: 0, Time elapsed: 0.021 sec

Testcase: testAddSuccess took 0.004 sec
Testcase: testAddFail took 0.003 sec
FAILED
```

That's pretty much all there is to JUnit! Although JUnit is a simple framework, it is powerful because you can have several test methods within each JUnit TestCase subclass (a *suite*). Furthermore, you can roll up the individual *suites* within other suites (with no limit). For example, you can create a class named `AllTests`, which calls the suites of all other Test classes in the test package.

Test First Design and Refactoring

Test-driven development (TDD) has brought the concept of *test first design* to the forefront. This approach has several benefits and hence we will write tests first in this book, whenever possible.

Writing tests first takes a little bit of getting used to, and many times, you will wonder if you really have the time to write tests given the pressure of deliverables. However, I find it is a nicer way to code (after you get the hang of it), particularly because it helps me think of how to design/develop my classes. Also, if you factor in the time you spend unit testing and fixing defects discovered during functional and user testing, you will find that this style of working can actually save time in the end.

Writing tests first has several benefits. For example, writing tests first ensures that you write only functional code that will actually be used; this is based on the assumption that you have written code to satisfy the unit tests, which themselves are based on the acceptance tests specified earlier in our business requirements. Second, if your code passes the unit and acceptance tests, you are done with that part of the code. Third, it can help you design your classes better because when you write the test first, you are experiencing firsthand how your actual classes/methods will be used. Last, test first can also help you to refactor with confidence because you can retest your refactored code quickly through JUnit unit tests to ensure that the refactored code works as the original version did (assuming there is little or no change to the external interface, as defined on refactoring. com).

Although, unit testing is only one part of the overall testing that occurs in corporations, it is something that developers should always do. Other testing includes functional testing, user acceptance testing (UAT), system integration testing (also known as interface testing), stress/load testing, and more.

We will use JUnit to implement our acceptance tests. The following are sample files to demonstrate our class-naming convention for test classes:

- `test/TimesheetListControllerTest.java`
- `test/TimesheetManagerTest.java`
- `test/ReminderEmailTest.java`

I have chosen to keep our JUnit test classes in a separate test package (that is, `com. visualpatterns.timex.test`) because I believe this is a cleaner design. However, I've also seen other developers keep the JUnit test classes in the same directory as the code being tested. For example, in this scenario, our `TimesheetListControllerTest. java` would be placed in our controller package.

Personal Opinion: Early Environment Setup Is Essential

After almost two decades of developing software, I am amazed how little some of the fundamental concepts have changed. Although the technologies have changed dramatically, underlying concepts such as environment setup, design, development, debugging, and so on remain fundamentally the same. One of things I have consistently found over the years is that the environment setup almost always involves more than people expect or plan for. So, getting the environment setup upfront is vital. Based on my personal experience, I like to recommend three things to my customers in regards to environment setup.

First, get the minimal but completely functional environment set up up front (directory structure and build scripts, for example). This should be consistent for all members of a software development team. Second, get a simple end-to-end demo working up front (for example, a user interface to database round-trip demo). Third, environment setup generally takes longer than people expect, so factor in enough time up front. This is one reason many Agile projects consider this iteration 0 (zero) or cycle 0 (Jim Highsmith), because a demo or environment setup doesn't produce anything tangible from a customer perspective; it merely gets the environment setup for developers and testers to work in.

Summary

In this chapter, we began the setup of our development environment with the following core tools required for Java development:

- Java development kit (JDK) setup
- Ant
- JUnit

However, we still have some environment-related setup remaining in the chapters ahead. For example, we need to install the database, the web server, Eclipse, and more. However, we will tackle each technology one at a time and as we need it, in the coming chapters.

Recommended Resources

The following websites are relevant to or provide additional information on the topics discussed in this chapter:

- Ant (built-in) Tasks   http://ant.apache.org/manual/tasksoverview.html
- Ant   http://ant.apache.org/
- Continuous Integration article   http://www.martinfowler.com/articles/continuousIntegration.html
- EasyMock   http://www.easymock.org/
- External Ant Tasks   http://ant.apache.org/external.html
- Framework for Integrated Test (FIT)   http://fit.c2.com/
- Full Life Cycle Object-Oriented Testing   http://www.ambysoft.com/essays/floot.html
- Java tutorial   http://java.sun.com/docs/books/tutorial/
- JDK   http://java.sun.com
- JUnit testing framework   http://junit.org

- Junit   http://junit.org
- Maven   http://maven.apache.org/
- Mock Objects   http://mockobjects.com
- Test Driven Development (TDD)   http://www.agiledata.org/essays/tdd.html
- Test First Guidelines   http://www.xprogramming.com/xpmag/
  testFirstGuidelines.htm

5

Using Hibernate for Persistent Objects

Release 1, Week 5, Iteration 2

Raj: When do you want to meet with Susan for the questions on the screens we are working on currently?

Steve: Let's just call her right now since it impacts our database persistence design. After all, she wants to be an active stakeholder since her department is paying for this application.

Within the first few years of my software development career, I came to realize more and more that information (data) is an organization's main asset; however, many developers tend to lose sight of this fact and get caught up in the latest cool tools.

We often use the words "information technology" (or simply, IT) but have you ever stopped to think about these two words? In my opinion, the definition is obvious: technology to manage information. Simply put, data is at the core of what we do in our industry because we are constantly moving data from point A to point B. No matter how many systems the data travels through, it originates on one end (point A; for example, a UI) and is typically viewed on the other end (point B; for example, reports). Furthermore, the data and its structure typically outlive the applications built around it; hence, it should arguably be the most important component of an overall software application's architecture.

Given my emphasis on data and databases, I will cover Hibernate before the other key products discussed later in this book, such as the Spring Framework and the Eclipse SDK.

What's Covered in This Chapter

In this chapter, we develop the classes we need to implement functionality for the first five user stories (page 63) for our sample application, Time Expression. So, we will do the following:

- Understand what object-relational mapping technology is and the benefits it offers.
- Install HSQLDB, a Java-based, lightweight relational database.
- Design our database.
- Write a Data Definition Language (DDL) script to create our database tables using Ant and test out some sample queries.
- Set up Hibernate, understand its basic concepts, and begin working with it.
- Demonstrate a simple and then a slightly more complex example (along with a corresponding unit test suite class) of using Hibernate for Time Expression's Department and Timesheet tables.
- Discuss advanced Hibernate areas for you to explore (should you need them).

> **Note**
> The complete code for the examples used in this chapter can be found within this book's code zip file (available on the book's website).

We will cover a lot of material in this chapter, so let's get started.

An Overview of Object-Relational Mapping (ORM)

It is no secret that relational databases are the most common type of databases in a majority of organizations today when compared to other formats (for example, object-oriented, hierarchical, network). Product names such as Oracle, Microsoft SQL Server, MySQL, IBM DB2, and Sybase are common terms used by developers in our line of work.

On the computer languages side of things, object-oriented (OO) programming has become the norm. Languages such as Java, C#, C++, and even OO scripting languages are common discussion topics among developers.

A majority of the software applications that use relational database and OO languages end up writing code to map the relational model to the OO model. This can involve anywhere from cumbersome mapping code (because of the use of embedded SQL or stored procedure calls) to heavy-handed technology, such as EJB's entity beans.

Because most of us seem to like both relational databases and OO, Object-Relational Mapping (ORM) has become a natural choice for working with POJOs (plain old Java objects), especially if you don't need the distributed and secure execution of EJB's entity beans (which also map object attributes to relational database fields).

Although you still need to map the relational model to the OO model, the mapping is typically done outside of the programming language, such as in XML files. Also, once this mapping is done for a given class, you can use instances of this class throughout your applications as POJOs. For example, you can use a `save` method for a given object and the underlying ORM framework will persist the data for you instead of you having to write tedious `INSERT` or `UPDATE` statements using JDBC, for example.

Hibernate is one such ORM framework and given its popularity in the world of Java today, we will use it for Time Expression. A few others, such as JDO, iBATIS, Java, and Apache ObJectRelationalBridge, are listed at the end of this chapter under "Recommended Resources."

Hibernate also supports the EJB 3.0 standard, so should you need to move to EJB 3.0, it'll be an easy transition (in fact, EJB 3.0 is based on many of the concepts and techniques found in Hibernate). EJB 3.0, as you might already know, aims to simplify working with EJB technology prior to this release; for example, EJB 3.0 provides a lighter-weight persistent API similar to the one provided by Hibernate. However, if you do not need the many services provided by EJB technology, you can use the Hibernate core technology by itself (without needing a big EJB container product such as an application server).

Before delving into Hibernate, let's review some basic concepts common across ORM technologies. Later we will look at lots of Hibernate Java code and XML file examples. After you have the hang of coding using an ORM framework, you will almost certainly not turn back to the old ways of working with relational databases.

Relationships and Cardinality

Database relationships are typically defined in terms of direction and cardinality (multiplicity in OO terminology). From an OO perspective, relationships are defined as association, inheritance, or aggregation. Many software development projects use ORM either with existing databases or are required to conform to standards established by a database group within the organization; hence, I will approach our relations discussion from a database perspective.

> **Note**
>
> Relationships can be viewed as unidirectional or bidirectional for objects. On the other hand, relations in a relational database are bidirectional by definition because related tables know of each other. However, if we were designing objects that map to the database, we would factor in both types of relations because object relationships have to be made bidirectional explicitly. So for the sake of our discussion on relationships and cardinality, we will pretend that the database can have both—unidirectional and bidirectional—relations.

Unidirectional is when one table knows of another, but not vice versa. For example, you might have a record that uses a unique primary key; this same primary key can be used as a foreign key by records in a child table, thereby establishing a unidirectional relationship. In a *bidirectional* relationship, records in both tables would know about each other. For example, assume we have two tables named Employee and Project to store information about which employees worked on which project. In the Project record, we might have an EmployeeId foreign key. On the flip side, we might have a ProjectId key in the Employee table.

Cardinality can be defined as *one-to-one*, *one-to-many* (or many-to-one depending on which direction you look at the relationship), and *many-to-many*. We look at each briefly:

- A one-to-one relationship is when a record in table 1 can have exactly one associated record in table 2. For example, a record in a Person table might have exactly one related record in a JobTitle table.

- A one-to-many relationship is typically seen in parent-child relationships where a parent record can have several related records in a child table (for example, related via the parent's primary key).

- A many-to-many relationship is where a record in table 1 can have several related records in table 2 and vice versa. For example, an Employee table might have more than one record in a Project table (because an employee can be involved in multiple projects). On the flip side, a record in the Project table might have several related records in the Employee table because a project can have multiple employees assigned to it. Also, this type of relationship is typically achieved by using an (extra) association table (for example, a ProjectEmployee table that contains foreign keys pointing to the two main tables).

> **Note**
> We will be looking at examples of relationships in this chapter from various perspectives, namely diagrams, code, and mappings. For example, Figures 5.1 and 5.2 show examples of one-to-many relationships.

Object Identity

An object identity (or simply, object id) is something that uniquely defines a persisted object (that is, a record in the database). It is commonly mapped to the primary key of a database table.

Cascade

Cascading can be defined as an action on a given entity flowing down to related entities. For example, if we wanted to maintain referential integrity between related parent-child tables in a database, we would delete records from a child table whenever its related parent is deleted, so that no orphan records are left lingering in the database. Similarly, when you read a parent record in, you may also want to read in all its children records. Cascading can be defined for each of the four CRUD operations—that is, create, read, update, and delete. Also, cascading is often handled via the use of database triggers.

Mapping

Before we can begin working with objects that store and retrieve data from a relational database, we must create mappings (usually in an XML file) between the database tables and Java classes. The mapping file typically contains properties, which essentially map an attribute (variable) in a class to a column in database. If you are new to some of these concepts, don't worry; after you see some examples later in this chapter, it'll start to become a bit clearer.

There are various mapping strategies we can employ, such as horizontal mapping, vertical mapping, and union mapping. In *vertical mapping*, each class in a hierarchy (abstract or concrete) is mapped to a different table. For example, if we have concrete classes named Dog and Cat, both inheriting from an abstract class named Animal, we would end up having three tables in the database—one for each class. In *horizontal mapping*, each concrete class is mapped to a table. In *union mapping*, many classes (presumably part of the same hierarchy) map to a single table.

Although vertical mapping is more flexible, it is also more complex because it requires multiple tables to extract all the data. Hence, we will use horizontal mapping because it is a simpler design and can provide faster performance, especially for simple to reasonably complex applications. To be more specific, our approach will involve one table per class mapping strategy.

In-Memory Versus Persisted Objects

When we are working with ORM technologies, there is a distinction between database objects we have in memory versus persisted ones. If the object does not exist in the database, or its attribute values do match the corresponding column values in the database, it is considered an in-memory object. For example, Hibernate distinguishes object states as persistent, detached, or transient (each is explained later in this chapter).

Another way to look at this distinction is that if we remove an object from memory (for example, by removing it from a Java collection), it does not necessarily mean the record has been physically deleted from the database (unless, of course, we mapped the collection in Hibernate to have automatic cascading during parent deletes).

Design of Our Sample Database

Now that we have covered some OR concepts, it is time to set up our database so that we can move one step closer to building an application's user interface with the help of the Spring Web MVC Framework.

As I mentioned in earlier chapters, the focus of this book is more on development and less on infrastructure. Given Java's vendor product portability (for example, operating system, web/application server, databases), in theory, it should be relatively easy to develop your application using one product but deploy to another application. In light of this, I chose the easiest (and consequently lightest-weight) products to set up. HSQLDB, a relational database, is one such product (discussed later in this chapter), and we will use it for Time Expression.

Denormalization

Before we look at HSQLDB, let's revisit our domain model from Chapter 3, "XP and AMDD-Based Architecture and Design Modeling," shown in Figure 5.1.

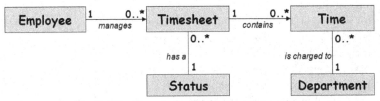

Figure 5.1 Domain model for Time Expression.

Given the simplicity of our sample application, Time Expression, and its domain model, we could create a physical database model (PDM), also known as an Entity-Relationship (ER) diagram, which contains entities identical to ones in our domain model, with the addition of columns and data types and other database constraints. However, let's denormalize it just a bit for performance and ease of development purposes.

Figure 5.2 shows a PDM, denormalized a bit from our Domain Model and with data types (for example, varchar) added to it. The denormalization is related only to the Timesheet and Time tables.

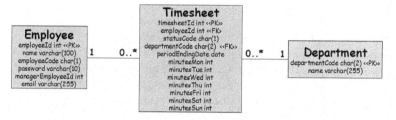

Figure 5.2   Physical database model for Time Expression.

Naming Convention

You will notice we are using Java-like naming conventions for the table and column names. This makes our job easier because we can use the same names across all artifacts related to Time Expression while also gaining consistency across them. In other words, we have matching names from User Story tag/name to controller classes to model (domain) objects to the Hibernate persistent bean Java code and finally, to the database tables and columns (shown in Figure 5.2).

This naming approach makes our job easier in two ways. First, we don't need to think about the naming convention for each layer, and second, it reduces the amount of mapping details we need to specify in our Hibernate class mapping files because we do not have to specify a corresponding column name for each property being mapped (as we will see later in this chapter).

However, in the real world, you might not have control over the database table/ column naming because a database group might have their own set of naming standards. In this case, it is easy to use Hibernate's *column* attribute to specify the database column name. I would also encourage following your organization's naming standards for consistency sake.

Note that for database objects (such as tables and sequences), I tend to use names starting with an uppercase letter, whereas column names start with a lowercase letter.

Database Design Disclaimers

The following are some disclaimers and/or explanations for the PDM we looked at in Figure 5.2.

Unused Columns

By combining the Timesheet and Time entities into one physical table, there is the possibility of wasted database space by unused columns. For example, there is a good chance that MinutesSat and MinutesSun will be less frequently used (unless employees in this company work most or all weekends). However, the advantages of the simpler design and performance arguably outweigh the disadvantages of a bit of wasted space.

Int Versus Float

We have used Minutes<Day> columns to store fractional hours worked (for example, 30 minutes or 0.5 hour) in the Timesheet table versus Hours<Day> columns or even float data types. The reason we did this is because I want to demonstrate how we can use the Spring Web MVC framework (in Chapter 7, "The Spring Web MVC Framework") to do automatic data conversions between the UI and the database. Also, an int will typically take up less physical storage space than a `float` will (for example, 2 bytes versus 4 bytes).

Password

We have a Password column in the Employee table. Typically, in larger organizations, you might end up using something like a central Lightweight Directory Access Protocol (LDAP) authentication service. However, this works well for our small (and sample) application, Time Expression.

DDL Script

Now that we have a PDM (see Figure 5.2), we can move to the next level down, which is to write a DDL script that can be used to create the actual databse. Our DDL script is embedded inside one of our Ant scripts, named `timexhsqldb.xml`. The table names, column names, and data types in our DDL script closely match the PDM in Figure 5.2, as they should.

Our DDL file primarily contains CREATE TABLE statements. However, I would like to point out a couple of additional notable items.

First, the primary key column of the `Timesheet` table is of data type `identity`, as shown in this code excerpt:

```
CREATE TABLE Timesheet
(
    timesheetId IDENTITY NOT NULL,
```

As you might already know, an `identity` is an auto increment database column (and is directly supported by Hibernate). For databases that do not support identity types, we can use a sequence type instead.

Second, we have seen some test data being inserted; this is for use by our JUnit test cases covered later in this chapter. For the sake of simplicity, I have not created any primary or foreign key constraints, as we typically should in a real-world application. Also, the focus of this chapter is to demonstrate features of Hibernate and not necessarily database design.

Where HSQLDB and Hibernate Fit into Our Architecture

Before we get too far along with HSQLDB and Hibernate, it is a good idea to revisit our architecture diagram that we developed earlier in this book. Figure 5.3 shows the diagram; notice where HSQLDB and Hibernate fit into the big picture (top-right).

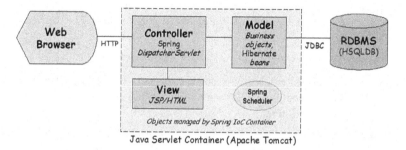

Figure 5.3   High-level architecture for Time Expression.

In later chapters, when we develop our web and schedule job-related code, we will need the classes and database we will create in this chapter.

HSQLDB

HSQLDB is a lightweight Java database engine that has been around since 2001. However, because it is a continuation of Thomas Mueller's closed Hypersonic SQL Project, it has actually been around longer than 2001. In short, the product is fairly mature.

HSQLDB provides a good amount of ANSI-92 SQL-compliant features (and many enhancements from more recent SQL standards)—more than we will need in this book. Furthermore, most of the features defined by JDBC 2, and some from JDBC 3, are also supported. HSQLDB's popularity has grown significantly since its inception a few years ago, and it is commonly found bundled with open source and commercial Java-related products such as JBoss, OpenOffice.org, Atlassian's JIRA, and many more.

At the time of this writing, the HSQLDB project was one of the top 50 ranking in more than 100,000 SourceForge.net projects.

HSQLDB can be found at http://hsqldb.org. There are ample setup instructions on this site to download, install, and configure it. I'm using version 1.8.x in this book.

HSQLDB Server and Convenient Ant Tasks

Now we need to start the HSQLDB server and create the database using our DDL file. However, first, let's copy the `hsqldb.jar` file from the HSQLDB install directory to our lib/ directory; for example, on my Microsoft Windows XP-based system, I typed the following:

```
copy \hsqldb\lib\hsqldb.jar \anil\rapidjava\timex\lib\
```

We will use our Ant script, `timexhsqldb.xml`, to start the server and also to create the database. This file is placed in the top-level directory of our sample application (in my case, this is `C:\anil\rapidjava\timex`).

Assuming our HSQLDB configuration is set up correctly, we can now type the **ant -f timexhsqldb.xml starthsql** command to start the HSQLDB server, as demonstrated here:

```
C:\anil\rapidjava\timex>ant -f timexhsqldb.xml starthsql
```

From another command window, we can type the **ant -f timexhsqldb.xml execddl** command to execute our DDL script for creating our database within HSQLDB, as demonstrated here:

```
C:\anil\rapidjava\timex>ant -f timexhsqldb.xml execddl
```

Before we move on, let's review parts of `timexhsqldb.xml`.

The following properties are related to HSQLDB; that is, the `hfile` property points to a local set of files under the `timex/data/` directory, the `halias` is the alias we will use in our client applications to connect to the HSQLDB server, and the `hport` is the port number the HSQLDB server will listen to:

```
<property name="hfile" value="-database.0 data/timexdb"/>
<property name="halias" value="timex"/>
<property name="hport" value="9005"/>
```

Next, the `starthsql` Ant target starts the HSQLDB server using the built-in Ant `java` task, as shown here:

```
<java fork="true"
    classname="${hclass}" classpath="${hjar}"
    args="${hfile} -dbname.0 ${halias} -port ${hport}"/>
```

The `execddl` Ant target uses the built-in `sql` task to execute our SQL DDL script, as shown here:

```
<sql classpath="${hjar}"
    driver="org.hsqldb.jdbcDriver"
    url="jdbc:hsqldb:hsql://localhost:${hport}/${halias}"
    userid="sa" password=""
    print="yes">
```

HSQLDB Database Manager and SqlTool

HSQLDB is bundled with two tools you should read about in the HSQLDB documentation: HSQL Database Manager (GUI) and SqlTool (command-line based). These are nice tools for working with our database. Meanwhile, you will find two convenient ant tasks in our `timexhsqldb.xml` file, `hsqldm` and `sqltool`, which can be used to start these two tools. For example, to start HSQL Database Manager, type the following on the command line:

```
ant -f timexhsqldb.xml hsqldm
```

After the Database Manager comes up, we can change the following parameters on the screen and work with our database in a GUI fashion, instantly (assuming the HSQLDB server is running in another window):

Type: HSQL Database Engine Server

URL: jdbc:hsqldb:hsql://localhost:9005/timex

HSQLDB Persistent and In-Memory Modes

Be sure to read about the various modes HSQLDB can run in (such as local versus server and in-memory versus persistent); we will use the server and persistent mode. For example, we could also use the very same HSQLDB database files (found under our `timex/data/` directory) as follows:

```
jdbc:hsqldb:file:${catalina.base}/webapps/timex/WEB-INF/data/timexdb
```

Incidentally, this is a feature that ties in nicely with the next section on bundling HSQLDB in an archive file.

Bundling HSQLDB in a Deployable Archive File

As an added benefit, HSQLDB has a small enough footprint to run entirely in memory. For example, we could deploy our sample application with HSQLDB, bundled in the same web archive (WAR) file, essentially making the WAR file a fully self-contained system with no need for an external database!

Personal Opinion: Data Is the Customer's Most Valuable Asset!

After all my years developing software, I still find that some people miss the whole point of Information Technology (IT). In my words, IT means technology for managing information. Information. As in data (databases).

Data is the customer's asset and hence the single most important component of a system. The data outlives most programs written to use it. This is precisely why the domain model, physical data model, and database refactoring are more important aspects of software development than, for example, *cool tools* or adding layers of unnecessary abstractions in your code.

When you're designing the database, one important thing to keep in mind is that the database can be used by multiple applications, not just a single, well-designed, object-oriented, n-tier application. For example, querying and reporting tools could also access the database for customer reports. So, as much as possible, the structure of the database should be somewhat independent of a single application. Furthermore, even the original application designed for the database can be retired after a few years, but the database will likely live on for a long time to come on.

For further reading on this matter, visit the agiledata.org website to learn more about database refactoring techniques. You may also want to visit the domaindrivendesign.org website, which is complementary to the AM website. For example, I found this line from an article by Eric Evans on this website, "the complexity that we should be tackling is the complexity of the domain itself—not the technical architecture, not the user interface, not even specific features."

To summarize, the data is the customer's asset, so focus on getting the domain model and database structure right using a combination of some upfront design and database refactoring as necessary.

Working with Hibernate

Hibernate has recently gained a lot of momentum in the world of Java database application development. Although products such as Toplink and others have been around for many years, Hibernate is open source (hence, free), stable, mature, well documented, and relatively easy to learn; these are probably just a few reasons why it is as popular as it is. Hibernate has been around for several years but was recently acquired by the JBoss group. (However, it continues to operate autonomously as an open source project.)

The Hibernate persistence framework can make working with relational databases using Java a pleasant experience. This is especially true if you have been developing using JDBC or using heavy-handed type entity beans. Defining the mappings can seem like a slight pain initially, but as you will see in later in this book, there are tools to generate these mapping files.

No Need for DAOs or DTOs

The extra work of defining mappings is well worth it because our persistence code will be cleaner and we will have automatically eliminated the need for Data Access Objects (DAOs), which typically are objects that know how to persist themselves. We also won't need Data Transfer Objects (DTOs), which are objects used to encapsulate business data and get transferred between layers of an application.

Supported Databases

As of the writing of this book, Hibernate supported the following databases (other databases are supported via community efforts):

- DB2
- HSQLDB
- Microsoft SQL Server
- MySQL

- Oracle
- PostgreSQL
- SAP DB
- Sybase
- TimesTen

Note

The databases are supported via Hibernate's *SQL Dialect* classes such as org.hibernate.dialect.HSQLDialect, org.hibernate.dialect.OracleDialect, org.hibernate.dialect.MySQLDialect, and so on.

Hibernate and EJB 3.x

One thing worth mentioning here is that members of the Hibernate/JBoss team are part of the EJB 3.0 expert group, a group that helped simplify the EJB specifications. It should come as no surprise, then, that the latest version of Hibernate supports the EJB 3.0 specification. However, we will not cover the EJB 3.0 here because it is outside the scope of this book. The focus of this book is on lighter-weight (and open source) frameworks, not heavy-handed specifications that require commercial application servers to use these features.

Simple Test for Hibernate Setup

Before diving into Hibernate concepts and terminology, let's look at a simple hibernate program and the setup involved. The following sections outline the steps required to get our first test program, SimpleTest, working. But first, let's take another look at the development directory structure we established in Chapter 3.

Figure 5.4 shows the development directory structure for Time Expression. It is important to review this again because we will create several files in this chapter and refer to them using their relative path names—for example, model/Department.java means file Department.java in the timex/src/java/com/visualpatterns/timex/model/ directory.

Hibernate XML Files and Related Java Files

We will place the three types of Hibernate files (discussed next), a Hibernate configuration file, related Java classes, and table mapping files, in the same directory. This is the practice recommended in Hibernate documentation and examples.

The naming convention for the Hibernate mapping files is typically the name of the Java class name with a suffix of .hbm.xml—for example, Timesheet.hbm.xml.

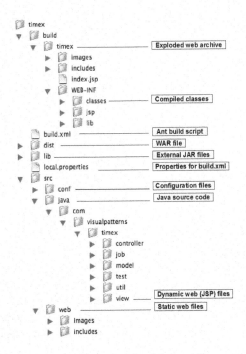

Figure 5.4   The Time Expression development directory structure.

Hibernate Configuration File (`hibernate.cfg.xml`)

First we will create a file named `hibernate.cfg.xml` in the `timex/src/java/com/visualpatterns/timex/model/` directory. This file will contain a SessionFactory definition (discussed later in this chapter) and reference to our first mapping file, `Department.hbm.xml`. Let's review some of the interesting lines from this file:

The following lines show the HSQLDB-related configuration (as we saw in `timexhsqldb.xml`, previously):

```
<property name="connection.driver_class">
    org.hsqldb.jdbcDriver
</property>
<property name="connection.url">
    jdbc:hsqldb:hsql://localhost:9005/timex
</property>
<property name="connection.username">sa</property>
```

The following lines from our `hibernate.cfg.xml` show the reference to the mapping files we will create in this chapter:

```
<mapping resource="Department.hbm.xml"/>
<mapping resource="Employee.hbm.xml"/>
<mapping resource="Timesheet.hbm.xml"/>
```

Using the complete `hibernate.cfg.xml` file, we will be able to create a Hibernate SessionFactory (discussed later in this chapter).

Mapping File (`Department.hbm.xml`)

We will create our first mapping file, `Department.hbm.xml`, in the `timex/src/java/com/visualpatterns/timex/model/` directory.

To keep things simple, I chose to start with the Department table because it is one of the simpler tables, and we will also use it in our slightly more complex example later in this chapter. Let's review the `Department.hbm.xml` file a bit closer.

The following line maps our Java class to the database table:

```
<class name="com.visualpatterns.timex.model.Department" table="Department">
```

The following line establishes `departmentCode` as the object id (as we discussed earlier) and the database primary key, and also maps the two:

```
<id name="departmentCode" column="departmentCode">
```

The `generator class="assigned"` value shown next tells Hibernate that we will be responsible for setting the value of this object id in our Java class, and Hibernate does not need to do anything special, such as get the next sequence from an auto-increment type column (for example, HSQLDB's identity data type):

```
<generator class="assigned"/>
```

This line maps the remainder of the Department table—that is, the name column to a name property in the `Department.java` class file (discussed next):

```
<property name="name" column="name"/>
```

Java Code

We will write two Java classes, one called `com.visualpatterns.timex.model.Department` and another called `com.visualpatterns.timex.test.HibernateTest`.

Department.java

The `Department.java` (under `src/java/com/visualpatterns/timex/model`) contains a simple JavaBean class, which provides *accessors* (*get methods* or *getters*) and *mutators* (*set methods* or *setters*) for these two variables:

```
String departmentCode;
String name;
```

HibernateTest.java

Now we will write some simple code to accomplish two things: test the Hibernate setup and also look at a basic example of how to use Hibernate. Let's review our `HibernateTest.java` file (under `src/java/com/visualpatterns/timex/test`) step-by-step.

The first few lines show how we obtain a Hibernate SessionFactory class and get a single Department record back for the departmentCode "IT":

```
SessionFactory sessionFactory = new Configuration().configure()
        .buildSessionFactory();
Session session = sessionFactory.getCurrentSession();
Transaction tx = session.beginTransaction();
Department department;
department = (Department) session.get(Department.class, "IT");
System.out.println("Name for IT = " + department.getName());
```

The following lines shows how to get and process a `java.util.List` of Department objects.

```
List departmentList = session.createQuery("from Department").list();
for (int i = 0; i < departmentList.size(); i++)
{
    department = (Department) departmentList.get(i);
    System.out.println("Row " + (i + 1) + "> " + department.getName()
        + " (" + department.getDepartmentCode() + ")");
}
```

The remaining notable line closes out theSessionFactory.

```
sessionFactory.close();
```

Note the `HibernateTest.java` file provides a simple example of using Hibernate by bunching all the code in a single (main) method. Later in this chapter, we will look at a better way of building a SessionFactory and subsequently obtaining Session objects from it.

Now we are going to try running our test using our Ant `build.xml` file, introduced in Chapter 4, "Environment Setup: JDK, Ant, and JUnit." Our Ant target, `hibernatetest`, is as follows:

```
<target name="hibernatetest" depends="build">
  <java fork="true" classpathref="master-classpath"
      classname="com.visualpatterns.timex.test.HibernateTest"/>
</target>
```

To run our test, we need to:

- Change (`cd`) to the `timex/` (top-level) directory.
- Type the **ant hibernatetest** command, as shown in Figure 5.5.

Notice that there are errors on the screen, such as `package org.hibernate does not exist`. This means it is time to download and set up Hibernate in our environment!

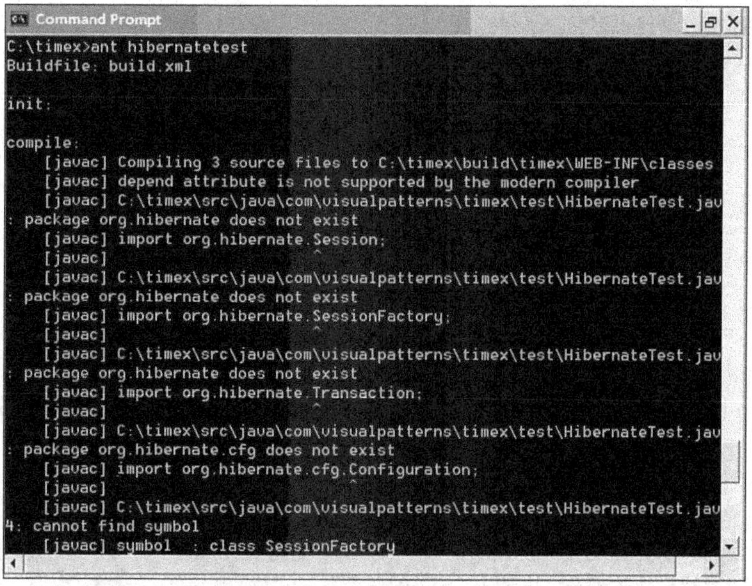

Figure 5.5 Ant errors due to missing `lib/hibernate3.jar`
file in classpath.

Installing Hibernate

Hibernate can be found at http://hibernate.org. At this point, we will follow the setup instructions provided on this site to download and install it to the recommended (or default) directory.

After we have the Hibernate installed, we will copy all the recommended libraries (for example, `hibernate3.jar` and `antlr.jar`) in the Hibernate documentation to the `rapidjava/lib` directory.

Note that I also needed to copy `ehcache-1.1.jar` and `antlr-2.7.6rc1.jar` (which was not mentioned in the Hibernate reference documentation at the time of this writing). Here is what I ended up with, in my `timex/lib/` directory:

- `antlr-2.7.6rc1.jar`
- `asm-attrs.jar`
- `asm.jar`
- `cglib-2.1.3.jar`
- `commons-collections-2.1.1.jar`
- `commons-logging-1.0.4.jar`
- `dom4j-1.6.1.jar`

- `ehcache-1.1.jar`
- `hibernate3.jar`
- `jta.jar`
- `log4j-1.2.11.jar`

Before rerunning our test, we need to temporarily alter the `hibernate.cfg.xml` file. Because we have only `Department.hbm.xml` implemented, we need to temporarily remove the following lines (to conduct this test) from our `hibernate.cfg.xml` file:

```
<mapping resource="Timesheet.hbm.xml"/>
<mapping resource="Employee.hbm.xml"/>
```

Finally, we can rerun the **ant hibernatetest** command. If we run the ant as shown earlier in Figure 5.5, this time our command is successful, as shown in Figure 5.6!

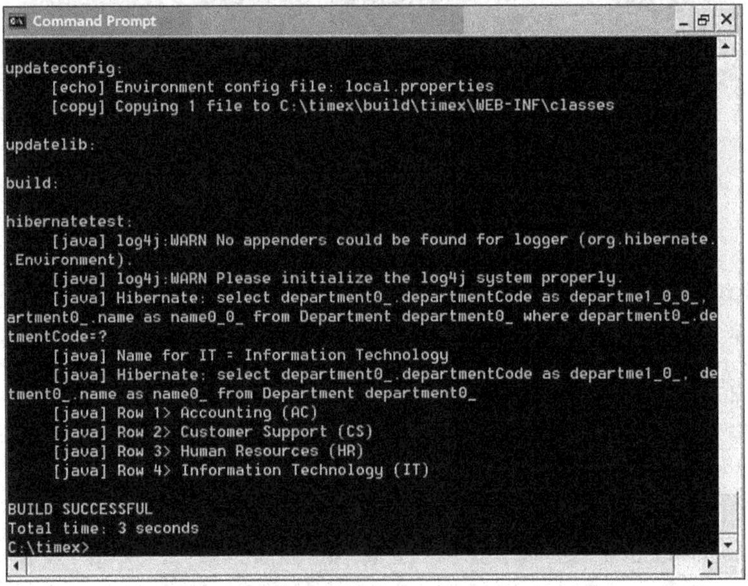

Figure 5.6   Output of the HibernateTest class.

At this point, we can reinsert the following two lines into the `hibernate.cfg.xml` file:

```
<mapping resource="Timesheet.hbm.xml"/>
<mapping resource="Employee.hbm.xml"/>
```

Notice the log4j warning messages in Figure 5.6. We could ignore these because they are harmless. However, we'll go ahead and create a minimal `log4j.properties` file (available in this book's code zip file) in our `timex/src/conf` directory. Logging will be discussed in more detail in Chapter 9, "Logging, Debugging, Monitoring, and Profiling."

Hibernate Basics

Now that we have looked at a small preview of Hibernate-related Java code and XML files, let's get a high-level understanding of some basic Hibernate concepts before we look at slightly more complex Hibernate code for the Time Expression application.

Dialect

Hibernate provides dialect classes for the various supported databases mentioned earlier. This is essentially to ensure that the correct and most optimized SQL is used for the database product being used. For example, we are using the `org.hibernate.dialect.HSQLDialect` class for HSQLDB.

SessionFactory, Session, and Transaction

SessionFactory, as you might guess, manages a collection of Session objects. Each SessionFactory is mapped to a single database. The Session object essentially is a wrapper for a JDBC connection and is also a factory for Transaction objects. A Transaction is a wrapper for the underlying transaction, typically a JDBC transaction.

Built-In Connection Pooling

A side but important benefit of using Hibernate is that it provides built-in database connection pooling—hence, one less thing for us to worry about. Connection pooling, as you might be aware, is used to create a specified pool of open database connections (see `connection.pool_size` property in our `hibernate.cfg.xml`). By using a pool of connections, we can achieve more efficiency in our use of the database because existing open connections are reused. Furthermore, we get performance gains because we reuse open connections, thereby avoiding any delays in opening and closing database connections.

Working with Database Records (as Java Objects)

Several methods available in Hibernate's org.hibernate.Session interface enable us to work with database records as objects. The most notable methods are *save, load, get, update, merge, saveOrUpdate, delete,* and *createQuery* (several of these are demonstrated later in this chapter).

Another noteworthy interface to mention is org.hibernate.Query, which is returned by calling the Session.createQuery Hibernate method in our `HibernateTest.java` file. The Query class can be used to obtain a group of records in the form of a java.util. Collection object (for example, Hibernate provides mapping elements such as an array, set, bag, and others).

One last interface worth mentioning here is org.hibernate.Criteria, which can be used for database queries in an OO fashion, as an alternative to the Query class (which is HQL based).

We will look at examples of most of these interfaces and methods in this chapter.

Object States

Hibernate defines three states for object instances: *persistent*, *detached*, and *transient*. *Persistent* objects are ones that are currently associated with a Hibernate session; as soon as the session is closed (or the object is *evicted*), the objects become *detached*. Hibernate ensures that Java objects in a persistent state for an active session match the corresponding record(s) in the database. *Transient* objects are ones that are not (and most likely, never were) associated with Hibernate session and also do not have an object identity.

Data Types

Hibernate supports a large number of Java, SQL, and Hibernate types—more than you will probably need for a typical application. Also, you can have Hibernate automatically convert from one type to another by using a different type for a given property in a entity/class mapping file.

The following is a partial list of types supported: integer, long, short, float, double, character, byte, boolean, yes_no, true_false, string, date, time, timestamp, calendar, calendar_date, big_decimal, big_integer, locale, timezone, currency, class, binary, text, serializable, clob, and blob.

Hibernate Query Language (HQL)

HQL is Hibernate's robust SQL-like query language, which is not case sensitive. HQL has many of the features defined in ANSI SQL and beyond, because it is fully object-oriented and supports OO concepts such as inheritance, polymorphism, and more. The following are some basic clauses and features supported in HQL. You will see some examples of these later in the chapter:

- SELECT, UPDATE, DELETE, INSERT, FROM, WHERE, GROUP BY, ORDER BY
- Joins (inner, outer)
- Subqueries
- Aggregate functions (for example, sum and count)
- Expressions and functions (mathematical, string, date, internal functions, and more)

Furthermore, Hibernate provides methods that enable you to use native SQL (discussed in Chapter 10, "Beyond the Basics") for the somewhat rare occasions when HQL is insufficient.

You will see basic examples of HQL throughout this chapter.

Unique Object Identifier (`<id>`)

Hibernate requires mapped classes to identify a table's primary key via the `<id>` element. For example, the following code excerpt from our `Department.hbm.xml` file shows departmentCode defined as the primary key (for the Department table mapping):

```
<id name="departmentCode" column="departmentCode">
   <generator class="assigned"/>
</id>
```

Notice the generator class of type "assigned" in this code excerpt; this means the application will provide a value for this id property prior to any database operations on this object.

Hibernate provides several ways to generate unique ids for inserted records, including increment, identity, sequence, hilo, seqhilo, uuid, guid, native, assigned, select, and foreign. The hibernate reference documentation provides ample explanation of each of these. We will use the assigned and identity generators for our examples.

Mandatory Hibernate Transactions

According to the Hibernate documentation related to working with this API, "transactions are never optional, all communication with a database has to occur inside a transaction, no matter if you read or write data."

Hence, you will find the following types of calls in all our Hibernate-related code:

- `session.beginTransaction()`
- `session.getTransaction().commit()`
- `session.getTransaction().rollback()`

HibernateUtil.java

The Hibernate reference documentation recommends the use of a helper class (named `HibernateUtil`, for example) for setting up a SessionFactory and providing access to it (via a getter method).

A sample `HibernateUtil.java` class file can be found under the `timex\src\java\com\visualpatterns\timex\test` directory. This helper class contains only a few lines of actual code. The first notable lines are the following, which build a SessionFactory object:

```
sessionFactory = new Configuration().configure()
                            .buildSessionFactory();
```

The only other interesting code in this class is a convenient getter method to return the SessionFactory, as shown here:

```
public static SessionFactory getSessionFactory()
{
   return sessionFactory;
}
```

Then we can obtain a Session object, as demonstrated in this code snippet, which fetches a list of Department database objects:

```
List departmentList=null;
Session session = HibernateUtil.getSessionFactory().getCurrentSession();
session.beginTransaction();
departmentList = session.createQuery("from Department ORDER BY name").list();
session.getTransaction().commit();
```

Further Reading

Again, we have looked only at high-level explanations of the various Hibernate concepts. I will refer you to the Hibernate documentation (found on their website) for detailed information on the concepts discussed here; however, we will be using many of these concepts in our examples, so I will provide additional explanations and code examples along the way.

Now that we have the basics covered, let's begin doing some real work by implementing a full-fledged example to exercise some of Hibernate's many features.

Developing TimesheetManager.java Using Hibernate

If you think about the business requirements of Time Expression, combined with the prototyped screens we looked at in Chapter 2, "The Sample Application: An Online Timesheet System," and the database model shown in Figure 5.2, you can easily see that the Timesheet table is at the heart of our sample application (Time Expression). Hence, I've chosen to use this table as an example in this chapter because our requirements will exercise both read and write type database operations on this table. For example, most screens in Time Expression will either modify data in this table or fetch data from it.

Based on the class/package design we defined in Chapter 3 and the Hibernate configuration files needed, here are the files we will end up with for the example to follow:

- test/TimesheetManagerTest.java
- model/TimesheetManager.java
- model/Timesheet.java
- model/Timesheet.hbm.xml

The following sections review each of these files in more detail.

TimesheetManagerTest.java

Let's begin by writing a little JUnit test class. Remember, write tests first whenever possible. We already looked at the reasons and benefits of writing tests *first* in Chapter 4, so I won't repeat the same information here.

The only class we need to write a unit test for is TimesheetManager because Timesheet.java is a JavaBean and hence has no *real* logic in its methods (just setters and getters).

If we analyze the following two screens from Chapter 2, we can come up with the type of functionality we need our TimesheetManager class to provide:

- Timesheet List—A list of Timesheet records for a given employeeId.
- Enter Hours—The capability to insert and update a single Timesheet record.

Let's look at an example of the functionality we need and how we might implement it. We know we need a list of Timesheet records for the Timesheet List screen (shown in Figure 5.7); this list will be fetched from the database using an employeeId (that is, the employee who is logged in) and also for the current pay period. Hence, I can already picture a method in the TimesheetManager class with a signature that looks something like this: getTimesheet(int employeeId, Date periodEndingDate). So, we can easily write a test case (method) such as testGetByEmployeeIdAndPeriod().

Timesheet List

Click here to add a new timesheet, or select one from the list below.

Period Ending	Hours	Timesheet Id
January 21, 2007	39.50	1234
January 14, 2007	43.00	1239
January 07, 2007	40.00	1242
December 31, 2006	40.00	1299

Figure 5.7   Timesheet list prototype screen (from Chapter 2).

This book's code zip file contains TimesheetManagerTest.java, a complete JUnit test suite class to exercise all the methods in our TimesheetManager class.

> **Note**
>
> Note that I didn't write the entire test class in one shot. As I mentioned earlier, unit testing and coding happen in the same sitting. So you would write a little test code (perhaps a few lines in a single method), write a little implementation code, compile, try, and repeat the steps until the method has been fully implemented. The idea is to write small methods, which can be tested relatively easily. This technique also enables us to write the minimal code required to satisfy our user requirements (nothing more, nothing less).

Let's review some of the test code behind this class next; we won't walk through the entire file because we only require fetching (get) of Timesheet objects and saving of individual ones, so let's review methods related to these operations next.

testGetByEmployeeId()

Let's start with the testGetByEmployeeId() method. The first few lines of this code ensure that we get a java.util.List of Timesheet objects back before proceeding:

```
List timesheetList = timesheetManager.getTimesheets();
assertNotNull(timesheetList);
assertTrue(timesheetList.size() > 0);
```

After we know we have at least one Timesheet object, we can fetch Timesheet records using the employeeId found in the first Timesheet object, as shown here:

```
int employeeId=((Timesheet)timesheetList.get(0)).getEmployeeId();
timesheetList = timesheetManager.getTimesheets(employeeId);
assertNotNull(timesheetList);
```

Now we can simply test each Timesheet object in the list to ensure that these records belong to the employeeId we requested, as demonstrated next:

```
Timesheet timesheet;
for (int i=0; i < timesheetList.size(); i++)
{
    timesheet = (Timesheet)timesheetList.get(i);
    assertEquals(employeeId, timesheet.getEmployeeId());
    System.out.println(">>>> Department name = "
                        + timesheet.getDepartment().getName());
}
```

testSaveSingle()

Let's review one more test method from our TimesheetManagerTest.java file, testSaveSingle. The first half of this method sets up a Timesheet object to save; however, the following lines are worth exploring:

```
timesheetManager.saveTimesheet(timesheet);
Timesheet timesheet2 = timesheetManager.getTimesheet(EMPLOYEE_ID,
        periodEndingDate);
assertEquals(timesheet2.getEmployeeId(), timesheet.getEmployeeId());
assertEquals(timesheet2.getStatusCode(), "P");
```

We essentially save a Timesheet object, and then fetch it back from the database and compare the two objects' attributes using the assertEquals method.

TimesheetManager.java

Next we will look at our bread-and-butter class (so to speak). We will use this class extensively in Chapter 7 when we implement our user interfaces (for example, Timesheet List and Enter Hours).

The key methods we will review here are getTimesheets, getTimesheet, and saveTimesheet.

Let's start with the TimesheetManager. getTimesheets(int employeeId) method. The key lines code essentially get a java.util.List of Timesheet objects from the database using the Hibernate Session.createQuery method, as shown here:

```
timesheetList = session.createQuery(
        "from Timesheet" + " where employeeId = ?").setInteger(0,
        employeeId).list();
```

The next method, `TimesheetManager.getTimesheet(int employeeId, Date periodEndingDate)`, is slightly different from the `getTimesheets(int employeeId)` method we just looked at; the key difference is the use of Hibernate's `uniqueResult` method, which is a convenient method to get only one object back from a query. The following code shows the notable lines from our *getTimesheet* method:

```
timesheet = (Timesheet) session.createQuery(
        "from Timesheet" + " where employeeId = ?"
            + " and periodEndingDate = ?").setInteger(0,
        employeeId).setDate(1, periodEndingDate).uniqueResult();
```

The last method in TimesheetManager that we will review here is `saveTimesheet(Timesheet timesheet)`. This is a very straightforward method, and the only code worth showing here is the Hibernate's `session.saveOrUpdate` method, which either does an INSERT or UPDATE underneath the covers, depending on whether the record exists in the database:

```
session.saveOrUpdate(timesheet)
```

`Timesheet.java` (and `Timesheet.hbm.xml`)

Before we can successfully compile and use `TimesheetManager.java`, we need to quickly write files it relies on, namely `Timesheet.java` and its mapping file, `Timesheet.hbm.xml` (both available in this book's code file). There is not much to these files; the Java code is a simple JavaBean and the XML file simply maps the bean's properties to the appropriate database columns.

Employee.* and DepartmentManager.java

The other files provided in this book's code zip file but not explicitly discussed here include the following as we will need these to implement our first five user stories (page 36).

At this point, we will create these files in our `src/java/com/visualpatterns/timex/model` directory:

- `DepartmentManager.java`
- `Employee.hbm.xml`
- `Employee.java`
- `EmployeeManager.java`

Files Required in Classpath

The various Hibernate files, such as the `hibernate.cfg.xml` and mapping files (for example, `Department.hbm.xml`) need to be in the CLASSPATH; accordingly our Ant script, `build.xml`, automatically copies these files to the `timex/build/timex/WEB-INF/classes` directory during a build process.

Running the Test Suite Using Ant

Now we can run our test suite (TimesheetManagerTest) discussed previously. However, before we can run the test suite, we need to run HSQLDB in server mode. We can either do it manually as shown here:

```
java -cp /hsqldb/lib/hsqldb.jar org.hsqldb.Server
➥   -database.0 data\time xdb -dbname.0 timex -port 9005
```

> **Note**
> I've assumed the HSQLDB directory is installed under the root directory (that is, `/hsqldb`); alter the `java` command shown here according to your environment.

Or we can run it using our handy Ant script, as follows:

```
ant -f timexhsqldb.xml starthsql
```

After we start up the HSQLDB server successfully and have all our files created in the correct directories, we can test our new classes by typing **ant rebuild test** on the command line (from the timex/ top-level directory). The output of this command is shown Figure 5.8.

Deleting Records

We covered database reads and writes. However, we have not covered deleting records, a basic need in any CRUD application. Deleting records is not part of our Time Expression application's requirement. Nevertheless, I've added one for demonstration purposes. The only thing different from what we have already seen is the Session.delete, which deletes a database record (object) and Session.load, which fetches a record from the database, as demonstrated here:

```
session.delete(session.load(Timesheet.class, new Integer(timesheetId)));
```

Alternatively, the delete code can be written using the `Query.executeUpdate()` method, useful for bulk processing, as shown here:

```
int updated = session.createQuery("DELETE from Timesheet"
                            + " where timesheetId = ?")
                .setInteger(0, timesheetId)
                .executeUpdate();
```

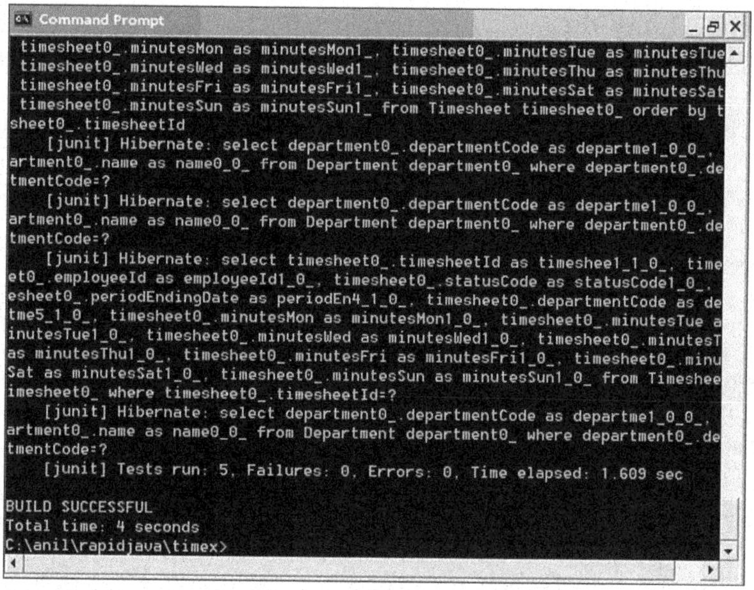

Figure 5.8   Running JUnit test suites via Ant.

Criteria Queries

Until now, we have utilized Hibernate's Query interface (via the `Session.createQuery` method) to fetch records from the database. However, there is a slightly more dynamic, and arguably cleaner, way of fetching records using Hibernate's Criteria interface. This provides a more object-oriented approach, which can result in fewer bugs because it can be type checked and can avoid potential HQL-related syntax errors/exceptions. This method is cleaner because developer does use a more object-oriented approach—more objects rather than simple text queries, hence, more type checking, hence fewer bugs, especially, QueryExceptions. It could be a problem though if query syntax is too complex.

The Criteria interface can be obtained using the `Session.createCriteria` method as shown in the following code excerpt:

```
timesheetList = session.createCriteria(Timesheet.class)
                    .add(Restrictions.eq("employeeId", employeeId))
                    .list();
```

In addition, Hibernate provides several classes in the org.hibernate.criterion package, which work with the Criteria interface to provide robust querying functionality using objects. Some examples of these classes are Restrictions, Order, Junction, Distinct, and several others.

Exception Handling

Most of the database-related exceptions thrown while using the Hibernate API are wrapped inside org.hibernate.HibernateException; more details on this can be found in Hibernate's reference manual. Meanwhile, the following strategy is recommended in Hibernate's reference manual for handling database exceptions:

"If the Session throws an exception (including any SQLException), you should immediately rollback the database transaction, call Session.close() and discard the Session instance. Certain methods of Session will not leave the session in a consistent state. No exception thrown by Hibernate can be treated as recoverable. Ensure that the Session will be closed by calling close() in a finally block."

We are following these guidelines, of course. However, you might also have noticed in our model code that we rethrow any caught exceptions. It is generally a good idea to pass exceptions up the call stack, so the top-level methods can determine how to process the exception. We will discuss exception handling in more detail in Chapter 10.

I think the problem with this piece of code may be that the developer will never know what exception has actually occurred, because all we do in the catch block is roll back the transaction. Some kind of logging mechanism or exception propagation mechanism to outer callers is necessary to make sure the exception is noticed and handled properly (otherwise, we'll never know about the failure details, except by knowing that timesheet did not get saved).

Other Hibernate Features

Up to now in this chapter, we have looked at some basic Hibernate features. Next, let's review some additional, slightly more advanced, Hibernate concepts.

Associations

The physical database design, the mapping, and the Java classes for Time Expression are all fairly straightforward. We have essentially used a one-class-per-table mapping strategy to keep the design simple and fast. However, we have utilized a many-to-one association to fetch the corresponding Department record, which we can use to obtain the name of the department. We will need this functionality on various Time Expression screens that display the full Department.name (versus just the Department.departmentCode).

Let's dissect the Java code and XML mapping related to this association.

First, the persistent attribute Java bean code can be found in Department.java file; an excerpt of it, is shown here:

```
private Department department;

public Department getDepartment()
{
    return department;
}
```

```
public void setDepartment(Department department)
{
    this.department = department;
}
```

Secondly, the many-to-one mapping can be found in our `Timesheet.hbm.xml` file:

```
<many-to-one name="department" column="departmentCode"
             class="com.visualpatterns.timex.model.Department"
             lazy="false" not-found="ignore" cascade="none"
             insert="false" update="false"/>
```

Finally, the code on how we obtain the department name can be found in our `TimesheetManagerTest.java` file:

```
System.out.println(">>>> Department name = " +
timesheet.getDepartment().getName());
```

Locking Objects (Concurrency Control)

Database locking can apply to any database applications, not just ones based on ORM technologies. There are two common strategies when dealing with updates to database records, *pessimistic locking* and *optimistic locking*.

Optimistic locking is more scalable than pessimistic locking when dealing with a highly concurrent environment. However pessimistic locking is a better solution for situations where the possibility of simultaneous updates to the same data by multiple sources (for example, users) is common, hence making the possibility of "data clobbering," a likely scenario. Let's look at a brief explanation of each of these two locking strategies.

Pessimistic locking is when you want to reserve a record for exclusive update by locking the database record (or entire table). Hibernate supports pessimistic locking (using the underlying database, not in-memory) via one of the following methods:

- `Session.get`
- `Session.load`
- `Session.lock`
- `Session.refresh`
- `Query.setLockMode`

Although each of the methods accepts different parameters, the one common parameter across all is the `LockMode` class, which provides various locking modes such as NONE, READ, UPGRADE, UPGRADE_NOWAIT, and WRITE. For example, to obtain a *Timesheet* record for updating, we could use the following code (assuming the underlying database supports locking):

```
public Timesheet getTimesheetWithLock(int timesheetId)
{
    Session session =
```

```
        HibernateUtil.getSessionFactory().getCurrentSession();
    session.beginTransaction();
    Timesheet timesheet = (Timesheet)session.get(Timesheet.class,
            new Integer(timesheetId), LockMode.UPGRADE);
    session.getTransaction().commit();
    session.close();0

    return timesheet;
}
```

Optimistic locking means that you will not lock a given database record or table and
instead check a column/property of some sort (for example, a timestamp column) to
ensure the data has not changed since you read it. Hibernate supports this using a
version property, which can either be checked manually by the application or automatically by Hibernate for a given session. For example, the following code excerpt is taken
verbatim out of the Hibernate reference documentation and shows how an application
can manually compare the oldVersion with the current version using a getter method
(for example, getVersion):

```
// foo is an instance loaded by a previous Session
session = factory.openSession();
int oldVersion = foo.getVersion();
session.load( foo, foo.getKey() );
if ( oldVersion!=foo.getVersion ) throw new StaleObjectStateException();
foo.setProperty("bar");
session.flush();
session.connection().commit();
session.close();
```

StaleObjectStateException, shown in the previous example, is an exception in the
org.hibernate package.

Lots More Hibernate

Although we covered a lot of material in this chapter, there is much more to Hibernate.
However, as I mentioned earlier, entire books exist on Hibernate, and we cannot cover
everything about this technology in one chapter. Nevertheless, I have given you enough
here to build some reasonably complex applications using Java, Hibernate, and relational
databases.

Other Hibernate advanced topics not covered here, but ones you might want to
explore, include

- Advanced mappings (for example, bidirectional associations, ternary associations,
  sorted collections, component mapping, inheritance mapping, and more)
- Advanced HQL
- Annotations (and XDoclet)
- Filters

- Hibernate SchemaExport utility
- Inheritance mapping
- Interceptors
- Locking objects
- Performance improvement strategies (for example, fetching strategies, second-level cache)
- Scrollable iteration and pagination
- Transaction management (advanced topics)
- Other areas such as using stored procedures, native SQL, and more

Summary

In this chapter, we developed the classes we need to implement functionality for the first five user stories (page 36). Furthermore, these classes are directly relevant to the code we will develop in Chapter 7 and the scheduled jobs in Chapter 10.

In this chapter, we accomplished the following:

- Learned what object-relational mapping technology is and the benefits it offers
- Installed HSQLDB
- Designed our database
- Used DDL script to create our database tables and some test data
- Setup Hibernate, covered its basic concepts, and began working with it
- Developed a simple and then a slightly more complex example (along with a corresponding unit test suite class) of using Hibernate for Time Expression's Department and Timesheet tables
- Discussed advanced Hibernate topics and other features for you to explore (should you need them)

However, we are not done with Hibernate just yet! For example, we will use some of the classes coded in this chapter in our web application in the next chapter. In addition, I will demonstrate how we can use an Eclipse plug-in to generate the Hibernate mapping files (in Chapter 8, "The Eclipse Phenomenon!").

For now, we are ready to dive into the next two chapters where we enter the world of user interfaces by using the Spring MVC web framework to develop our web UI.

We will also begin working with the Eclipse SDK in Chapter 8 and see how much time IDEs can save. Till now, I have intentionally used the command line because I truly believe learning the fundamentals first by using the manual way will help you better understand how things work behind the scenes. It can also help you drop back to the command line in case the IDE does not provide a certain functionality or it has a known bug.

Recommended Resources

The following websites are relevant to and provide additional information on the topics discussed in this chapter:

- Agile Data   http://www.agiledata.org
- Agile Modeling   http://www.agilemodeling.com
- Apache ObJectRelationalBridge (OJB)   http://db.apache.org/ojb/
- Introduction to Concurrency Control   http://www.agiledata.org/essays/concurrencyControl.html
- Cocobase   http://www.thoughtinc.com/
- Database refactoring   http://www.agiledata.org/essays/databaseRefactoring.html
- Domain-Driven Design   http://domaindrivendesign.org/
- Hibernate forums   http://forum.hibernate.org/
- Hibernate   http://hibernate.org/
- HSQLDB   http://hsqldb.org/
- iBATIS Java   http://ibatis.apache.org
- JDO and EJB 3.0   http://java.sun.com
- JORM   http://jorm.objectweb.org/
- Object Data Management Group   http://www.odmg.org/
- SimpleORM   http://www.simpleorm.org/
- The Castor Project   http://www.castor.org/
- Cocobase   http://www.thoughtinc.com/

6

Overview of the Spring Framework

Release 1, Week 5, Iteration 2

Steve: Susan, we are working on iteration 2 and had a couple of questions about these screens. For example, how many decimal places should we display in this field?

Susan: Let's go with 2 decimal places. I would also like to move the top section to the middle and the drop-downs have the wrong values. Overall, it is going in the right direction. I like the fact that I can see the progress of this application every two weeks. This ensures that we only implement the features we need and we get to realize potential problems sooner rather later.

WHEN SUN MICROSYSTEMS INTRODUCED the Enterprise JavaBean (EJB) 1.0 specification a few years ago, I was excited at first and even wrote a relatively lengthy article in 1999 for JavaWorld.com (http://www.javaworld.com/javaworld/jw-04-1999/jw-04-middleware.html), essentially summarizing this specification in one article. The article was well received and I was proud of my work.

A year later I wrote a much shorter article, also for JavaWorld.com, titled "Do You Really Need Enterprise JavaBeans?" (http://www.javaworld.com/javaworld/jw-10-2000/jw-1006-soapbox.html).

My motivation for writing this article came from the many projects I ran across that were using EJBs in the wrong manner. For example, I saw nondistributed use of this distributed technology. I even saw simple web applications use EJBs when they could have easily used plain old Java objects (POJOs) in a well-designed application with a clear separation of the tiers (presentation and business tiers, for example).

Furthermore, the role I played in my company required me to interview many developers, and that enabled me to gauge what the mainstream companies, projects, and developers were using. Over a three-to-four-year period, it also enabled me to listen to personal opinions of probably a hundred or so developers about EJBs (and other JEE components). The common theme I saw was that a large majority were using only stateless session beans and the remainder were using a mix of entity beans and message-driven beans; I can't recall anyone using stateful session beans.

So, what is the point of this story? Simple. In my opinion, Sun had defined a standard that was possibly more applicable to the complex applications and less applicable to applications that did not require the many facilities provided by JEE. Furthermore, using EJB on a project meant needing an EJB container—which can sometimes translate into an expensive, application server, if your organization chooses to go the commercial route versus using open source products such as JBoss Application Server (jboss.com) or Apache Geronimo (geronimo.apache.org).

When I came across the Spring Framework some time ago, I was thrilled to see that I could work with POJOs and still have many of the services (similar to JEE/EJB) available to me, if I chose to use them. For example, Spring provides robust declarative transaction management.

Dedicating two full and some partial chapters to the Spring Framework does not do it justice because there is so much to cover. However, as you will soon see, the Spring Framework does not take an all-or-nothing approach; that is, you can pick and choose which modules are applicable to you. In this book, we are using Spring for two main features: its web framework and of course, the inversion of control (IoC; also referred to as *dependency injection*) services. In addition, we will use Spring for scheduling jobs and sending emails. We will not use Spring AOP directly, but indirectly when we use the Spring Web MVC Framework.

Note
From this point, I will refer to the Spring Framework simply as Spring in many places. Also, I will use the terms *dependency injection* and *IoC* interchangeably (more on this later in this chapter).

What's Covered in This Chapter

The focus of this chapter is to get a high-level understanding of the Spring Framework and some related concepts (for example, dependency injection). We will look at the Spring Web MVC Framework in the next chapter, and we'll look at other features such as job scheduling and emailing in later chapters. In this chapter, we will

- Get a clear understanding of what the Spring Framework is, its fundamental concepts, how it is organized, and the many benefits of using this framework

- Learn about the basic Spring concepts such as dependency injection, beans and bean factory, application context, property editors, and more

- Understand how the Spring Framework is packaged, from development and deployment perspectives

What Is Spring?

When people ask me what Spring does, I have to stop and think about how to answer it in one sentence, which is not easy to do as you will see shortly. So, let me first start by quoting an excerpt directly out of the Spring Framework Reference Documentation (springframework.org) because it describes the framework well:

"...Spring provides a light-weight solution for building enterprise-ready applications, while still supporting the possibility of using declarative transaction management, remote access to your logic using RMI or web services, mailing facilities and various options in persisting your data to a database. Spring provides an MVC framework, transparent ways of integrating AOP into your software and a well-structured exception hierarchy including automatic mapping from proprietary exception hierarchies.

Spring could potentially be a one-stop shop for all your enterprise applications, however, Spring is modular, allowing you to use parts of it, without having to bring in the rest..."

Let's explore the "modular" aspect of Spring a bit further. Figure 6.1 (also taken directly out of the Spring Framework Reference Documentation) is probably the best way to get an immediate understanding of the various things Spring can do, and it shows precisely why it is difficult to describe the entire Spring Framework in a short sentence.

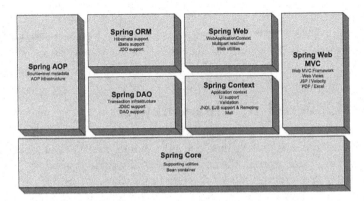

Figure 6.1 Overview of the Spring Framework (taken directly from the Spring Framework Reference Documentation found on springframework.org).

In this book, I use Spring Framework 2.0 RC1.

Spring Packaging for Development

The Spring *modules*, shown in Figure 6.1, are essentially conceptual groups of functionality provided by the extensive list of Spring's Java packages and underlying classes.

Figure 6.2 shows the various top-level Spring packages. (Note: The shaded packages are ones we will use for our sample application, again demonstrating that Spring does not take an all-or-nothing approach.)

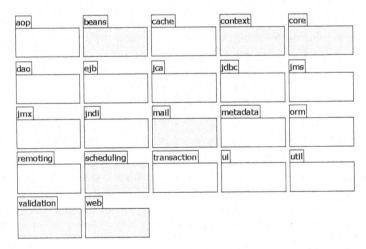

Figure 6.2 Spring's top-level Java packages under org.springframework.

> **Overwhelmed by the Size of the Spring Framework?**
>
> The Spring Framework contains something along the lines of 130+ Java packages and 1,200+ Java classes. However, do not be overwhelmed by this number; here is why.
>
> First, you may want to use only Spring's IoC features, so you could essentially ignore most of the APIs. Second, although there are lots of classes and there's lots of Javadoc, many of these classes are for internal use by the framework itself. Third, Spring enables you to select the modules you want to use and ignore the rest. For example, we will use only a handful of these for our sample application, Time Expression—this is proof that Spring's design is highly modular.

Spring Packaging for Deployment

The modular aspect of Spring extends to deployment as well, because you can deploy your application with only the subset of Spring JAR files you need (for example, spring-jdbc.jar). Table 6.1 shows how Spring provides the packages using various JAR files. Notice how the spring.jar is bigger than others, because it is the complete package. I tend to include the complete spring.jar file in my applications because 1.7MB isn't considered very large these days, especially for server-side applications.

Table 6.1   **Spring's Complete or Separate JAR Files**

JAR File	Size (KB)
spring.jar	1,731
modules/spring-beans.jar	258
modules/spring-aop.jar	224
modules/spring-jdbc.jar	210
modules/spring-webmvc.jar	208
modules/spring-support.jar	189
modules/spring-remoting.jar	166
modules/spring-web.jar	138
modules/spring-core.jar	129
modules/spring-context.jar	111
modules/spring-dao.jar	103
extmodules/spring-hibernate3.jar	102
extmodules/spring-portlet.jar	97
extmodules/spring-hibernate2.jar	85
extmodules/spring-mock.jar	69
extmodules/spring-jdo.jar	61

Table 6.1   **Continued**

JAR File	Size (KB)
extmodules/spring-toplink.jar	55
extmodules/spring-ojb.jar	27
aspects/spring-aspects.jar	10

Overview of the Spring Modules

Now that we have seen a very high-level preview of Spring, let's look at a brief description of each module. First, we will begin with the two most important modules and then look at the remaining ones in an alphabetical order. Again, we will use only a subset of the modules described next, so do not get overwhelmed by how extensive this framework is.

Spring Core

The core module is essentially the foundation for Spring. It provides fundamental features such as *dependency injection* (which we will look at later in the chapter) and management of beans. Some of the top-level packages that fit under this module are `org.springframework.beans`, `org.springframework.core`, and `org.springframework.util`.

Spring Context

The context module is perhaps the second most important module in Spring, after the Spring Core module. It contains key classes such as `ApplicationContext` (explained later in this chapter) and `WebApplicationContext`, which we will use in Time Expression (loaded from our `timex-servlet.xml` file, which is explained in the next chapter). In addition, we will use the `org.springframework.mail` (for sending emails) and `org.springframework.validation` (for validating web UI fields) packages, which are also considered part of this module.

Other packages, primarily used for remote/distributed functionality (EJB and JNDI, for example), are outside the scope of this book.

Spring AOP

We will not write AOP code directly using Spring. However, indirectly we will end up using Spring AOP-based facilities, such as interceptors for our web application and declarative transaction management. In fact, the Spring reference documentation mentions the same point; that is, if the prepackaged functionality provided in Spring is sufficient for your needs, you do not need to use Spring AOP (to write custom aspects, for example).

Personal Opinion: Projects Not Ready for AOP

Aspect-Oriented Programming (AOP) in some ways is a whole new world, even though it complements OO. Like many other creative innovations, the AOP concept originated at Xerox PARC. Gregor Kiczales originated the AOP concept and, along with his team, also developed AspectJ, the first AOP language and probably still the most popular, or at least the most feature-rich AOP framework or toolkit available today.

AOP essentially provides a cleaner way of modularizing an application into distinct parts (known as *separation of concerns*). Each layer of an application (business object layer, for example) focuses on its core functionality and does not contain overlapping functionality with other layers. Things such as logging, security, transaction management, and testing are the most common examples of concerns that can easily be separated from the business object layer, for example, via the use of interceptors.

Typically, an implementation of an AOP language seeks to encapsulate these types of crosscutting concerns (such as logging, security, transactions) through the introduction of a new construct called an aspect. An *aspect* can alter the behavior of the base code (the non-aspect part of a program) by applying advice (additional behavior) over a quantification of join points (points in the structure or execution of a program), called a pointcut (a logical description of a set of join points).

Although AOP offers some obvious advantages and holds a lot of promise for the way we modularize our software applications (using separation of concerns), in my personal opinion, a majority of the software projects are not ready for AOP; hence, it won't become mainstream for another one to two years. Furthermore, I find that AOP's fundamental problem is its core terminology. Terms such as *concern*, *advice*, *jointpoint*, *pointcut*, and *aspect* will take many developers some time to adjust to.

Granted, this sounds like a silly reason, but I have always felt that people need to feel comfortable with the basics of a new technology or approach before moving to a more advanced level.

Again, this is my personal opinion and not the state of AOP in the industry, because AOP as a technology is ready and can significantly help your projects if applied correctly.

Spring DAO

Because we are already using Hibernate for database persistence, we do not need this module. However, this module is worth checking out if you like, or need, to work with JDBC but don't like all the tedious `try-catch-finally` blocks, opening/closing connections, and more. In addition, Spring goes one step further by providing a consistent exception hierarchy, which can convert vendor-specific checked exceptions into more consistent runtime exceptions that can be caught only in the layer of your application you want and ignore it in other places (thereby eliminating the need for cumbersome try/catch/finally code blocks).

Spring for Persistence

It is important to realize that Spring provides a complete persistence functionality. In other words, you could use Spring without an ORM product such as Hibernate and still get the benefits of an easier and cleaner persistence mechanism than plain JDBC (although it won't provide some of the benefits of ORM frameworks that we discussed in Chapter 5, "Using Hibernate for Persistent Objects").

In addition, you get a consistent exception-handling mechanism and other related benefits. We are using ORM framework because so we can work with database records as Java objects.

Spring ORM

Spring's Object-Relational Map (ORM) module provides integration support for popular ORM products used by Java developers, such as Hibernate, JDO, Oracle TopLink, Apache OJB, and iBATIS SQL Maps.

Some of the benefits of using Spring's ORM support include ease of testing (via dependency injection), common data exceptions, persistent resource management (for example, Hibernate's SessionFactory), integrated enterprise-class transaction management, and more.

Spring Web and Web MVC

Among all the Spring modules mentioned here, the web modules are where we will spend the most time in this book. However, we will work with only a few of the classes and packages. For example, we will not have a need for packages that support Sun Microsystem's JavaServer Faces (JSF) standard and others.

Some examples of classes found in these packages, and applicable to Time Expression, are `SimpleUrlHandlerMapping`, `InternalResourceViewResolver`, `SimpleFormController`, `Validator`, and many others. We will look at these and other classes in more detail in the next chapter.

Note

There are many other Java packages that we have not touched on, and none of these are unimportant—they are just outside the scope of this book.

A couple more classes worth mentioning are `org.springframework.scheduling.quartz.CronTriggerBean` and `org.springframework.mail.javamail.JavaMailSenderImpl`. We will use these in Chapter 10, "Beyond the Basics," to satisfy the automatic email sending requirements we defined in Chapter 2, "The Sample Application: An Online Timesheet System." Furthermore, we will use classes found in the `org.springframework.mock.web` package to help us unit test our code using mocked web objects. (For general information about mock objects, visit mockobjects.com.)

Where Spring Framework Fits into Our Architecture

Before discussing the various benefits and concepts of Spring, it is a good idea to revisit our architecture diagram (from Chapter 3, "XP and AMDD-Based Architecture and Design Modeling") to see where we will use Spring. Figure 6.3 shows the diagram. Notice that we will use Spring web controllers (discussed in detail in Chapter 7, "The Spring Web MVC Framework"), job scheduling, sending emails (in Chapter 10), and more. At the core of our application, we will use Spring's IoC services.

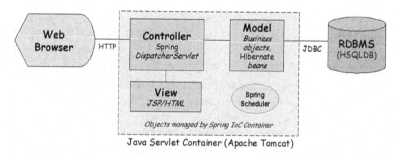

Figure 6.3   High-level architecture for Time Expression.

Benefits of Using Spring

By now, you should have a pretty good idea about what Spring is, how it is logically organized (into modules), and the types of functionality it provides. Although the benefits may appear somewhat obvious, the following is an explicit list:

- POJOs—My favorite benefit is that Spring enables me to develop enterprise-class applications using POJOs. The benefit of using only POJOs is that you do not need an EJB container product such as an application server if your application doesn't require all the capabilities that such products provide. With Spring, you have the option of using only a robust servlet container such as Tomcat or some commercial product.

- Modular—As we have already discussed, Spring is organized in a modular fashion. Even though the number of packages and classes is substantial, you have to worry only about ones you need (see the sidebar "Overwhelmed by the Size of the Spring Framework?"). Hence, phasing Spring into an existing or new project can be done on a case-by-case and module-by-module basis.

- Complementary—I like the fact that Spring does not reinvent the wheel; instead, it truly complements some of the existing work out there. For example, it complements several ORM frameworks, JEE, Quartz and JDK timers, other view technologies, and more.

- Testing—Testing an application written with Spring is simple because environment-dependent code is moved into this framework (versus JNDI lookups embedded in code, for example). Furthermore, by using JavaBean-style POJOs, it becomes easier to use dependency injection for injecting test data (perhaps by using an XML file as the source of test data). In addition, Spring's mock classes can help you simulate classes such as an HTTP request object. This is primarily true because dependency injection works with setter and getter methods. Hence it is easy to inject test data into your objects and unit test your code using a product such as JUnit. This also includes testing of web components developed using Spring's web MVC framework, as you will see in the next chapter.

- Singletons—Spring eliminates the need to maintain your own singleton classes. Instead, you write a class as a normal POJO (without the need for static variables/methods), and Spring ensures that you always get access to the same object, unless you override the default by defining a class as nonsingleton.

- Web framework—Spring's web framework is a well-designed web MVC framework, which provides a great alternative to web frameworks such as Struts or other overengineered or less popular web frameworks. It enables you to develop no-form screens, simple-form screens, wizardlike screens, and much more. It can also bind HTML form fields directly to the business objects instead of having to write custom classes that extend the web framework's classes. Spring Web MVC is also view agnostic, so it can work with JavaServer Pages (JSP), Velocity, JavaServer Faces (JSF), and others. In addition, the Spring Web Flow subproject can be used to develop web applications that require state management across several HTTP requests (an online airline-booking website, for example).

- Consistent exception hierarchy—Spring provides a convenient API to translate technology-specific exceptions (thrown by JDBC, Hibernate, or JDO, for example) into consistent, unchecked exceptions (`org.springframework.dao.PessimisticLockingFailureException`, for example).

- Enterprise-class transaction management—Spring provides a consistent transaction management interface that can scale down to a local transaction (using a single database, for example) and scale up to global transactions (using JTA, for example). Spring also provides application server-specific integration, for instance, with BEA's WebLogic Server and IBM's WebSphere. Spring's transaction management can be used programmatically or declaratively. We will use the declarative version in Chapter 10.

- Lightweight container—IoC containers tend to be lightweight, especially when compared to EJB containers, for example. This can be beneficial, perhaps for developing and deploying applications on computers with limited memory and CPU resources.

We saw some of the benefits here, particularly ones that are applicable to Time Expression. However, if you decide to use Spring more extensively, you are likely to come up with your own list of benefits.

Fundamental Spring Concepts

We have covered a lot of introductory material on Spring already. However, this only reflects what Spring can do for you and how it is organized. We still need to cover some basic concepts that Spring is built on. Let's do that now before jumping into Spring code related to Time Expression (in the next chapter).

Dependency Injection Pattern (and IoC Containers)

In 2004, Martin Fowler published an article (http://www.martinfowler.com/articles/injection.html) discussing inversion of control (IoC) containers. Martin Fowler, some people involved with the PicoContainer, Rod Johnson (founder of the Spring Framework), and others collectively defined the *dependency injection pattern*. Dependency injection is a style of IoC; another style uses a template/callback technique. In both cases you are giving control to something else (hence, the term inversion of control). We will, of course, use the dependency injection style.

What is dependency injection exactly? Let's look at these two words separately. First, there is the *dependency* part; this basically translates into an association between two classes. For example, class A might need class B to get its job done. In other words, class A is dependent on class B. Now, let's look at the second part, *injection*. All this means is that class B will get *injected* into class A by the IoC container. This injection can happen in the way of passing parameters to the constructor or by post-construction using setter methods. (Both are described in more detail later in this chapter.)

Figure 6.4 shows an association between two classes we will see in our examples for Time Expression (in the next chapter). The associations shown in this diagram are exactly the dependencies we will map in the Spring application context file. In other words, `TimesheetListController` depends on `TimesheetManager`; hence, we will use Spring to automatically create a single instance of the `TimesheetManager` and *inject* (set) it via the `TimesheetListController.setTimesheetManager` method.

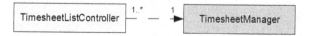

Figure 6.4   Sample association to use for determining bean class dependencies for use with Spring.

You might not be fully convinced of the benefits of using the design pattern approach for developing applications. However, after you begin working in this fashion, you probably won't want to go back to constructing objects using new statements, which not only clutters your Java code more than using dependency injection, but also couples your associated classes a bit more.

Two Injection Styles

There are two key types of dependency injection styles: one via arguments passed to the constructor when an object is created and the other via the setter methods of a JavaBean style class, after the object has been created.

Spring advocates the use of setter-based dependency injection (in the Spring Reference Documentation), because passing many arguments to the constructor can get cumbersome. Martin Fowler, on the other hand, argues (also at http://www.martinfowler.com/articles/injection.html) that if you have too many constructor arguments, your object might be too busy, and it's worth considering splitting the class up.

Although there are pros and cons to both approaches, considering that we are using Spring, we will go with Spring's recommendation and accordingly use setter-based injection for Time Expression. Also, I prefer the JavaBean style of injecting and obtaining property values—that is, using setters and getters. For some reason, this feels a bit more natural to me while coding in Java, but you might disagree. To further confuse things, the Pico Container team prefers the constructor-based injection and provides some valid reasons for it on their website (http://www.picocontainer.org/Why+Constructor+Injection).

Either way, it is nice to know that Spring supports both styles, which we will review shortly.

> **Note**
>
> Fowler also suggests a third type, *interface injection*, which isn't covered here, but you can read about it at http://www.martinfowler.com/articles/injection.html.

Beans, BeanFactory, and ApplicationContext

The `org.springframework.beans.factory.BeanFactory` interface is the actual IoC container! It is an interface that essentially manages the application's configuration by instantiating and managing beans defined via code or, in our case, XML files. *Beans* can be any type of objects, but commonly are JavaBean style classes—that is, classes with getters and setters.

The `org.springframework.context.ApplicationContext` essentially extends BeanFactory and adds additional facilities such as resource bundles, integration with Spring AOP, message resource handling, event broadcasting, and more. Furthermore, `WebApplicationContext` extends `ApplicationContext` by adding web application-specific context. Although you can use an implementation of the BeanFactory interface (for example, XmlBeanFactory), it is recommended that you use ApplicationContext for server-side applications.

This book's code zip file shows `springtest-applicationcontext.xml`, a sample Spring application context file. This example demonstrates both the setter-based injection using the `<property>` element and constructor-based injection using the `<constructor-arg>` element. In this example, notice that the bean `springtestmessage` depends on bean `stringmessage`, as shown here:

```
<bean id="springtestmessage"
    class="com.visualpatterns.timex.test.SpringTestMessage"
    lazy-init="false" init-method="printMessage">
    <property name="message" ref="stringmessage" />
</bean>
```

Notice also that we have an initialization method using the `init-method` attribute; this is a nice way to invoke initialization and termination methods on objects. This relationship (or association) is established using the `<property>` element and the injection occurs via the `SpringTestMessage.setMessage` method, as shown here:

```
public void setMessage(String message)
{
    this.message = message;
}
```

Our `SpringTest.java` class (also in the book's code zip file) shows how simple it is to load an entire application context file and immediately begin using the various beans, with all the collaborator classes autowired by Spring's IoC container, as demonstrated here:

```
public static void main(String args[]) throws Exception
{
    FileSystemXmlApplicationContext factory =
        new FileSystemXmlApplicationContext(
            "src/conf/springtest-applicationcontext.xml");

    SpringTestMessage stm = (SpringTestMessage) factory
            .getBean("springtestmessage");
}
```

Note

I chose FileSystemXmlApplicationContext for the sake of simplicity in my example. However, ClassPathXmlApplicationContext is generally a better class to use because it searches not only for context definition files in the classpath but also embedded within JAR files.

Before we move to the next section, the following list describes a couple of additional notes about beans:

- Beans can be created by Spring via the constructor (as you normally would using a new statement) or via static factory methods of another class.

- Each bean must have a unique id (for example, `springtestmessage`).
- Beans can be of two types, Singleton and Prototype (nonsingleton). By default, all beans are singletons, but you can make them prototypes by specifying an attribute such as `singleton="false"`. We will use only singletons for Time Expression because Spring cannot manage the life cycle of a prototype bean after it has been created and handed off to (injected in) the objects that depend on it. Also, by specifying `singleton="false"` for a given bean definition, you are instructing Spring to create a new instance of the bean every time there is a request for this bean. Last, almost 100% of the time, using singleton beans is sufficient.
- You can inject values in a setter method or constructor as single objects or as collection elements (for example, List, Set, Map, and Properties).

This is all we will discuss about `BeanFactory` and `ApplicationContext` classes in this chapter. After we move to the Spring Web MVC Framework (in the next chapter), we will not have to worry about creating either of these objects manually.

However, you might want to familiarize yourself a bit more about how all this works by reading the Spring Reference Documentation (springframework.org). For example, you might want to better understand constructor argument resolution, dependency checking, autowiring of collaborator beans, programmatically interacting with the `BeanFactory`, injecting `null` values, method-based injection, and much more. You will also see additional examples of several of these things in the next chapter and in later chapters in this book.

The `spring-beans.xsd` (or the older `spring-beans.dtd`) file provides the XML schema for the Spring Framework's application context file. Looking at one of these files in the Spring's software directories might give you some additional insight into the various elements and properties that can be specified in the application context file.

Property Editors

Spring makes heavy use of the `java.beans.PropertyEditor` interface by allowing *custom property editors* to be registered, which convert an object into readable text, and vice versa. For example, in the next chapter, we will use it to convert the hours entered on our Enter Hours web page.

Spring Subprojects

Just when you thought you had heard enough about Spring, there is more.

What we have looked at so far are modules and packages that are part of the Spring's core distribution. There are also other subprojects hosted by the Spring team that can be found via the springframework.org website:

- Acegi Security System for Spring—This project provides comprehensive security services for the Spring Framework (for example, HTTP security, object instance security, security taglib, password encoding, and more).

- Spring BeanDoc—This tool facilitates documentation and graphing of a Spring application's bean factories and application context file. A very useful, easy, and flexible tool to use.

- Spring IDE for Eclipse—This is a graphical user interface for the configuration files used by a Spring-based application. We will see a preview of this in Chapter 8, "The Eclipse Phenomenon!"

- Spring Rich Client—I have not personally worked with this project, so I will quote the Spring website, which claims that this is a "viable option for developers that need a platform and a 'best-practices' guide for constructing Swing applications quickly."

- Spring Web Flow—This project is based on the concepts similar to the Spring Web MVC Framework, essentially providing wizardlike screen functionality to implement a business process. This project has been getting a lot of attention recently and is worth checking out if you need the type of functionality it provides.

Summary

In this chapter, we

- Got a clear understanding of what the Spring Framework is, its fundamental concepts, how it is organized, and the many benefits of using this framework.

- Learned about basic Spring concepts such as dependency injection, beans and bean factory, application context, property editors, and more.

- Understood how the Spring Framework is packaged, from development and deployment perspectives.

We covered a lot of material in this chapter on the fundamentals of the Spring Framework. In the next chapter, we will take a closer look at Spring's web-related modules. In later chapters, we will also take a look at the following features of Spring:

- Declarative transaction management
- Scheduling jobs
- Sending emails

Now it is time to develop a couple of Time Expression's screens using the Spring Web MVC Framework!

One last note before we move on: You might have noticed that the Spring Reference Documentation was mentioned multiple times. This is a well-written document. However, if you cannot find the information you are looking for in there, try the Spring Framework API JavaDocs, which are well documented and complement the reference documentation quite nicely.

Recommended Resources

The following websites are relevant to or provide additional information on the topics discussed in this chapter:

- Acegi Security System for Spring   http://acegisecurity.org/
- Apache Geronimo   http://geronimo.apache.org
- AOP Alliance (Java/JEE AOP standards)   http://aopalliance.sourceforge.net/
- Dependency injection   http://www.martinfowler.com/articles/injection.html
- Eclipse SDK   http://www.eclipse.org/aspectj/
- Excalibur   http://excalibur.apache.org/
- HiveMind   http://jakarta.apache.org/hivemind/
- JBoss Application Server   http://www.jboss.com
- Mock Objects   http://mockobjects.com
- PicoContainer   http://www.picocontainer.org/
- Software Practices Lab   http://www.cs.ubc.ca/labs/spl/
- Spring discussion forums   http://forum.springframework.org/
- Spring IDE   http://springide.org/project
- The Spring Framework   http://springframework.org

7

The Spring Web MVC Framework

Release 1, Week 6, Iteration 3

Steve: Raj, isn't life great? The users accepted iteration 2, Spring is here, the leaves are growing back, and there is an eclipse later this week.

Raj: Sounds great, Steve. By the way, this integrated development environment I'm reading about sounds pretty cool. Also, it has hundreds of open source and commercial plug-ins available for it. Can't wait to check it out!

(c) Visual Patterns, Inc.

I N THE PREVIOUS CHAPTER, I gave you an overview of the Spring Framework. We looked at what Spring is, how it is packaged, and the various modules it contains. I also mentioned that with Spring, you do not have to take an all-or-nothing approach when trying to decide whether you should use Spring. In other words, based on your needs, you can phase in the Spring Framework one module at a time (along with any dependencies). In this chapter, I will demonstrate how to use Spring Web MVC Framework (module), to build Time Expression, our sample web application.

Note that from this point on, I will refer to the Spring Web MVC Framework as simply Spring MVC, in most places.

What's Covered in This Chapter

In this chapter, we will

- Look at the various benefits of using Spring MVC
- Take an in-depth look at the Spring Web MVC Framework
- Build three of the screens in Time Expression using Spring MVC: a no-form controller, two form controllers, and a Spring HTTP interceptor.

> **Note**
> The complete code for the examples used in this chapter can be found within this book's code zip file (available on the book's website).

This is an exciting chapter, so I won't waste any more time boring you with introductory material. Let's spring into action!

Benefits of the Spring Web MVC Framework

The Spring Web MVC Framework is a robust, flexible, and well-designed framework for rapidly developing web applications using the MVC design pattern. The benefits achieved from using this Spring module are similar to those you get from the rest of the Spring Framework. Let's review a few of these. I will demonstrate some of these benefits later in this chapter.

- Easier testing—This is a common theme you will find across all the Spring classes. The fact that most of Spring's classes are designed as JavaBeans enables you to inject test data using the setter methods of these classes. Spring also provides mock classes to simulate Java HTTP objects (`HttpServletRequest`, for example), which makes unit testing of the web layer much simpler.
- Bind directly to business objects—Spring MVC does not require your business (model) classes to extend any special classes; this enables you to reuse your business objects by binding them directly to the HTML forms fields. In fact, your

controller classes are the only ones that are required to extend Spring classes (or implement a Spring controller interface).

- Clear separation of roles—Spring MVC nicely separates the roles played by the various components that make up this web framework. For example, when we discuss concepts such as controllers, command objects, and validators, you will begin to see how each component plays a distinct role.

- Adaptable controllers—If your application does not require an HTML form, you can write a simpler version of a Spring controller that does need all the extra components required for form controllers. In fact, Spring provides several types of controllers, each serving a different purpose. For example, there are no-form controllers, simple form controllers, wizardlike form controllers, views with no controllers, and even prepackaged controllers that enable you to write views without your own custom controller.

- Simple but powerful tag library—Spring's tag library is small, straightforward, but powerful. For example, Spring uses the JSP expression language (EL) for arguments to the `<spring:bind>` tag.

- Web Flow—This module is a subproject and is not bundled with the Spring core distribution. It is built on top of Spring MVC and adds the capability to easily write wizardlike web applications that span across several HTTP requests (an online shopping cart, for example).

- View technologies and web frameworks—Although we are using JSP as our view technology, Spring supports other view technologies as well, such as Apache Velocity (jakarta.apache.org/velocity/) and FreeMarker (freemarker.org). This is a powerful concept because switching from JSP to Velocity is a matter of configuration. Furthermore, Spring provides integration support for Apache Struts (struts. apache.org), Apache Tapestry (jakarta.apache.org/tapestry), and OpenSymphony's WebWork (opensymphony.com/webwork/).

- Lighter-weight environment—As I mentioned in the previous chapter, Spring enables you to build enterprise-ready applications using POJOs; the environment setup can be simpler and less expensive because you could develop and deploy your application using a lighter-weight servlet container.

Spring Web MVC Concepts

The world of Java has seen many MVC design pattern-based web frameworks crop up in the past few years (several are listed at the very end of this chapter). MVC was originally conceived at XEROX PARC around the 1978–79 time frame and was later implemented in the Smalltalk-80 class library (also at XEROX PARC). It is a relatively simple concept to grasp and provides for a clean separation of presentation and data, as I'll explain briefly here.

First, let's look at our architecture diagram established earlier in the book and shown here in Figure 7.1.

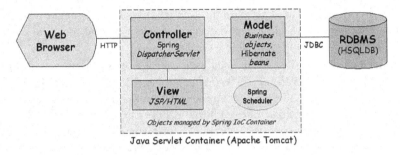

Figure 7.1   High-level architecture diagram for Time Expression.

As you can see, all incoming HTTP requests from a web browser are handled by Controllers. A *controller*, as the name indicates, controls the view and model by facilitating data exchange between them. The key benefit of this approach is that the model can worry only about the data and has no knowledge of the view. The view, on the other hand, has no knowledge of the model and business logic and simply renders the data passed to it (as a web page, in our case). The MVC pattern also allows us to change the view without having to change the model.

Let's review some basic Spring MVC concepts. First, we will look at the concepts related to Java coding, and then we will look at the configuration required to make all this work.

Spring MVC Java Concepts

Figure 7.1 provided us a high-level view of the architecture for Time Expression. Now let's take a slightly more detailed and focused look at the Spring MVC components. Figure 7.2 shows an end-to-end flow for a typical screen in Time Expression. This diagram shows many of the concepts we will discuss next.

Controller

Spring provides many types of controllers. This can be both good and bad. The good thing is that you have a variety of controllers to choose from, but that also happens to be the bad part because it can be a bit confusing at first about which one to use.

The best way to decide which controller type to use probably is by knowing what type of functionality you need. For example, do your screens contain a form? Do you need wizardlike functionality? Do you just want to redirect to a JSP page and have no controller at all? These are the types of questions you will need to ask yourself to help you narrow down the choices.

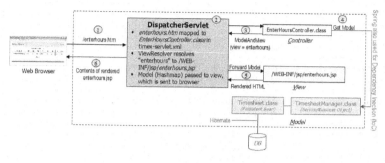

Figure 7.2   End-to-end flow for Enter Hours screen using
Spring and Hibernate.

Figure 7.3 shows a class diagram of some of the more interesting controllers that are part
of Spring MVC. Table 7.1 provides brief descriptions on the interface and classes shown
in Figure 7.3. (Note: The descriptions provided in this table are taken directly out of
the Spring Framework Javadocs.) I tend to use `SimpleFormController`,
`UrlFilenameViewController`, and `AbstractController` most often. We will see examples of these later in this chapter.

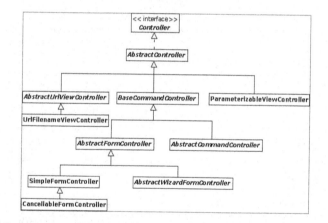

Figure 7.3   Class diagram showing a partial list of Spring controllers.

Table 7.1   **Description of Various Spring Controllers**

Controller	Description (Taken Directly from the Spring Javadocs)
AbstractCommandController	Abstract base class for custom command controllers.
AbstractController	Convenient superclass for controller implementations, using the Template Method design pattern.

Table 7.1   **Continued**

Controller	Description (Taken Directly from the Spring Javadocs)
AbstractFormController	Form controller that autopopulates a form bean from the request.
AbstractUrlViewController	Abstract base class for Controllers that return a view name based on the URL.
AbstractWizardFormController	Form controller for typical wizard-style workflows.
BaseCommandController	Controller implementation that creates an object (the command object) on receipt of a request and attempts to populate this object with request parameters.
CancellableFormController	Extension of SimpleFormController that supports "cancellation" of form processing.
Controller	Base Controller interface, representing a component that receives HttpServletRequest and HttpServletResponse like a HttpServlet but is able to participate in an MVC workflow.
ParameterizableViewController	Trivial controller that always returns a named view.
SimpleFormController	Concrete FormController implementation that provides configurable form and success views, and an onSubmit chain for convenient overriding.
UrlFilenameViewController	Controller that transforms the virtual filename at the end of a URL into a view name and returns that view.

Model and View

Many of the methods in the Controller related subclasses return a `org.springframework.web.servlet.ModelAndView` object. This object holds the model (as a `java.util.Map` object) and view name and makes it possible to return both in one return value from a method. We will see examples of this later in this chapter when we build two of the screens for Time Expression.

Command (Form Backing) Object

Spring uses the notion of a command object, which essentially is a JavaBean style class that gets populated with the data from an HTML form's fields. This same object is also passed to our validators (discussed next) for data validation, and if the validations pass, it is passed to the `onSubmit` method (in controller related classes) for processing of valid data. Given that this command object is a simple JavaBean-style class, we can use our business objects directly for data binding instead of writing special classes just for data binding. I will demonstrate this benefit later in this chapter.

Validator

A Spring validator is an optional class that can be invoked for validating form data for a given command (form) controller. This validator class is a concrete class that implements the `org.springframework.validation.Validator` interface. One of the two methods required by this interface is the `validate` method, which is passed a `command` object, as mentioned previously, and an `Errors` object, which can be used to return errors. I will demonstrate an example of a Validator class later in this chapter. Another notable validation class is `org.springframework.validation.ValidationUtils`, which provides convenient methods for rejecting empty fields.

Spring Tag Library (`spring:bind`)

The spring bind tag library is simple yet powerful. It is typically used in JSP files via the `<spring:bind>` tag, which essentially binds HTML form fields to the `command` object. Furthermore, it provides access to special variables within JSP, such as `${status.value}`, `${status.expression}`, and `${status.errorMessages}`, which we will look at later in the chapter.

Spring MVC Configuration Concepts

In this section, we will review some core concepts related to configuring the Spring Web MVC Framework.

DispatcherServlet

`DispatcherServlet` (part of the `org.springframework.web.servlet` package) is the entry point to the world of Spring Web MVC, as depicted in Figure 7.2. It essentially dispatches requests to the controllers. If you have worked with Java web applications before, you will not be surprised to find out that this class is configured in the `web.xml` file, as shown in the following excerpt from the complete `web.xml` for Time Expression:

```
<servlet-class>
org.springframework.web.servlet.DispatcherServlet
</servlet-class>
```

We will discuss `DispatcherServlet` in detail later in this chapter.

Handler Mappings

You can map handlers for incoming HTTP requests in the Spring application context file. These handlers are typically controllers that are mapped to partial or complete URLs of incoming requests. The handler mappings can also contain optional interceptors, which are invoked before and after the handler. This is a powerful concept. I will demonstrate an example of this later in this chapter when we use such a web interceptor for authentication and close our Hibernate session for the given HTTP request.

The following code excerpt taken from our complete `timex-servlet.xml` file shows how a handler can be mapped to a partial URL:

```
<bean id="urlMap"
      class="org.springframework.web.servlet.handler.SimpleUrlHandlerMapping">
    <property name="urlMap">
        <props>
            <prop key="/signin.htm">signInController</prop>
            <prop key="/signout.htm">signOutController</prop>
        </props>
    </property>
</bean>
```

View Resolvers

Spring uses the notion of view resolvers, which resolve view names to the actual views (enterhours to enterhours.jsp, for example). We will use Spring's `InternalResourceViewResolver` class to resolve our view names. (This is covered in the next section.)

Spring Setup for Time Expression

Now that I have provided you some fundamental concepts for Spring MVC, let's begin setting it up for development of Time Expression screens.

We need a couple of components to get Spring up and running for us. Figure 7.1 showed the Time Expression high-level architecture we established early in this book. As you can see, we need a servlet container that Spring can run within for our web application. So let's start with the installation of a Servlet container first, and then we will download and install the Spring Framework.

Installing a Servlet Container (Apache Tomcat)

I have chosen to use Apache Tomcat (http://tomcat.apache.org/) as the Servlet container for the Time Expression application. However, you can use any other product you want; this can be a servlet-container-only product, such as Tomcat, or a full-blown application server, such as JBoss Application Server, BEA WebLogic, or IBM Websphere.

> **Note**
>
> If you have been following along the examples in this book, you will recall the `timex/local.properties` file used by our Ant `build.xml` file (both files are provided in this book's code zip file). Note the `deploy.dir` property in the `timex/local.properties` file; this can be adjusted to point to your servlet container's deployment directory. For example, in my case, the `deploy.dir` property is set up as shown here:
>
> ```
> deploy.dir=/apache-tomcat-5.5.15/webapps
> ```

Now we can run the `ant deploy` from a command line using our `build.xml` file. By running this ant command, a fresh new `timex.war` web archive file will be built and deployed to the specified directory (in `deploy.dir`).

Hot Deploying WAR Files and HTTP Mock Style Testing

In 2001, I wrote an article titled "How Many Times Do You Restart Your Server During Development?" (http://www.javaworld.com/javaworld/jw-04-2001/jw-0406-soapbox.html). Although various servlet containers or application servers handle reloading of applications differently, restarting the server every time you make a change to your application can become a waste of time. Much of this has to do with the way Java's class loading works, but it still doesn't make it any less frustrating.

If your server doesn't (hot) redeploy your war files successfully, you could consider tweaking your style of coding and testing. One good alternative (discussed in this chapter) is to use Spring's mock classes to simulate a HTTP request and use JUnit to unit test the code instead of relying completely on the web application server for your testing.

Incidentally, I recently came across an option for Apache Tomcat that will enable to us to avoid restarts when deploying our application. This can be activated by setting the following attributes in the `conf/context.xml` file found under the Tomcat install directory, `<Context antiJARLocking="true" antiResourceLocking="true">`.

Documentation on these attributes can be found at http://tomcat.apache.org/tomcat-5.5-doc/config/context.html#Standard%20Implementation.

Alternatively, we could use the Tomcat Ant deploy tasks; however, I wanted to keep our `build.xml` generic for most web servers. Nevertheless, documentation on these tasks can be found at the tomcat.apache.org website.

Installing the Spring Framework

By now, you should have a thorough understanding of what Spring can do for you. Next, it is time to download Spring, install it, and begin using it!

The Spring Framework can be downloaded from http://springframework.org. We will now follow the instructions provided on the website to download and install it.

The following are one-time setup steps we will need to follow to get Spring set up for our environment. From here, you might add external jars for added Spring functionality as needed to the `timex/lib/` directory. (In Chapter 10, "Beyond the Basics," we will add OpenSymphony's `quartz.jar` file to our directory.)

- Spring—Copy `spring.jar` to the `timex/lib/` directory of Time Expression, based on the directory structure we established in Chapter 3, "XP and AMDD-Based Architecture and Design Modeling," and shown here in Figure 7.4.

- JSTL—We also need to obtain JavaServer Pages Standard Tag Library (JSTL), which is part of the Jakarta taglibs project and can be downloaded from http://jakarta.apache.org/taglibs/. After downloading this package, copy the jstl.jar and standard.jar files to the timex/lib/ directory. JSTL helps eliminate (or at least significantly reduces) the amount of embedded scriptlet code in our JSP files. For example, JSTL provides tags for iterations/loops (<forEach>, for example), conditional tags (<if>, for example), formatting tags (fmt:formatDate, for example), and several other tags. You will see examples of many of these tags in this chapter.

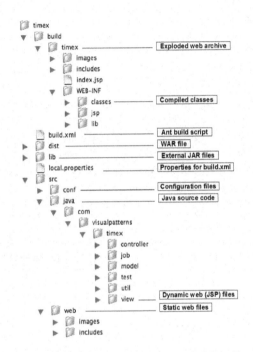

Figure 7.4   Development directory structure for Time Expression.

Running Our SpringTest

Incidentally, the three files we discussed in the previous chapter can now be created in the following paths, and we could run ant springtest (from our timex/ top-level directory) to test that we can use Spring in our code. The complete code for these files can be found in this book's code zip file:

- src/conf/springtest-applicationcontext.xml
- src/java/com/visualpatterns/timex/test/SpringTest.java
- src/java/com/visualpatterns/timex/test/SpringTestMessage.java

Configuring Spring MVC

Now that we have the servlet container and Spring software installed, we need to configure Spring MVC so that we can begin developing and deploying the Time Expression sample application.

Configure `DispatcherServlet` in `web.xml`

The very first thing we need to do is to have all incoming HTTP requests (that match a certain pattern) forwarded to Spring MVC, by Tomcat.

The following excerpt from our `web.xml` file demonstrates how we can configure all requests ending with an `.htm` extension to be processed by the Spring's `org.springframework.web.servlet.DispatcherServlet` class:

```
<servlet>
    <servlet-name>timex</servlet-name>
    <servlet-class>
        org.springframework.web.servlet.DispatcherServlet
    </servlet-class>
    <load-on-startup>1</load-on-startup>
</servlet>
<servlet-mapping>
    <servlet-name>timex</servlet-name>
    <url-pattern>*.htm</url-pattern>
</servlet-mapping>
```

Later on we will see how requests with a `.jsp` extension are handled by Spring's `DispatcherServlet`.

Note

Our Spring application context file, `timex-servlet.xml`, will automatically be searched for and loaded by Spring for us.

This file is stored under `timex/src/conf` but automatically copied to the `timex/build/timex/WEB-INF/` directory by our Ant `build.xml` file when the build, dist, or deploy targets are used.

Create Spring's Application Context XML File (`timex-servlet.xml`)

Now we need to create our application context XML file, `timex-servlet.xml`. We will review various parts of this file throughout the remainder of this chapter. You will see how this file quickly becomes an essential part of working with Spring MVC.

The following excerpt from `timex-servlet.xml` shows how we configure a Spring view resolver to resolve logical view names to the physical view (JSP) file:

```
<bean id="viewResolver"
class="org.springframework.web.servlet.view.InternalResourceViewResolver">
    <property name="viewClass">
        <value>org.springframework.web.servlet.view.JstlView</value>
```

```
    </property>
    <property name="prefix">
        <value>/WEB-INF/jsp/</value>
    </property>
    <property name="suffix">
        <value>.jsp</value>
    </property>
</bean>
```

> **Note**
>
> By storing our JSP files in the `build/timex/WEB-INF/jsp/` directory, we are essentially *hiding* these files so they cannot be accessed directly from a web browser using their actual filenames (that is, only views ending with `.htm` are mapped to these files). To access `.jsp` files directly, they must be placed a couple of levels up, under `build/timex/`, the same location where our welcome file, `index.jsp`, will reside.
>
> Hiding files is a security precautionary measure. Appendix D, "Securing Web Applications," provides additional security guidelines.

Developing Time Expression User Interfaces with Spring

Now that we have Tomcat and Spring installed and set up, we can go through the steps required to develop our sample screens. Let's look at two Time Expression screens we will develop in this chapter—one a nonform screen and the other an HTML form screen.

Timesheet List Screen

Figure 7.5 shows the Timesheet List screen, which is a nonform screen (that is, it contains no input fields a user can fill in because it is a display-only screen). From the perspective of coding a controller, this is the most basic screen that you can develop using Spring MVC; we will review the code behind this shortly.

Enter Hours Screen

Figure 7.6 shows the Enter Hours screen, a form screen (that is, it contains input fields a user can fill in). This is a little more complicated than the Timesheet List screen because we will have to bind the HTML form fields to our Java code, perform validations on the data entered, display errors, and so on.

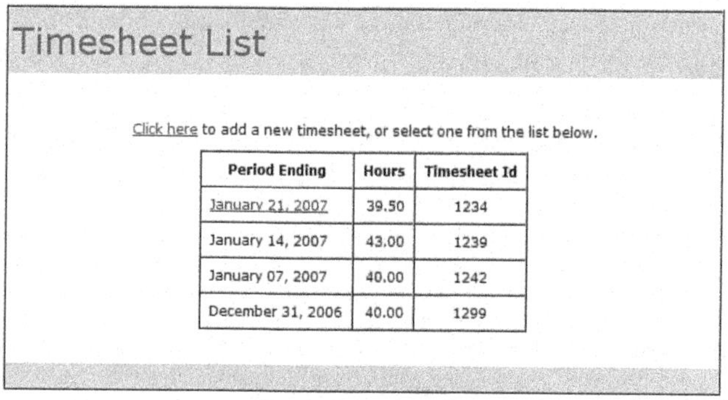

Figure 7.5   Time Expression's Timesheet List web page
(view name: timesheetlist).

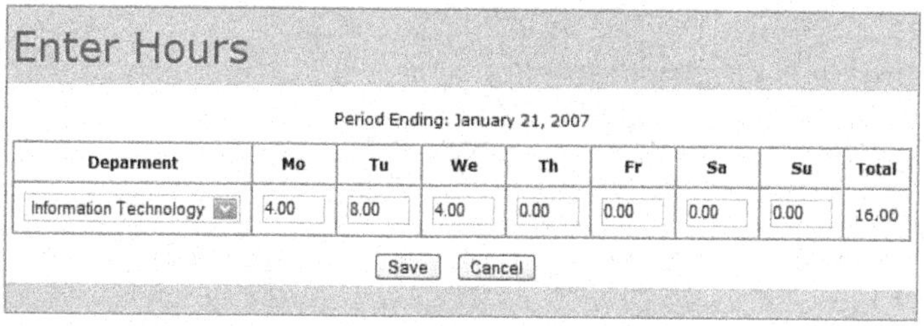

Figure 7.6   Time Expression's Enter Hours web page (view name: enterhours).

Java Files

By now we have enough information to come up with filenames for our Java classes and
JSP (view) filenames. Table 7.2 shows a map of the view, controller, and collaborator
(model) classes required to complete the two screens shown in Figures 7.5 and 7.6. You
might recall that we designed this map in Chapter 3 (see Table 3.5).

Table 7.2   **Sample Application Flow Map (from Chapter 3)**

Story Tag	View	Controller Class	Collaborators	Tables Impacted
Timesheet List	timesheetlist	TimeSheetListController	TimesheetManager	Timesheet
Enter Hours	enterhours	EnterHoursController	TimesheetManager	Timesheet Department

Note that the collaborator classes mentioned here were already developed in Chapter 5, "Using Hibernate for Persistent Objects," so we need to develop the view and controller classes now.

Figure 7.7 shows a rudimentary class diagram on how the controller and model related classes fit together.

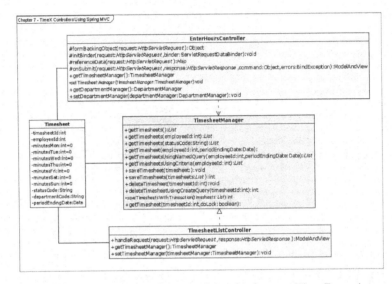

Figure 7.7   Class diagram showing relationship between Time Expression model and controller classes.

If you have developed web applications in Java before, you might question the placement of .jsp files under the same directory structure as my Java classes (that is, java/com/visualpatterns/timex/); this is purely a personal preference because I like to see my MVC files grouped together under the same parent directory.

Let's look at how to develop the Timesheet List and Enter Hours screens, step-by-step. We will later look at how to develop the Sign In screen because it is a special case because of the authentication (sign in) required.

Cascading Style Sheet (CSS)

Other than the Java and JSP files we discussed, we are also using a cascading style sheet (CSS) file named timex.css (placed in our src/web/includes directory). CSS provides a consistent look-and-feel across our user interfaces; furthermore, it helps reduce the size of our JSP/HTML code because we don't have as much formatting code in our view (JSP) files.

Timesheet List Screen: A No-Form Controller Example

Developing a *no-form* controller in Spring is a relatively straightforward process. Let's look at the steps involved to do this.

Step-by-Step Configuration

The following are Spring-related items we need to configure in `timex-servlet.xml`, our Spring application context file.

Map Handler

The first thing we need to do is to map the incoming request URL to an actual controller, which will handle the request. The following excerpt from the `timex-servlet.xml` file shows how we can map the `timesheetlist.htm` URL to an internal bean reference named `timesheetListController` (discussed next) with the help of Spring's `SimpleUrlHandlerMapping` class:

```
<bean id="urlMapAuthenticate"
    class="org.springframework.web.servlet.handler.SimpleUrlHandlerMapping">
    <property name="interceptors">
        <list>
            <ref bean="httpRequestInterceptor" />
        </list>
    </property>
    <property name="urlMap">
        <props>
            <prop key="/timesheetlist.htm">
                timesheetListController
            </prop>
```

Also, notice the `interceptors` property; by configuring this, we can intercept HTTP requests, for example, to implement authentication (interceptors are discussed in detail later in this chapter).

Define Controller and Associated Class

The next step is to define the controller class referenced by the map handler. The following excerpt from the `timex-servlet.xml` file demonstrates how this is done:

```
<bean name="timesheetListController"
    class="com.visualpatterns.timex.controller.TimesheetListController">
    <property name="timesheetManager">
        <ref bean="timesheetManager" />
    </property>
    <property name="applicationSecurityManager">
        <ref bean="applicationSecurityManager" />
    </property>
```

```
      <property name="successView">
          <value>timesheetlist</value>
      </property>
</bean>
```

Notice the `ref` attributes. As you might guess, these are references to other beans defined in our application context, as shown in this XML excerpt:

```
<bean id="timesheetManager"
    class="com.visualpatterns.timex.model.TimesheetManager"/>
<bean id="applicationSecurityManager"
    class="com.visualpatterns.timex.util.ApplicationSecurityManager" />
```

We already developed the `TimesheetManager` class in Chapter 5; we will develop the `ApplicationSecurityManager` class later in this chapter.

This is all we need to configure for the Timesheet List screen. Now we need to write the controller and view code, referenced here. Let's look at that next.

Step-by-Step Coding

The Timesheet List screen is a relatively simple screen and will be developed using the most basic type of Spring controller because it contains no form fields; therefore, it will not require things such as Command and Validator classes. Basically, if we look at this from an MVC design pattern perspective, the files for this screen will include the following:

- Model—`TimesheetManager.java` and `Timesheet.java`
- View—`timesheetlist.jsp`
- Controller—`TimesheetController.java`

We already developed the model files in the previous chapter, so all we need to develop here are the controller and view files. Let's dissect and review parts of our complete code.

Let's begin by writing the unit test code for our controller class.

Writing Our Test First with Mock Objects

The next few code excerpts from our `TimesheetListControllerTest.java` file show how we can unit test controller classes. We will create this in the `timex/src/java/com/visualpatterns/timex/controller` directory.

We start by creating an instance of the `org.springframework.mock.web.MockHttpServletRequest` class to simulate a real HTTP request. This class not only provides the benefit of being able to unit test our code but also reduces the need to deploy the application and potentially restart the servlet container (Tomcat, for example) each time we want to test something.

```
mockHttpServletRequest = new MockHttpServletRequest("GET",
"/timesheetlist.htm");
```

Next, we will create some test dependency objects and *inject* them, as Spring will do for us at runtime:

```
Employee employee = new Employee();
employee.setEmployeeId(EMPLOYEE_ID);
applicationSecurityManager.setEmployee(mockHttpServletRequest,
        employee);

// inject objects that Spring normally would
timesheetListController = new TimesheetListController();
timesheetListController.setTimesheetManager(timesheetManager);
timesheetListController
        .setApplicationSecurityManager(applicationSecurityManager);
```

In our test code, we instantiated our own TimesheetManager class for the sake of simplicity. However in real-world applications, you might want to use Spring's FileSystemXmlApplicationContext or ClassPathXmlApplicationContext classes to instantiate your classes. This way, you not only get an instance of a class but also have its dependent objects loaded and injected by Spring.

Now we can complete our test by checking the `java.util.List` we just retrieved; our test ensures that list is not empty and also that it contains `Timesheet` objects for the employee we requested the records for:

```
ModelAndView modelAndView = timesheetListController.handleRequest(
        mockHttpServletRequest, null);

assertNotNull(modelAndView);
assertNotNull(modelAndView.getModel());

List timesheets = (List) modelAndView.getModel().get(
        TimesheetListController.MAP_KEY);
assertNotNull(timesheets);

Timesheet timesheet;
for (int i = 0; i < timesheets.size(); i++)
{
    timesheet = (Timesheet) timesheets.get(i);
    assertEquals(EMPLOYEE_ID, timesheet.getEmployeeId());
    System.out.println(timesheet.getTimesheetId() + " passed!");
}
```

That's about it for our unit test class; now let's review the actual TimesheetListController class.

Writing Unit Test and Actual Code in the Same Sitting

This book's code zip file shows the complete code for our `TimesheetListControllerTest.java` class, which is the JUnit test case for `TimesheetController.java`. As I've preached previously in this book, development of a unit test and the actual code works best when it is done in the same sitting. For example, I wrote the `TimesheetListControllerTest.java` and `TimesheetListController.java` in the same sitting; that is, I coded a little, compiled and tested a little, and then repeated these steps until my controller class provided all the functionality I needed. The obvious benefit of this approach was that my code was unit tested by the time I was done!

Furthermore, our controller class will now contain only the code we need—nothing more, nothing less.

Another notable benefit worth mentioning is that at times I find myself getting programmer's block (similar to writer's block). But starting out with the unit test code helps me get going. Note that what I have mentioned here is a personal style of working, but hopefully you will find value in it and give the test-first approach a try (if you don't already do so).

One thing I do want to stress is that like everything else, you need to find the right balance. Although I believe in the test-first approach, there are times when it isn't feasible for me to write a unit test code that becomes more complicated than the actual code or is cumbersome to write. After all, you are writing Java code to test other Java code, which raises an obvious question—do we also test the test code? Of course, I'm kidding here, but my point is to find the right balance and in most cases, unit tests work out pretty well.

Last, unit testing works best if you write small methods that can be unit tested relatively easily.

Controller Code

Now it is time to review the code behind our controller class for the Timesheet List screen, `TimesheetListController.java`. We will create this in the `timex/src/java/com/visualpatterns/timex/controller` directory.

For starters, notice that we are implementing the `org.springframework.web.servlet.mvc.Controller` interface; this is perhaps the most basic type of controller you can develop using Spring.

```
public class TimesheetListController implements Controller
```

The next interesting thing to note is the `handleRequest` method; this is the only method we must implement to satisfy the requirements of the Controller interface.

```
public ModelAndView handleRequest(HttpServletRequest request,
                         HttpServletResponse response)
```

The `handleRequest` method returns a `ModelAndView` object, which contains the view name and the model data (a `java.util.List`, in our case). The view name is resolved by `JstlView`, which we defined in the `timex-servlet.xml` file we saw earlier in this chapter.

```
        return new ModelAndView(VIEW_NAME,
                MAP_KEY,
                timesheetManager.getTimesheets(employeeId));
```

There are a few more variations to how you can construct the `ModelAndView` class, as shown in the following list (see the Spring Framework API Javadocs for details):

- `ModelAndView()`

- `ModelAndView(String viewName)`

- `ModelAndView(String viewName, Map model)`

- `ModelAndView(String viewName, String modelName, Object modelObject)`

- `ModelAndView(View view)`

- `ModelAndView(View view, Map model)`

- `ModelAndView(View view, String modelName, Object modelObject)`

View/JSP Code

We already prototyped the screens in Chapter 2, "The Sample Application: An Online Timesheet System," so we now need to add some code to the related view (`.jsp`) files. This book's code zip file contains the before file, `timesheetlist.html` (prototyped, static HTML), and the after file, `timesheetlist.jsp` (dynamic/JSP), versions of this file.

Let's review our `timesheetlist.jsp` a bit closer. For starters, we will create this in the `timex/src/java/com/visualpatterns/timex/view` directory. Now let's look at some JSP code.

The following excerpt from our `timesheetlist.jsp` file shows the dynamic code used for populating the HTML table on the Timesheet List screen; this is done in a loop using JSTLs `forEach` tag. Within each loop, we are generating the HTML table's rows and columns (and also formatting the hours) using the JSTL core library.

```
<c:forEach items="${timesheets}" var="timesheet">
    <tr>
        <td align="center"><a
            href='enterhours.htm?eid=<c:out
            value="${timesheet.employeeId}"/>&amp;tid=<c:out
            value="${timesheet.timesheetId}"/>'><fmt:formatDate
            value="${timesheet.periodEndingDate}" type="date"
```

Now let's look at another interesting piece of code from our view file, `timesheetlist.jsp`:

```
<c:if test="${not empty message}">
    <font color="green"><c:out value="${message}"/></font>
    <c:set var="message" value="" scope="session"/>
</c:if>
```

All this code does is check for any messages stored in the `message` session attribute. This message is set by the Enter Hours controller upon a successful save in the `onSubmit` method, as you will see later in the chapter.

We just looked at how to configure and code the Timesheet List screen. Now it is time to review more complex Spring MVC features.

Enter Hours Screen: A Form Controller Example

The Timesheet List screen example we just looked at demonstrated how to develop a simple no-form controller. Now let's look at a slightly more complex example using the Enter Hours screen shown in Figure 7.6.

As you can see from Figure 7.6, the Enter Hours screen enables users to enter their hours and select the department these hours should be charged to (using a drop-down list). This functionality will require us to get a list of department names, bind the HTML form fields to a Java object, validate data entered on the screen, and display error/status messages on the screen.

Step-by-Step Configuration

The following are steps required to configure the Enter Hours screen in our `timex-servlet.xml` file. For the sake of brevity, I will not provide detailed explanations for the same steps we covered previously for the Timesheet List screen.

Map Handler

The following line provides the mapping for the Enter Hours view to the controller class:

```
<prop key="/enterhours.htm">enterHoursController</prop>
```

Define Controller and Associated Classes

The configuration for the Enter Hours controller is a bit more involved than the Timesheet List controller, so let's take a closer look at it.

First, you will notice that we have two model classes and one security-related (utility) class; these are required for the Enter Hours screen to function, which are configured as follows:

```
<property name="timesheetManager">
    <ref bean="timesheetManager" />
</property>
<property name="departmentManager">
    <ref bean="departmentManager" />
</property>
<property name="applicationSecurityManager">
    <ref bean="applicationSecurityManager" />
</property>
```

The following lines configure the command class for the `EnterHoursController`:

```
<property name="commandClass">
    <value>com.visualpatterns.timex.model.Timesheet</value>
</property>
```

The remainder of the configuration for this controller is Spring specific. For example, you will notice the validator property, which is an optional configuration but one we will use to validate the input data from the screen. The `formView` is the name of the actual form view and `successView` is the view you want Spring to redirect to upon a successful form submittal. The `sessionForm` property allows us to keep the same instance of the command object in the session versus creating a new one each time.

```
<property name="formView">
    <value>enterhours</value>
</property>
<property name="successView">
    <value>redirect:timesheetlist.htm</value>
</property>
<property name="validator">
    <ref bean="enterHoursValidator" />
</property>
```

ResourceBundle

One other configuration item we should look at is related to externalizing string messages for internationalization and other purposes, as shown here:

```
<bean id="messageSource"
    class="org.springframework.context.support.ResourceBundleMessageSource">
    <property name="basenames">
        <list>
            <value>messages</value>
        </list>
    </property>
</bean>
```

The `ResourceBundleMessageSource` Spring class relies on JDK's `java.util.ResourceBundle` class; we will use this to externalize our error and status messages in a file called `messages.properties` (placed in our `timex/src/conf` directory), which contains the following messages:

```
typeMismatch.int=Invalid number specified in a numeric field
error.enterhours.missingdepartment=Please select a department
error.login.invalid=Invalid employee id or password
message.enterhours.savesuccess=Timesheet saved successfully
```

Alternatively, Spring also provides a class named
`ReloadableResourceBundleMessageSource`, which can be used to reload the properties
periodically using its `cacheSeconds` parameter setting. This can come in handy during
development, when the messages file can change often.

Step-by-Step Coding

The following is Spring-related Java code we need to write for our form controller. By
the end of this Enter Hours example, we will end up with the following files (under our
`timex/src` directory):

- `conf/messages.properties`
- `java/com/visualpatterns/timex/controller/EnterHoursController.java`
- `java/com/visualpatterns/timex/controller/EnterHoursValidator.java`
- `java/com/visualpatterns/timex/controller/MinutesPropertyEditor.java`
- `java/com/visualpatterns/timex/view/enterhours.jsp`

Controller Code

Let's start by developing the controller. For starters, notice that instead of implementing
the `org.springframework.web.servlet.mvc.Controller` interface as we did for the
`TimesheetListController`, we are extending Spring's `org.springframework.`
`web.servlet.mvc.SimpleFormController` (concrete) class.

```
public class EnterHoursController extends SimpleFormController
```

`SimpleFormController` implements the Controller interface but also is part of a
hierarchy of various abstract controller-related classes (as we saw in Figure 7.3). It can
also automatically redirect the user to the default form view in case of errors and to a
different (or same) view if the form submission is successful; this is controlled using the
`successView` and `formView` properties we set in our `timex-servlet.xml` for the
`enterHoursController` Spring bean, as we saw earlier.

Let's take a look at the various Spring-related methods for form processing. However,
before looking at each method, let's look at the order in which these methods are called.

Figure 7.8 shows three boxes: the first box is essentially when the user first enters the
screen; the second box is when the user submits the form with invalid fields (that is, validation fails), and the third/last box shows which methods are called when the validation
is successful. Now let's review the type of code that goes into each of these methods.

The first method I will discuss is the `formBackingObject`, which returns a command
object that is used to hold the input data from the HTML form fields. Notice that we
fetch an existing `Timesheet` record from the database if parameters are passed into the
controller, indicating it is an edit operation versus an add operation, in which case, we
construct a new command object (which, incidentally, is a Time Expression domain/
business object).

```
protected Object formBackingObject(HttpServletRequest request)
{
    if (request.getParameter(TID) != null
            && request.getParameter(TID).trim().length() > 0)
        return timesheetManager.getTimesheet(Integer.parseInt(request
                .getParameter(TID)), false);

    Timesheet timesheet = new Timesheet();
    Employee employee = (Employee) applicationSecurityManager
            .getEmployee(request);
    timesheet.setEmployeeId(employee.getEmployeeId());
    timesheet.setStatusCode("P");
    timesheet.setPeriodEndingDate(DateUtil.getCurrentPeriodEndingDate());
    return timesheet;
}
```

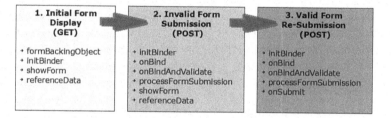

Figure 7.8   Life cycle of `EnterHoursController`.

Binding Directly to Domain (Business) Objects

One vital benefit of Spring MVC is the capability to bind the form fields directly to a domain object (Timesheet, for example)! This is one of the things that separates Spring from many other web frameworks.

Next up is the `initBinder` method, which provides a good place to register custom property editors (discussed shortly), as shown here:

```
binder.registerCustomEditor(int.class, new MinutesPropertyEditor());
```

The `referenceData` method is a good place to return read-only data for forms, typically for drop-down lists on the screen, as we have done by returning a list of departments for the Enter Hours screen:

```
model.put("departments", departmentManager.getDepartments());
```

Last, but not least, let's look at one of the most important methods in our controller class, the `onSubmit` method, shown next. As we saw in Figure 7.8, this method is called only after all validations have passed through successfully:

```
protected ModelAndView onSubmit(
        HttpServletRequest request,
        HttpServletResponse response,
        Object command,
        BindException errors)
{

    Timesheet timesheet = (Timesheet) command;
    timesheetManager.saveTimesheet(timesheet);
    request.getSession().setAttribute(
            "message",
            getMessageSourceAccessor().getMessage(
                    "message.enterhours.savesuccess"));
    return new ModelAndView(getSuccessView());

}
```

Also, notice the following code in the `onSubmit` method, which returns a successful message via the HTTP session. This message is extracted from the `messages.properties` file (using the `message.enterhours.savesuccess` key) and displayed on the Timesheet List screen.

This is about all we will cover for the controller class. Now, let's look at the other related classes used by this controller.

Custom Property Editor

As I mentioned earlier in this chapter, Spring makes heavy use of JavaBean style property editors (that is, `java.beans.PropertyEditorSupport`).

We will write a custom property editor class, `MinutesPropertyEditor`, to convert the hours entered on the screen to minutes because that is how our database is designed. The code for this class should be fairly straightforward because it performs the conversion from minutes to hours and vice versa (that is, multiplying or dividing by 60 minutes).

Validation

Our validation example is very also fairly straightforward. The main code really is in the `validate` method of this class, as shown in the following code excerpt:

```
Timesheet timesheet = (Timesheet)command;
if (timesheet.getDepartmentCode() == null ||
    timesheet.getDepartmentCode().trim().length() < 1)
    errors.reject("error.enterhours.missingdepartment");
```

The `error` variable shown here is of type `org.springframework.validation.Errors`, which provides several `reject` methods. The example I have shown here is useful for displaying global messages for the entire screen; I tend to use this method rather than the field-specific ones. For example, one of the field-specific `reject` methods has the following signature: `rejectValue(String field, String errorCode)`.

Also, you might have noticed an `onBindAndValidate` method in Figure 7.8. This method has the following signature:

```
onBindAndValidate(HttpServletRequest request,
                  Object command,
                  BindException errors)
```

This method is called by Spring automatically after the `validator` object has been invoked. This is a great place to do additional validations—for example, validations based on parameters sent in via HTTP request or database validations using one of the injected model classes, perhaps to check for duplicate records in the database.

View/JSP Code

Now that we are done looking at Java classes for the Enter Hours screen, we can look at the corresponding view code, located in our `enterhours.jsp` file. We will inspect a few excerpts here.

The first interesting block of code in our view is the displaying of error messages set in our `EnterHoursValidator` class, as shown here:

```
<spring:bind path="command.*">
    <c:if test="${not empty status.errorMessages}">
        <c:forEach var="error" items="${status.errorMessages}">
                        <font color="red"><c:out value="${error}"
escapeXml="false"/></font><br/>
        </c:forEach>
    </c:if>
</spring:bind>
```

This is the first time we are seeing the `spring:bind` tag, so let me explain a few things about it.

The key class behind the spring bind tag library is `org.springframework.web.servlet.support.BindStatus`. This tag enables you to bind the HTML form fields to the command object (Timesheet, in our case). However, it also provides access to a special variable named *status*. The `status` object contains some of the following attributes, which can be used in the JSP code:

- status.value—The value of a given attribute in the command object
- status.expression—The name of a given attribute in the command object
- status.error—A Boolean flag indicating whether an error exists
- status.errorMessage—A field-specific error message
- status.errorMessages—Global error messages for the view
- status.displayValue—Get a string value suitable for display using `toString`

Now let's look at how fields are bound. The following code shows how the departmentCode JSP/HTML variable is bound to the matching variable in our Command object (that is, Timesheet.departmentCode).

```
<spring:bind path="command.departmentCode">
```

That is really all there is to enterhours.jsp; some of the code I have not explained here is because we already covered similar code for the Timesheet List screen example earlier in this chapter (such as looping through code using the JSTL forEach tag).

I wish I could tell you there is more to Spring's bind tag library, but as I mentioned earlier, this library is fairly simple; but what you can do with it is quite powerful.

Binding to Custom (Nonbusiness) Command Objects

One of the key benefits of Spring MVC is that it enables you to bind HTML form fields directly to your domain object. Spring refers to these objects as *command* objects, perhaps based on the "Command" design pattern, which basically involves encapsulation of a request in an object. Another way to view the concept of a command object is to view it as our *form object* because it can hold all the values entered on the HTML form. However, because we can bind our HTML form fields directly to our business objects or have other data stored in this object, the term *command* is more appropriate.

For the Time Expression screens, we bind directly to Timesheet, our domain object. However, you always have the option to create a custom Command class, which could, for example, extend or contain the Timesheet class and provide some additional methods. For instance, I worked on a project where I need to assemble and disassemble a java.util.Date object because the HTML form had separate drop-downs for month, date, and year. In that case, I used methods such as assembleDate and disassembleDate in a custom command class.

There are a couple of ways you can approach a custom command class. For example, we could have done something like the following:

```
public class TimesheetCommand extends Timesheet
```

By doing this, you can still bind directly to the setter/getter methods of our business object, but also extend it by adding additional methods, as needed. Also, to construct a custom command class, you would need to specify it in the timex-servlet.xml file and also construct/return an object of this type in the formBackingObject method.

The other approach is to have the TimesheetCommand class contain a reference to the Timesheet object. For example, this class could have a constructor as follows:

```
public TimesheetCommand(Timesheet timesheet) {...}
```

Using this approach, you would bind the HTML form fields to the *Timesheet* object using a notation similar to this:

```
command.timesheet.minutesMon
```

The one problem you run into with this approach is related to JavaScript validation checking because JavaScript gets confused with the dots in HTML field names. For example, `command.timesheet.minutesMon` would translate into `timesheet.minutesMon` for the HTML input text field name if we used `${status.expression}` to fill in the name of this input field.

DateUtil.java

The one other notable file is `DateUtil.java`; this file provides some utility type date methods. For example, our `EnterHoursController` class uses one of these methods in its `formBackingObject` method:

```
timesheet.setPeriodEndingDate(DateUtil.getCurrentPeriodEndingDate());
```

JSP Taglib Directives

The one thing I haven't pointed out explicitly until now are the following lines of code you might have noticed in our JSP files:

```
<%@ taglib prefix="c"      uri="http://java.sun.com/jsp/jstl/core" %>
<%@ taglib prefix="fmt"    uri="http://java.sun.com/jsp/jstl/fmt" %>
<%@ taglib prefix="spring" uri="http://www.springframework.org/tags" %>
```

These directives are required before using a JSP tag library. More information on this and other JSP features can be found on the java.sun.com website.

Views with No Controllers

There might be times when you do not need or want to write a controller. For example, suppose we want to implement a help screen for Time Expression. We want this help screen to be accessible as `/help.htm` and have the real file (`help.jsp`) hidden in `/WEB-INF/jsp`. In this case, we would first define `UrlFilenameViewController` in `timex-servlet.xml`, as shown next:

```
<bean id="urlFilenameController"
class="org.springframework.web.servlet.mvc.UrlFilenameViewController"/>
```

Then we can reference `urlFilenameController` in our handler mapping (the `urlMap` bean in `timex-servlet.xml`, for example):

```
<prop key="/help.htm">urlFilenameController</prop>
```

Spring HandlerInterceptors

Until now, we developed our Timesheet List and Enter Hours screens without worrying about authentication. However, one of our fundamental requirements from Chapter 2 is that employees can see only their own timesheets, which brings us to our Sign In and Sign Out features.

Spring provides the concept of interceptors for web application development; these enable you to intercept HTTP requests. We will use this feature to provide authentication for Time Expression.

To implement our sign in/out features, we will need to create the following files under the `src/java/com/visualpatterns/timex` directory:

- `controller/HttpRequestInterceptor.java`
- `controller/SignInController.java`
- `controller/SignInValidator.java`
- `controller/SignOutController.java`
- `util/ApplicationSecurityManager.java`
- `util/DateUtil.java`
- `view/signin.jsp`

Authentication for Time Expression

The authentication for Time Expression is enabled by having all HTTP requests requiring authentication to be mapped as they go through our interceptor class, `HttpRequestInterceptor.java`. The following code excerpt demonstrates how an intercepted request can be preprocessed:

```
public class HttpRequestInterceptor extends HandlerInterceptorAdapter
{
    private ApplicationSecurityManager applicationSecurityManager;

    public boolean preHandle(HttpServletRequest request,
                             HttpServletResponse response,
                             Object handler)
        throws Exception
    {
        Employee employee =
            (Employee)applicationSecurityManager.getEmployee(request);
        if (employee == null)
        {
            response.sendRedirect(this.signInPage);
            return false;
        }

        return true;
```

Notice the use of `ApplicationSecurityManager` here (and referenced several times earlier in this chapter). The complete code for this class should be fairly straightforward to follow because it essentially provides methods for seting, getting, and removing a HTTP session attribute named user (of type `Employee`, one of our domain objects), as demonstrated in the following code excerpt, which sets this attribute:

```
public static final String USER = "user";
public void setEmployee(HttpServletRequest request, Object employee)
{
    request.getSession(true).setAttribute(USER, employee);
}
```

The `SignInController` class validates the login and also sets the `Employee` domain object using the `ApplicationSecurityManager.setEmployee` method, as shown next:

```
Employee formEmployee = (Employee) command;
Employee dbEmployee = (Employee) command;
if ((dbEmployee = employeeManager.getEmployee(formEmployee
        .getEmployeeId())) == null)
    errors.reject("error.login.invalid");
else
    applicationSecurityManager.setEmployee(request, dbEmployee);
```

Our `SignOutController` class signs the user out by removing the Employee attribute from the session, as shown here:

```
applicationSecurityManager.removeEmployee(request);
```

Note

Our application uses a minimal index.jsp file, which will serve as our welcome file; this is placed under our src/web directory and forwards the request to the our `signin.htm` URL, as shown here:

```
<c:redirect url="signin.htm"/>
```

Our Sample Application—in Action!

Now that we have our web user-interface components (controller and view) and our model code developed, we have a completely functional application that can be built, deployed, and test driven!

For example, we can now type ant deploy on the command line and have it (hot) deploy to our Tomcat webapps directory. After deployment, the application can be accessed from a web browser using a URL such as http://localhost:8080/timex/. Figures 7.9 through 7.11 show our screens in action.

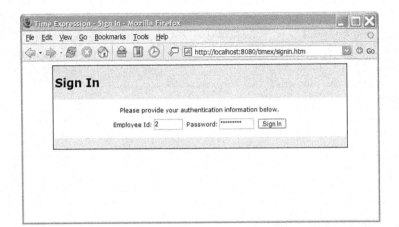

Figure 7.9 Sign In screen.

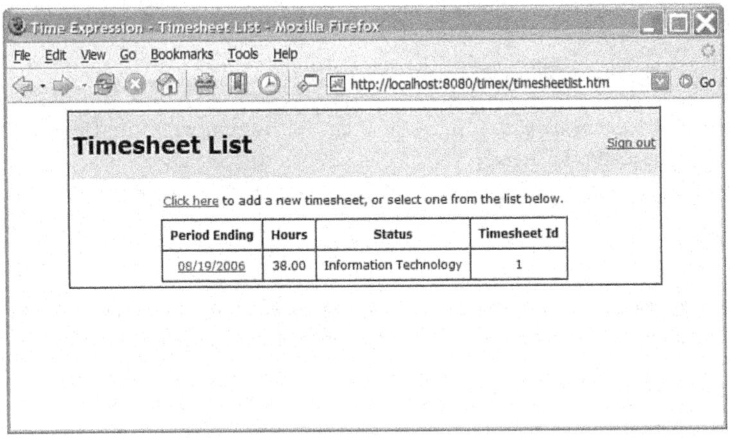

Figure 7.10 Timesheet List screen.

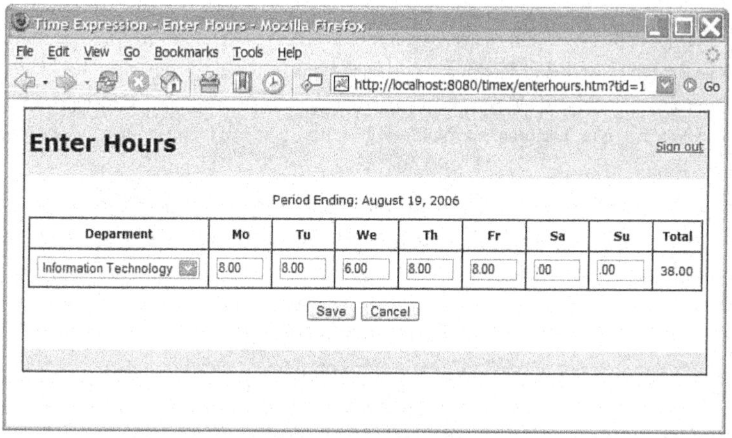

Figure 7.11 Enter Hours screen.

Personal Opinion: Designing and Coding with Interfaces

The Spring reference documentation and many articles on the web recommend designing and coding with interfaces. Spring supports both interface-based and class-based beans.

You might have noticed in Time Expression's class design that I have not used Java interfaces. This is related to my philosophy on when and where to use interfaces.

Let me start out by saying that I like programming with Java interfaces a lot! However, similar to the way many people jumped on the EJB bandwagon a few years ago, I see people jumping on the interface bandwagon recently. So, allow me to share my thoughts on this matter; you may agree or disagree with them. I would like to begin by telling you a little story on the topic of designing and coding with interfaces.

I have been using interfaces since 1996 and love the concept behind them. In 1997, I developed a 100% pure Java-based backup software named BackOnline (http://visualpatterns.com/backonline/). This product was mentioned in several well-known trade journals and won a Best Client award at JavaOne; it was even nominated by Scott McNealy (CEO, Sun Microsystems) for a Computerworld-Smithsonian award. BackOnline is a client-server product; the server is a multithreaded and multiuser server that essentially receives the files and stores them using an implementation class for an interface named DataStore. The DataStore interface has FTP-like methods, such as get, put, open, close, and so on; these, had to be implemented by concrete classes. The BackOnline software (which is no longer being sold) came prepackaged with two default DataStore implementation classes, DataStoreFileSystem and DataStoreJDBC (the fully qualified implementation class names were specified in a configuration file and dynamically loaded at runtime). DataStoreFileSystem essentially used the java.io package to store the files using the local file system. DataStoreJDBC used JDBC to store the file contents as Binary Large Objects (BLOBs) in a relational database.

I provided Javadoc and additional technical documentation for the DataStore interface, so Internet Service Providers (ISPs) and products vendors who signed an OEM (original equipment manufacturer) with my company could write their own custom implementations, if necessary. For example, an ISP might have wanted to take advantage of the native operating system's features, such as extended file permissions.

For the BackOnline example I just went through, using interfaces was an obvious choice. Also, many times I find that interfaces work well for lower-level APIs, such as the one I described for BackOnline or ones you find in frameworks such as the JDK or the Spring Framework (for example, `java.util.Collections` or `java.sql.Connection`). Furthermore, interfaces are great, if you think the underlying implementation can change (such as logging, authentication service, and OS specific functionality). Of course, with remote technologies (EJB, for example), you have no choice but to use interfaces.

For business applications, more times than not, especially on smaller projects, I have found that you need only one implementation of domain (business) objects or service objects (such as the TimesheetManager class for Time Expression). Furthermore, it doesn't make sense to have interfaces for domain objects (such as Timesheet.java, for example).

Creating one interface file for each implementation class amounts to unnecessary overhead, in my opinion. For large projects, this can amount to lots of extra `.java` (and `.class`) files without potentially adding much value. On the flip side, there are times when using interfaces makes sense. For example, in Chapter 2, we discussed multiple user types (roles) for the Time Expression application, such as Employee, Manager, and Executive. These could easily be created as concrete classes that implement an interface named Person or Role. On the other hand, given the common behavior in these objects, an abstract class would also make a lot of sense because the common methods could be pulled up into a super (parent) class (called Person, for example).

In summary, given the right opportunity, you should use interfaces—but do not use them because it has been preached in some book or article as the right thing to do. Furthermore, you should not feel at fault for not using interfaces for each and every concrete class you write. Focus more on having a sound design for your application—for example, clean separation of layers, good database design, easy-to-follow code, appropriate use of architecture/design patterns, and so on. I hope I do not sound dismissive about interfaces because that is certainly not my intention; my point is to use everything in moderation and appropriately.

New Tag Libraries in Spring Framework 2.0

At the time of this writing, the Spring team was getting close to releasing additional tag libraries to make it simpler to work with Spring with JSP. However, the design of these new tag libraries was still evolving, so I was unable to cover this with accuracy.

A Word About Spring Web Flow and Portlet API

Two additional user-interface Spring technologies might be of interest to you, if you have the need for features they provide.

Spring Web Flow

Spring Web Flow, based on similar concepts as Spring Web MVC Framework, essentially provides wizardlike screen functionality to implement a business process. Good examples of such applications include an online shopping site such as amazon.com, which requires you to go through several screens before the transaction is considered complete. This type of functionality requires session/state management, which provides the capability to go back and forth through the screens without losing the information you have already entered. This is precisely the type of functionality Web Flow eases. However, our application, Time Expression, does not require such a feature and would not be a good example for the Spring's Web Flow.

Even though Web Flow is not covered in this book, given the scope of this book, I highly recommend that you give this technology a serious look if your requirements call for this type of functionality.

Spring Portlet API

The Spring Portlet API is a new addition to Spring 2.0. It essentially implements the JSR-168 Portlet Specification defined on the Java Community Process (JCP) website (http://www.jcp.org/en/jsr/detail?id=168). According to this, the Portlet API can be used for "Portal computing addressing the areas of aggregation, personalization, presentation and security." Another way to look at this is that *portlets* are part of a *portal* website, which might contain several portlets. Portlets are different from servlets in that they do not redirect or forward any requests from or to the browser; instead, they are managed by a portlet container.

If you are interested in this API, you should check out the JCP website. Also, you might want to check out Apache's Pluto, a reference implementation for the Portlet API.

Summary

In this chapter, we

- Looked at the various benefits of using Spring MVC
- Took an in-depth look at the Spring Web MVC Framework
- Built three of the screens in Time Expression using Spring MVC: one as a no-form screen, the others as form screens

We covered a lot material in this chapter, but we aren't done with Spring just yet. In the next few chapters, we will touch on various additional facets of the Spring Framework, including

- The Spring IDE plug-in for Eclipse
- Job Scheduling
- Emailing

Meanwhile, if you want to dig into more Spring, take a look at Spring's JPetstore example and Reference Documentation, both part of the Spring distribution software.

In the next chapter, we will look at Eclipse, which will completely change the way we have been working in this book! In other words, we will change from command-line programming to a sophisticated Integrated Development Environment (IDE), which will make coding, unit testing, and debugging much easier—in short, agile Java development!

Recommended Resources

The following websites are relevant to or provide additional information on the topics discussed in this chapter:

Websites for competing technologies to ones discussed in this chapter:

- Apache Jakarta Tapestry   http://jakarta.apache.org/tapestry/
- Apache Jakarta Turbine   http://jakarta.apache.org/turbine/
- Apache Struts   http://struts.apache.org/
- Apache Tapestry   http://jakarta.apache.org/tapestry/
- Apache Tomcat   http://tomcat.apache.org/
- Apache Tomcat `antiJARLocking` and `antiResourceLocking` configuration attribute   http://tomcat.apache.org/tomcat-5.5-doc/config/context.html#Standard%20Implementation
- Apache Tomcat Ant Tasks   http://tomcat.apache.org/tomcat-5.0-doc/catalina/docs/api/org/apache/catalina/ant/package-summary.html
- Apache Velocity   http://jakarta.apache.org/velocity/
- FreeMarker   http://www.freemarker.org/
- JavaServer Faces   http://java.sun.com/j2ee/javaserverfaces/
- Jetty Servlet Container   http://jetty.mortbay.org/jetty/
- Mock Objects   http://mockobjects.com
- OpenSymphony WebWork   http://www.opensymphony.com/webwork/
- Spring Discussion Forums   http://forum.springframework.org/
- Spring Framework   http://springframework.org
- The original MVC   http://heim.ifi.uio.no/~trygver/themes/mvc/mvc-index.html

8

The Eclipse Phenomenon!

Release 1, Week 6, Iteration 3

Susan: Happy birthday, Steve. How does it feel to be one year older?

Steve: Oh, it feels great and not just because it's my birthday but also because we just deployed our app into production. Raj figured out the transaction management problem. Also, the eclipse I've been waiting on for so long, is tonight. You guys should check it out, I believe you will enjoy the experience.

(c) Visual Patterns, Inc.

U P TO THIS POINT IN THE BOOK, we have been working on the command line (to run Ant and JUnit, for example). Working on the command line could be viewed as contrary to *agile* development by some. However, I'm a big believer that you need to understand the fundamentals first—in other words, what is happening underneath the covers. Furthermore, many developers prefer the command line and are highly effective working in this fashion, so I wanted to provide value to those developers as well. Now it is time to kick things into high gear by using the Eclipse SDK!

The Eclipse SDK is a useful and highly effective Integrated Development Environment (IDE) for programming in Java and so much more, as you will see shortly. Although the Eclipse SDK is quite robust in itself, what truly makes the Eclipse SDK so powerful is that it is also a platform with well-defined standards for developing plug-ins, small applications that run inside Eclipse. Hundreds of plug-ins are available for Eclipse. For example, at the time of this writing, a query on google.com for the words "eclipse" and "plug-in" resulted in millions of hits!

If you already use the Eclipse SDK or have used other products such as Mozilla Firefox browser (http://mozilla.com), you will appreciate the power of plug-ins. In my opinion, the plug-in paradigm is taking open source to a new level, primarily because an organization such as the Eclipse Foundation can put its muscle behind a platform. But the community as a whole completes and enhances the platform by adding to it (using plug-ins, for example).

In this chapter we will take a close at the Eclipse SDK and various plug-ins useful for rapid Java development.

This is a special chapter because I have learned so much more about Eclipse while researching for this chapter; in fact, my entire perspective on Eclipse has changed. I will share with you information about the history behind the Eclipse Foundation, the Eclipse platform, the enormous number of plug-ins, and how tremendously active the Eclipse community is. I hope by the end of this chapter, you will have one word to say about the Eclipse phenomenon—*wow!*

What's Covered in This Chapter

In this chapter, we will take an in-depth look at Eclipse and how to leverage it for our sample application, Time Expression. By the time this chapter is complete, we will have shifted every single technology we have covered so far in this book into Eclipse, using a variety of free and sophisticated plug-ins. In this chapter we will learn about

- The Eclipse Foundation
- The Eclipse platform and projects
- Eclipse SDK concepts
- Installing Eclipse
- Setting up Eclipse for Time Expression
- The Java Development Tools (JDT) plug-in
- Eclipse Web Tools Platform Project (for Tomcat support, JSP editing, and other JEE support)
- Using Eclipse for Time Expression (starting Tomcat and connecting to HSQLDB, for example)

- Eclipse team support using CVS
- Plug-in directories for both free and commercial plug-ins
- Eclipse tips and tricks
- Results of a 30-minute comparison to IntelliJ and NetBeans

Why SDK and Not IDE?

SDK (Software Development Kit) typically implies an API, whereas IDE (Integrated Development Environment) typically indicates a coding and debugging environment. The Eclipse documentation refers to its IDE as the Eclipse SDK (perhaps because it is also an API for developing plug-ins). However, it is perfectly okay to call it the Eclipse IDE; many people do.

The Eclipse Foundation

Let me start by quoting some material directly from the Eclipse website, eclipse.org, because this will give you an immediate background on the Eclipse Foundation, its history, and the major players behind this foundation.

"Eclipse is an open source community whose projects are focused on providing a vendor-neutral open development platform and application frameworks for building software. The Eclipse Foundation is a not-for-profit corporation formed to advance the creation, evolution, promotion, and support of the Eclipse Platform and to cultivate both an open source community and an ecosystem of complementary products, capabilities, and services."

The website goes on to say:

"Industry leaders Borland, IBM, MERANT, QNX Software Systems, Rational Software, Red Hat, SuSE, TogetherSoft and Webgain formed the initial eclipse.org Board of Stewards in November 2001. By the end of 2003, this initial consortium had grown to over 80 members."

Eclipse was originally developed by Object Technology International (OTI), which was later purchased by IBM. IBM subsequently donated the Eclipse technology (reportedly worth $40 million) to open source and recruited the various corporations mentioned previously to jointly develop highly integrated products for this platform (in the form of plug-ins).

The Eclipse Foundation is similar to the Apache Foundation in that it provides open-source tools. However, the one underlying difference is that Eclipse tools tend to be more graphical in nature versus Apache's tools, which tend to be more text based, such as servers, APIs, and tools (Ant and Tomcat, for example). I think this is a refreshing change. In my opinion, the Java tools vendors are beginning to finally get it (see the sidebar later in this chapter, "The GUI Development Tools Battle Has, Only Now, Begun!"). Why it took so long is beyond my comprehension, considering robust GUI development/debugging tools for other programming languages have been around for a couple of decades.

Personal Opinion: The Java Versus Microsoft Thing

This chapter isn't about a Java versus Microsoft comparison or battle, but I must deviate a bit here.

I have a love-hate relationship with Microsoft because, on one hand, I hate how they tried to derail Java a few years ago; on the other hand, I also love many products they produce, one example being Microsoft Windows Media Center Edition. Having said this, let me clearly state that Eclipse is the first tool I have seen in the Java community that comes even close to competing with Microsoft's Visual Studio software. This is what excites me about Eclipse compared to other Java products.

What makes Eclipse such a powerful product isn't just that it is an awesome GUI development tool, which it is. Other products, such as JetBrain's IntelliJ and Sun Microsystem's NetBeans, are just as good. However, what truly makes the Eclipse phenomenon so compelling is the sheer number of sophisticated plug-ins available in the marketplace and the passion behind this platform from the commercial and open-source communities. From hundreds of free plug-ins to a large and quickly growing commercial plug-in market, the Eclipse community is growing by leaps and bounds. One such example includes myeclipseide.com, which offers a unique yearly subscription-based model and provides every plug-in under the sun that you will need for enterprise software development. Also, the Eclipse consortium had more than 80 members in 2003 and is growing quickly with major players such as Borland, Rational Software, Red Hat, SUSE, and TogetherSoft. In fact, in early 2005, Borland announced that going forward, their Java development flagship product, JBuilder, would be based on the Eclipse platform.

A couple of juicy facts you might find interesting are related to Ward Cunningham and Erich Gamma. Ward, the inventor of Wiki, co-inventor of CRC cards, and a significant contributor to Extreme Programming, left Microsoft's Patterns and Practices Team to join the Eclipse Foundation. Erich is the coauthor of the popular Gang of Four *Design Patterns* book and the JUnit testing framework. He is one of the key people involved in the JDT Project. It is comforting to know that the Eclipse foundation is able to recruit such well-respected, innovative leaders in our industry.

In short, the Eclipse community has been growing at a rapid pace, but in my opinion, it is about to experience exponential growth!

The Eclipse Platform and Projects

The Eclipse platform is an open source, cross-platform, and extensible IDE built using Java. The Eclipse platform is essentially a framework that provides a set of services that other plug-ins can build on (as depicted in Figure 8.1). Each plug-in is developed to the same platform, which translates into a set of highly integrated tools.

Eclipse: A Consolidated Toolbox

The Eclipse platform, combined with the large number of highly integrated plug-ins available, essentially serves as a consolidated software development environment. For example, there are plug-ins available for UML diagramming, coding, debugging, database management, unit testing, application server management, documentation, and much more. You could think of Eclipse as a toolbox, analogous to a carpenter's toolbox, which has many types of tools to get the job done.

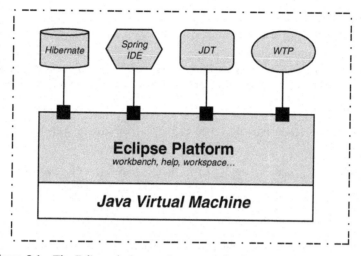

Figure 8.1   The Eclipse platform and some sample plug-ins (for example, JDT).

Eclipse comes bundled with the Java Development Tools (JDT), which is of high interest to us, given the nature of this book. However, Eclipse doesn't stop at Java; plug-ins are available for languages including HTML, C/C++, COBOL, and Eiffel. In addition, you will find third-party plug-ins for other languages such as PERL, PHP, and Ruby on Rails.

You can also develop your own custom plug-in to extend Eclipse. Although I have not personally done this, others who have suggest that it is not that difficult to do because you develop the plug-ins in Java. Also, you will typically hear about Eclipse in the context of development tools, plug-ins are under development for functionality other than programming, such as content management and other tools, from companies such as webMethods, SAS, Hitachi Software, and many more.

Eclipse Platform Objectives

Let's take a look at the objectives for the Eclipse platform, set by the Eclipse Foundation. It is a good idea to know these because it'll help tie things together when we see the enormous functionality provided by Eclipse in this chapter. Some of Eclipse's objectives are

- To provide a robust platform for highly integrated application development tools
- To enable viewing or editing of any content type (Java, JSP, XML, C/C++, Word documents, and others, for example)
- To attract a large community of developers to develop plug-ins for this platform

Eclipse Projects

To give you a better idea of the growing scope of the Eclipse Foundation, Table 8.1 shows the Eclipse projects underway at the time of this writing. Note that every project is overseen by a Project Management Committee (PMC). Each project can be divided into subprojects with each having a leader. Furthermore, each subproject, in turn, can have one or more components.

Table 8.1   Eclipse Projects (Organized by Topics) at the Time of This Writing

Topic	Project(s)
Application Development	Application Lifecycle Management Framework Model Driven Development Infrastructure Eclipse Communications Framework Buckminister Component Assembly Project Eclipse SDK Platform EJB 3.0/Java Persistence API Development Tools (Dali-ORM)
	Task Focused UI (Mylar Project) Parallel Development Tools Business Intelligence and Reporting Tools (BIRT) Project Voice Tools Project Eclipse Web Tools Platform Project
Editors	Graphical Editor Framework (GEF) Visual Editor (VE) Eclipse Web Tools Platform Project (HTML, JSP)
Modeling	Generative Model Transformer Graphical Modeling Framework EMF Modeling Framework UML2—EMF-based implementation of UML 2.0
Performance and Testing	Eclipse Test and Performance Tools Platform Project
Programming Languages	COBOL AspectJ Development Tools Project C/C++ IDE Photran project (Fortran) JDT—Java Development Tools Java/JSP—Eclipse Web Tools Platform Project

Eclipse SDK Concepts

When people use Eclipse for the first time, they often find it slightly confusing because of their unfamiliarity with the concepts. This was the case with me, as well. However, I found that I needed to understand only three to five basic concepts about Eclipse to instantly become productive with this tool. So, let's review these here. Note that I have intentionally provided brief descriptions here because we will look at these concepts in practice when we set up Time Expression in Eclipse.

Disclaimer: Screenshots of Eclipse in This Chapter

Almost all the screenshots of the Eclipse SDK are taken in 800×600 resolution in this chapter for the sake of legibility. However, most developers prefer a higher resolution, such as 1024×768. I use 1600×1050, for example. Therefore, the screenshots here do not do Eclipse justice because I'm unable to show how one would *practically* use Eclipse—that is, with lots of editors and views stacked in the workbench at one time.

Workspace

Considering how vital the term workspace is to Eclipse, let's begin with this concept first.

Simply put, a *workspace* is a directory for your projects. It is essentially the top-level (parent) directory under which your project-related files (.java files, for example) are organized. In my personal case, I used C:\anil\rapidjava, as you will see later in the chapter. So, everything under this directory (timex/ and the various subdirectories, that is) is considered part of the same workspace.

Workbench, Perspectives, Editors, and Views

The Eclipse workbench is the first thing we see when we start Eclipse. In other words, it essentially is the Eclipse platform plus some basic functionality such as management of projects. The actual work, such as editing and viewing, is handled by the plug-ins (the JDT, for example).

A workbench contains an arrangement of editors and corresponding views; this task-specific arrangement is called a *perspective*. Figure 8.2 shows a representation of how a user can switch between one perspective to another, using a single click or shortcut key combination (Ctrl+F8, for example).

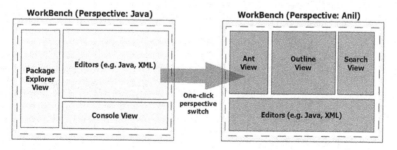

Figure 8.2 Diagrammatic representation of the Eclipse SDK.

Perspectives

A *perspective* is a collection of views and editors arranged in the fashion you like. A workbench can consists of several perspectives, but only one can be visible at time; however, we can quickly switch between perspectives with the click of a button or by using Ctrl+F8 (COMMAND+F8 on Mac OS X). Perspectives provide a nice way to arrange task-specific views and editors of your choice. For example, in the Debug perspective, it makes sense to have the Breakpoints view, whereas in the Java Browsing view, it doesn't. Note that the views can be arranged as attached (tiled or stacked as tabs) and detached windows.

There are some predefined perspectives such as Java, Java Browsing, Debug, and others. Furthermore, we can create custom perspectives. For example, I tend to create my own perspective using an existing perspective (such as Java), altering it by adding/removing views and then saving it as a perspective named Anil (I know, not the most creative name but it certainly doesn't conflict with the prepackaged perspective names). Figure 8.3 shows Eclipse using my own custom perspective, and Figure 8.4 shows a predefined Debug perspective.

Editors and Views

Editors, as you would expect, allow us to open, edit, save, and close files. By the end of this chapter, we will have editors for plain text, .java files, .jsp files, XML files, and more.

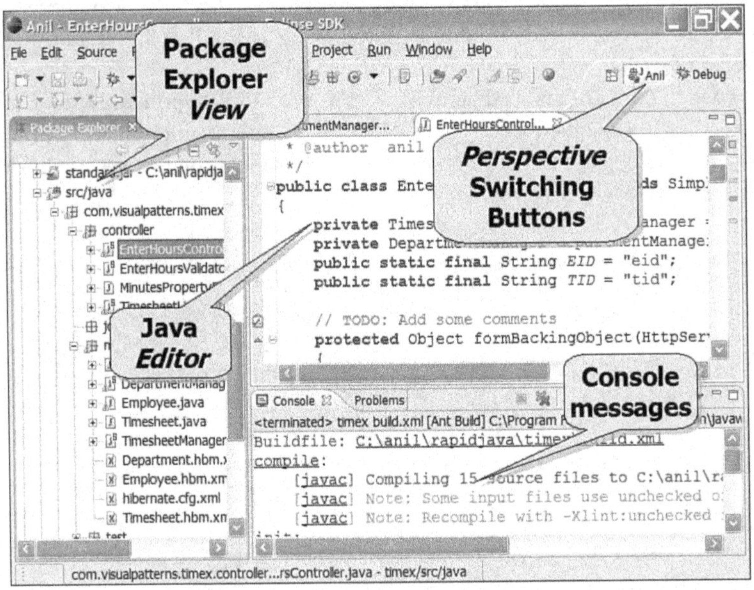

Figure 8.3   Custom perspective (Anil).

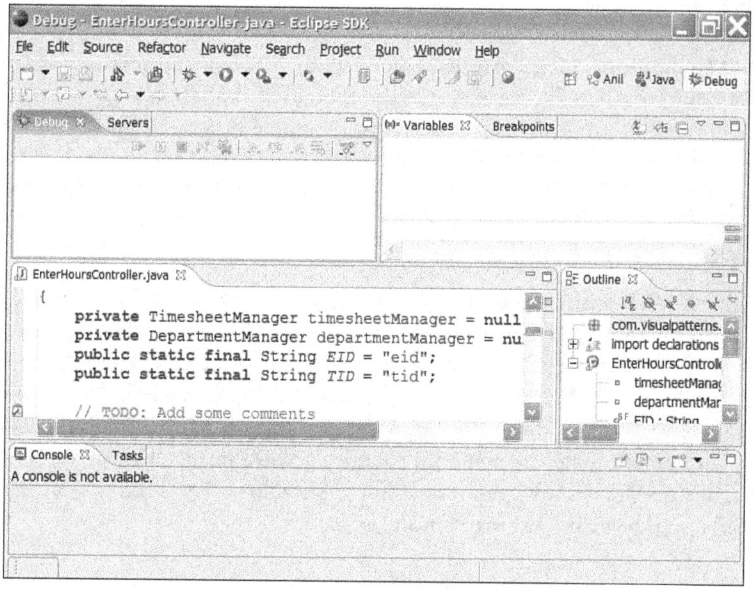

Figure 8.4   Predefined Debug perspective.

Views supplement editors by providing read-only information, typically about the file being edited in the editor. For example, the Outline view provides a list of methods for the Java file being edited. However, for an XML file, you would see the various XML elements and attributes for the file being edited.

The Eclipse platform, combined with the JDT, comes prepackaged with various views such as Ant, Console, Breakpoints, Package Explorer, and so on. Others include Bookmarks, Properties, Tasks, Problems, Progress, Call Hierarchy, and many more.

Several editors and views can be grouped together using tabs. For example, Figure 8.4 shows the Console and Task view with tabs grouped together at the bottom part of the screen.

Project

A *project* is a collection of your files that you manipulate, such as .java, .xml, and so on. In addition, Eclipse provides the capability to work with multiple projects of different types (for example, simple Java versus a web application) under the same workspace, each with project-specific configuration versus a default, workbenchwide configuration.

Because we will be setting up Time Expression in Eclipse shortly, we will edit all the Time Expression files from a single place by navigating the files and directories with the help of the Package Explorer or Navigator views. In other words, we can work with all our .java, .xml, .properties, .jsp, and other files from a single place.

Plug-ins

Plug-ins are applications (programs) that can easily be installed and used inside the Eclipse platform/workbench. For example, the JDT itself is a plug-in. However, when many people think of plug-ins, they think mini or simple programs. This is not the case with Eclipse, as you will most definitely see later in this chapter when we discuss the JDT in-depth and install and use the Eclipse Web Tools Platform (WTP) set of plug-ins.

Wizards

As we begin to work with Eclipse more and more, you will notice that there are wizards galore in Eclipse! Figure 8.5 shows a partial list of wizards you see when we select the File, New, Other option (or when we use the OS-specific hot key, such as Ctrl+N on Microsoft Windows). By the time we are done with this chapter, we will have approximately 100 wizards available to us, including plug-ins for setting up Tomcat, creating Hibernate configuration and mapping files, working with Spring application context files, managing HSQLDB, and even others not applicable to Time Expression, such as creating EJBs, web services, and many more!

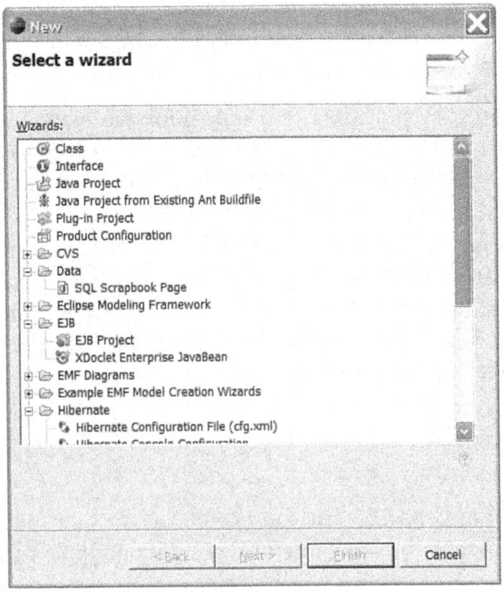

Figure 8.5   Eclipse wizards.

Installing Eclipse

Now that we have some background information on the Eclipse Foundation, the Eclipse platform, and its architecture, let's have some fun with Eclipse.

Before you can run Eclipse, a compatible JRE (v1.3 or later) must be installed on your system (see the sidebar Java Runtime Environment [JRE] Required by Eclipse"). If you already have a compatible JRE installed on your system or you installed it in Chapter 4, "Environment Setup: JDK, Ant, and JUnit," you should be okay. You may want to run `java -version` on the command line to verify that the Java VM is installed and that you have the appropriate version.

Java Runtime Environment (JRE) Required by Eclipse

According to the Frequently Asked Questions (FAQ) on the Eclipse website (eclipse.org), if Eclipse does not run on your system, "the number one reason is that the JRE cannot be located to run Eclipse. You must have a Java Runtime Environment (JRE) installed on your computer. Eclipse requires version 1.3 or 1.4 of a Java 2 Standard Edition JRE. The Eclipse SDK does not ship with a JRE." For more information, refer to the Eclipse website.

Before we go through the setup steps, let's take another look at the directory structure (shown in Figure 8.6) that we established in Chapter 3, "XP and AMDD-Based Architecture and Design Modeling," because we will be working with it in Eclipse.

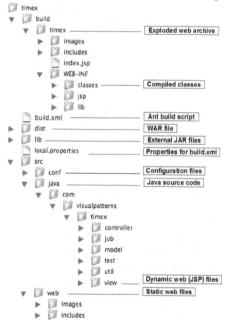

Figure 8.6   Development directory structure for Time Expression.

Now, it is time to run Eclipse! The following simple steps should get us up and running with Eclipse within minutes (assuming that you have the correct JRE installed and a fast Internet connection to download Eclipse).

Let's download the latest version of Eclipse SDK from http://www.eclipse.org/. The version used through this chapter is 3.1.2 (which was the latest version available at the time of this writing). Note that the prebuilt Eclipse SDK binaries include platforms such as Microsoft Windows, Linux, Solaris, AIX, HP-UX, and Mac OS X. At first, you might find the eclipse.org website confusing or overwhelming because there are so many projects and mirror sites; I typically start with the Downloads section, which can be accessed directly from the home page.

After we have unpacked the Eclipse SDK archive (.zip or .tar.gz, for example), run the Eclipse application from the /eclipse directory. (Depending on your platform, this executable file will be named eclipse.exe, eclipse.app, or simply eclipse).

Right after the eclipse command, we should see a Select a Workspace prompt similar to what is shown in Figure 8.7. Notice that I have entered C:\anil\rapidjava for my Windows directory; this is one level above the actually timex directory shown in Figure 8.6. After specifying the correct directory, click OK to proceed.

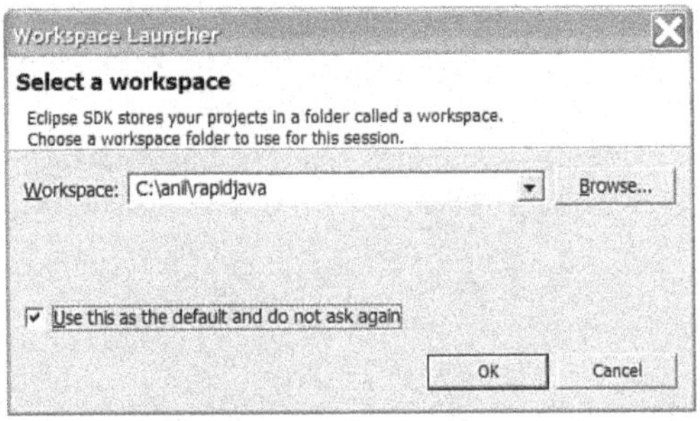

Figure 8.7   Select a Workspace prompt.

Next, we see the welcome screen shown in Figure 8.8. Close this by clicking the X next to the Welcome tab or the Workbench icon at the top-right.

Is Eclipse Itself Developed in Java?

One of the things you will notice with Eclipse is how snappy this product's user interface is (unlike older first-generation Java-based tools). In fact, you might even wonder if it is developed in Java given how fast and responsive this application is. The short answer is, yes and no. The Eclipse SDK uses the Java-based Standard Widget Toolkit (SWT), which in turn uses the native operating system's GUI widgets.

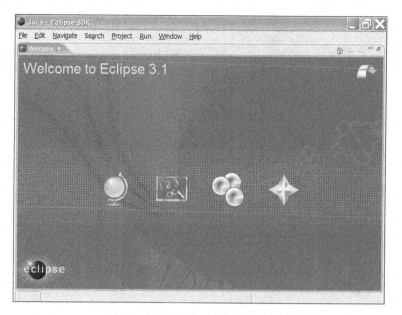

Figure 8.8   Eclipse welcome screen.

Setting Up Eclipse for Time Expression

So far I have provided you with a basic understanding of Eclipse, enough to move forward with setting Time Expression. Now we can build an Eclipse Project using our existing Ant `build.xml` file. This is done via the File, New, Project menu option. Figure 8.9 shows the New Project Wizard screen. Select Java Project from an Existing Ant Buildfile from the options and click Next.

Figure 8.10 shows the next screen where we actually specify our existing Ant `build.xml` file. This is the big moment for us because after this step we can begin working with all our existing source code within Eclipse; no more command line! So, we can click the Finish button.

Figure 8.11 shows the first screen we should see immediately after the new project has been created, named `timex`. However, as you might notice, we have a few (more like 100) problems as shown in the Problems view. This is related to the way I chose to set up the source and output directories for Time Expression.

I could have demonstrated a smooth working example here that used Eclipse's default directory structure; however, I intentionally wanted to demonstrate this because there are good chances you (or the organization you work for) already have a standard way of establishing your directory structures. Anyway, we can easily fix this problem as explained next.

Figure 8.9   The New Project, Select a Wizard screen.

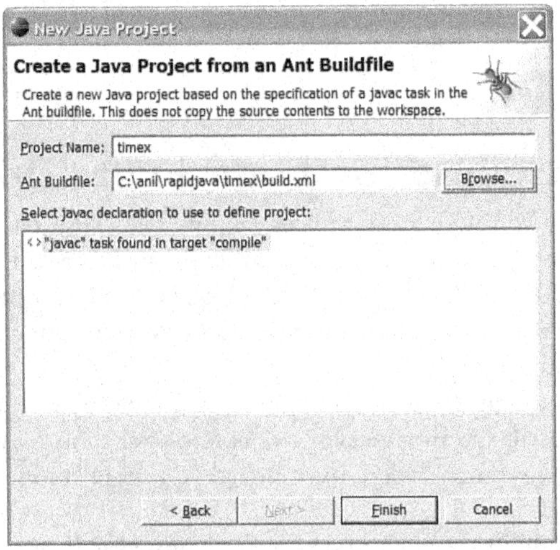

Figure 8.10   The New Java Project, Create a Java Project from an Ant Buildfile Wizard.

Let's expand the `timex` project's file/directory hierarchy tree in the Package Explorer view (on the left side of the screen). Locate the src directory in the tree and right-click it to show the context menu. Select Build Path, Remove from Build Path, as shown in Figure 8.12.

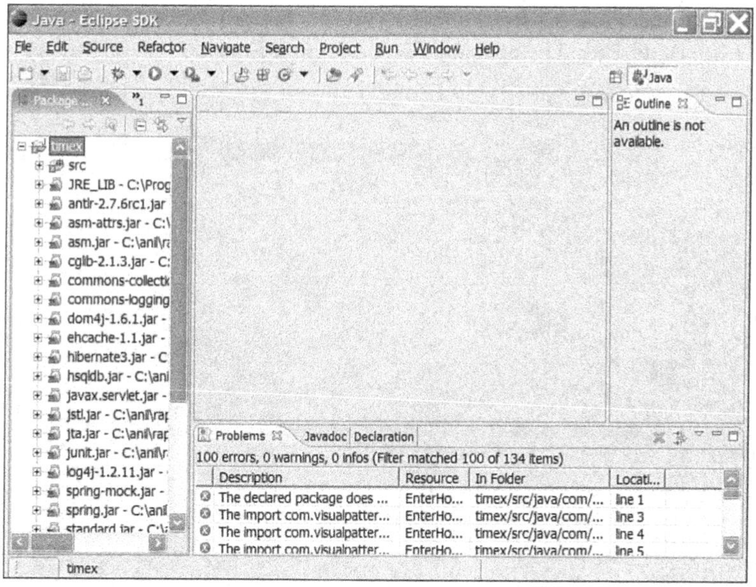

Figure 8.11 Newly created timex project.

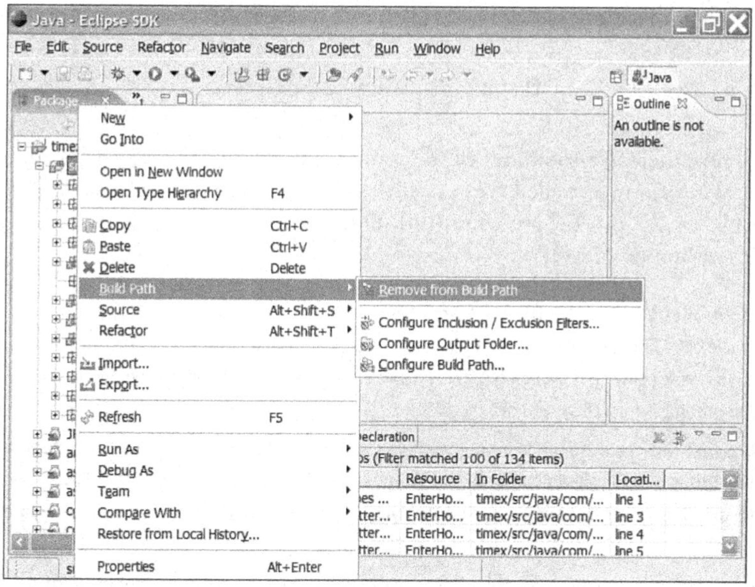

Figure 8.12 Remove src/ from build path.

After we do this, the src directory reappears on the list, but with a different icon. Note that we did not actually delete the directory, just removed it from the build path. Now, we will expand the src directory, locate the java subdirectory underneath it; right-click it and select the Build Path, Use as Source Folder option from the context menu, as shown in Figure 8.13.

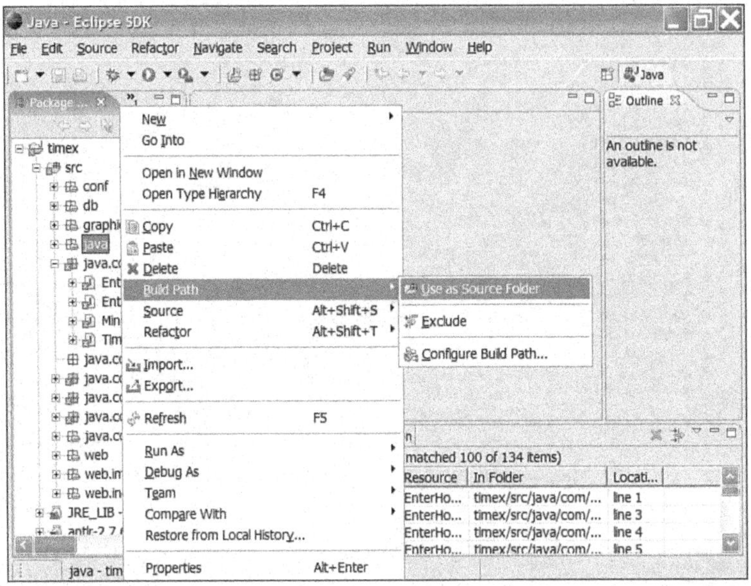

Figure 8.13   Use as Source Folder.

We are almost there. We took care of the source directory; now we need to adjust the output folder for our compiled (.class) files, so we can use our Ant build.xml file to compile classes and also Eclipse's built-in Builder feature (see the sidebar "Save Compiles Within the Blink of an Eye!").

Save Compiles Within the Blink of an Eye!

If you have been programming for some time now, you are probably used to the trial-and-error technique—that is, you write some code, compile it, fix compile errors, recompile, fix more compiler errors, recompile, run, find runtime errors. Okay, you get the picture.

Eclipse comes with a built-in builder for compiling your .java files to .class files every time you save your file. This is perhaps one of the most important, yet least advertised, features of Eclipse (it is a personal favorite of mine). The compilation is so fast that you won't even know the compilation took place. Pretty cool, huh?

If I press Ctrl+S to save my .java file, I instantly have a .class file generated for me within the blink of an eye (so to speak). Of course, the compilation takes place only if the source code is without errors (warnings are okay).

To change the default output folder, we right-click the src/java directory in the Package Explorer view and select the Build Path, Configure Output Folder context menu option, as shown in Figure 8.14.

We should now see a screen similar to what's shown in Figure 8.15. Notice that we have changed the default output folder to build/timex/WEB-INF/classes. This is relative to the workspace we specified earlier (shown in Figure 8.7).

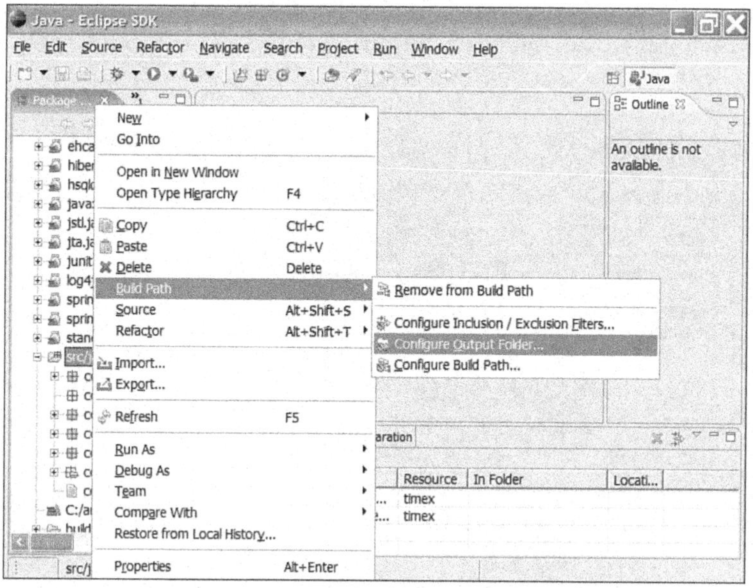

Figure 8.14   Configure output folder.

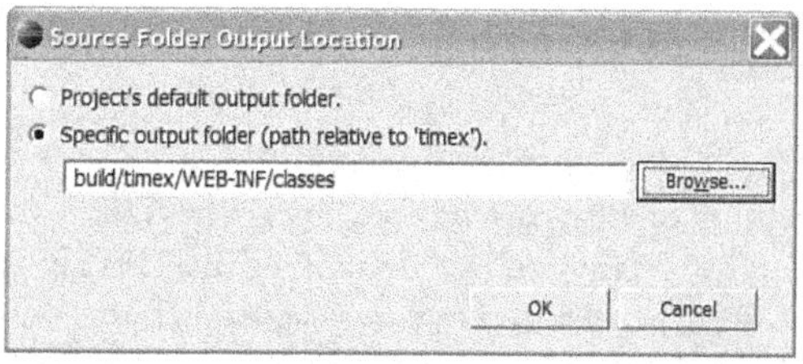

Figure 8.15   Specify output folder location.

Now we are actually ready to use Eclipse for our development! However, let's take care of a couple more cleanup steps. These are optional, but we don't want to leave any unnecessary remnants lingering out there.

When we changed the source folder to src/java, Eclipse compiled the .java files to its default output folder (timex/bin/, that is). We can manually delete this subfolder, but let's adjust a configuration item so that Eclipse doesn't create this directory again. To do so, right-click any entry (file, directory, or project name, for example) in the Package Explorer view and select Build Path, Configure Build Path. Figure 8.16 shows the Project Properties screen for our application, Time Expression. Notice that we have changed the default output folder (toward the bottom of the screen) to `timex/build/timex/WEB-INF/classes`. This is the same output folder as the one we chose for our `src/java` directory. Again, this is an optional step because we are working only with a single source directory, so the default and source directory output folder are the same. After this, we can right-click the `bin/` directory in the Package Explorer view and safely delete it.

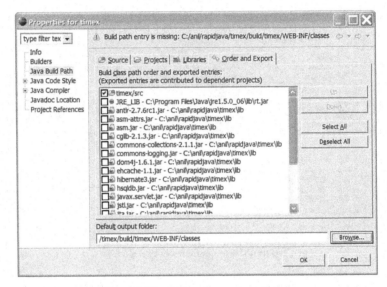

Figure 8.16   Project Properties window.

Also, you might have noticed an entry in the Package Explorer view with a directory name that looks something like `C:/anil/rapidjava/timex/build/timex/WEB-INF/classes`; this might indicate (unknown) at the end of the ToolTip when you hover your mouse over this entry. We can safely remove this; right-click this entry and choose Build Path, Remove from Build Path.

Now Eclipse is fully set up to develop Time Expression!

By the way, I tried this setup on my Mac OS X and Linux and it worked as advertised. Figure 8.17 shows the Eclipse workbench on a Mac OS X, with the Time Expression project open. Figure 8.18 shows Eclipse on Linux (using bootable Knoppix Linux CD). Impressed yet? We have only begun; there is much more to come.

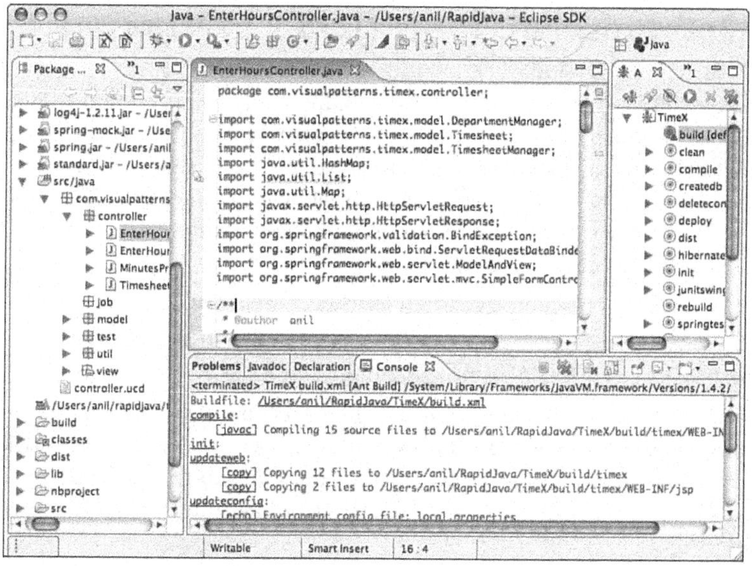

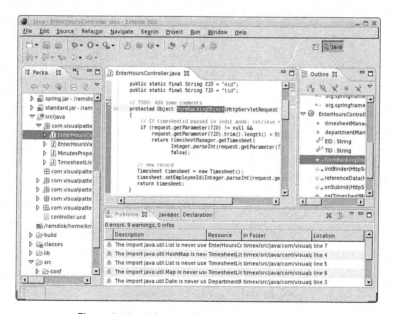

Figure 8.17   Eclipse with `timex` project on Mac OS X.

Figure 8.18   Eclipse with `timex` project on Linux
(using Knoppix bootable CD).

Java Development Tools (JDT) Features

The JDT plug-in builds on the Eclipse platform by adding robust Java-related capabilities to Eclipse. The JDT is such a core part of the Eclipse SDK that it is bundled with it.

The Eclipse platform combined with the JDT plug-in provides so many features that it would fill up an entire book. Hence, for the sake of conciseness, I will list the numerous features provided by plug-ins next, with a brief description of each. The online help bundled with Eclipse provides more detail on how these features work (the Eclipse help system is covered later in this chapter).

- Management of Java projects and files such as `.java`, `.class`, `.jar`, and Javadocs.

- Java source editing with keyword/syntax highlighting, truly intelligent content (code) assist, quick fix, import organization, and more.

- A variety of Java views. For example, Figure 8.19 shows a sample of the Java Browsing perspective, which allows us to browse Java packages, types (classes, interfaces), members, and variables; this is also a great way to browse other jar files (for example, spring.jar). Other Java views include JUnit, Ant, Package Explorer, and more.

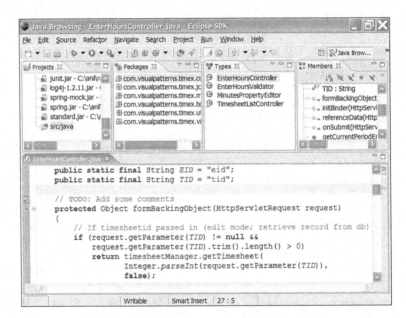

Figure 8.19   Java Browsing perspective.

- Every time we save a `.java` file, it is instantly compiled to a `.class` file (see the sidebar "Save Compiles Within the Blink of an Eye!").

- Intelligent quick fix (Ctrl+1) and content assist (Ctrl+spacebar)—If there are two keyboard shortcuts you should remember in Eclipse, these are the ones! Use one of these when you are stuck or are feeling lazy about typing. Try them anywhere and everywhere while coding, because these keys do too many things to list here. The assistance will be provided based on your cursor position, in the way of an intelligently narrowed applicable list of choices. For example, Ctrl+spacebar can fill in the remainder of your line of code, provide a drop-down list of choices, show us the signature of the method we are calling, and much more. Again, there are too many features to list here, but the Eclipse online help provides detailed information on these keys.

- Generation of code using prepackaged or custom templates (for code snippets), surround code with try/catch, add imports automatically, and more. Figure 8.20 shows the Source context menu. Generate setters/getters.

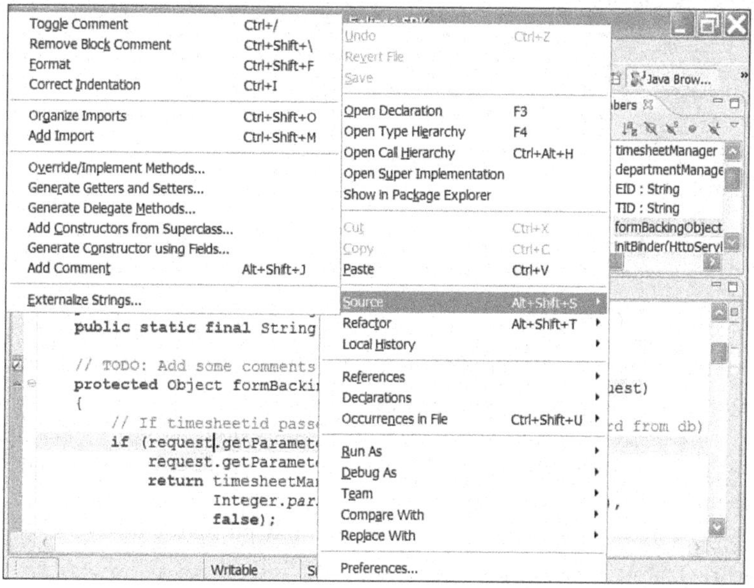

Figure 8.20   Source context menu.

- Eclipse JDT provides so many code formatting options that it can overwhelm you at first. If I had to take a guess about how many customization options are available to enable us to format our code, I would probably say about 100 or more. Figure 8.21 shows a sample of what I'm referring to. Notice all the options on the first tab; now multiply that by the eight tabs shown on this screen (you get the picture—there are a lot of options).

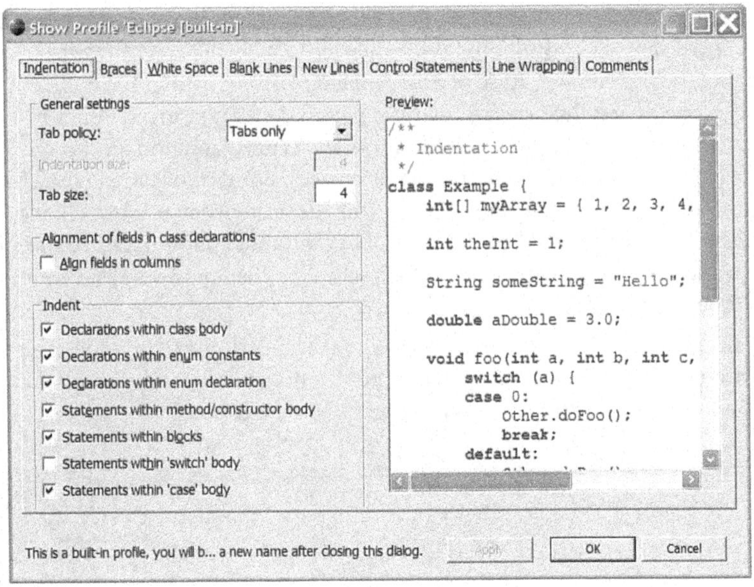

Figure 8.21   Java code formatting options.

- Compiler warnings and errors are displayed in the left and right side of the margins of the editor windows. Red is for errors and yellow is for warnings. Figure 8.22 shows an intentional error I generated. The marker on the left margin is the position on the page level; the indicator on the right margin is the position in the file. Also, notice that the warnings and errors are displayed in the Problems view.

- JDT provides all the debugging features you would expect, such as breakpoints, variable inspection, watch expressions, and more. Eclipse also provides a hotswap feature if your JRE supports it; this allows us to change code in the debugger and have it reloaded instantly, without the need to restart your debugging session (a very cool feature!). We will cover debugging in depth in the next chapter.

- The JDT provides reliable renaming of methods or classes and their references across a project. For example, if we rename a class, Eclipse will attempt to update all references to this class in Java code and XML files.

- Powerful searching using Java method signatures and more is another feature provided by the JDT. Figure 8.23 shows the Search dialog box. Notice that we can do file searches, Java searches, and even plug-in searches. In addition, we have other options for searching and repeating previous searches.

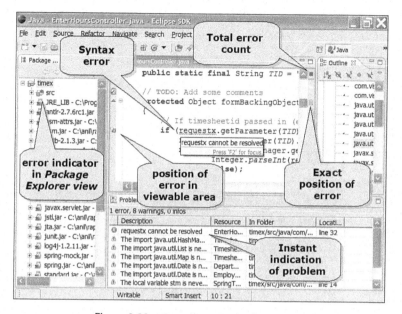

Figure 8.22   Compiler errors and warnings.

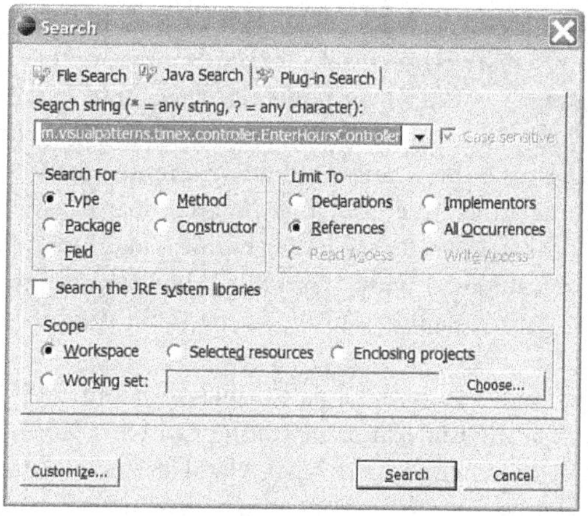

Figure 8.23   Search dialog box.

- The JDT goes beyond syntax highlighting and debugging by providing such features as the capability to add comments with the word TODO (we can choose other words as well) and have it appear in the Tasks view (Figure 8.24), which shows us every single TODO item we have in all the source files.

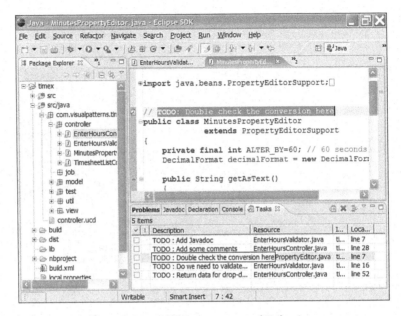

Figure 8.24   TODO comments and Tasks view.

As I mentioned earlier, Eclipse provides many types of wizards. The JDT-specific wizards include the capability to create classes, packages, annotations, simple files, and more. Each of these wizards is powerful in their own respect. For example, Figure 8.25 shows the Class Wizard. Notice how we can specify just about everything we need to create a skeleton class belonging to some package, extending another class or implementing various interfaces, containing a main method, inheriting constructors from the super class, and more. Now if Eclipse could only write our business logic, we would all be set.

The JDT comes preconfigured with JUnit. The JUnit plug-in provides a wizard and a view to create and test classes. Figure 8.26 shows the JUnit Wizard. We will use the JUnit view later in this chapter.

As you would guess, Ant is an integral part of Eclipse. Figure 8.27 shows the Ant view for running Ant tasks and the Ant editor for editing Ant build XML files (notice the Ctrl+spacebar-based context help for the XML elements and attributes). Also, the Console view shows the output of the Ant command with clickable filenames that take us directly to the point of the error!

Eclipse's Export feature provides the capability to export many types of files. I like the fact that any exportable files by any plug-ins show up in one place. Also, *export* is a term used loosely here because we can even create JAR files using this option. Figure 8.28 shows the list of files we can export to (in our setup so far).

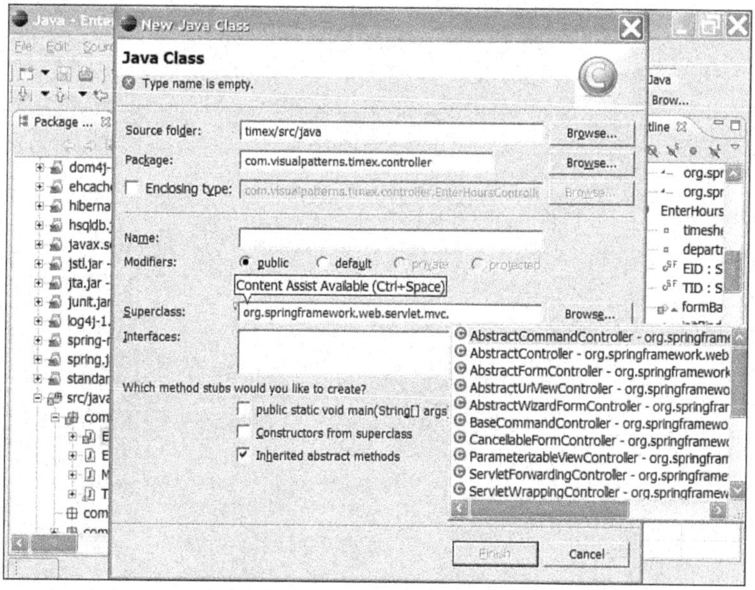

Figure 8.25 New Java Class Wizard.

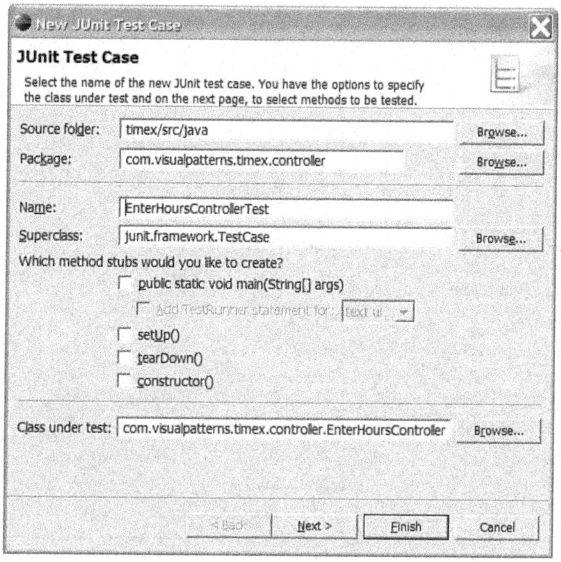

Figure 8.26 New JUnit Test Case Wizard.

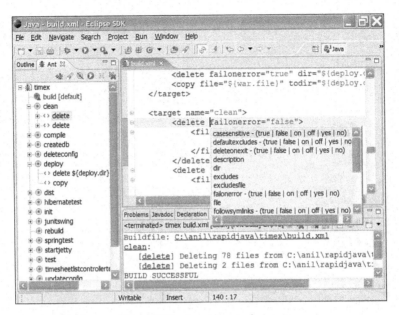

Figure 8.27   Ant editor and view.

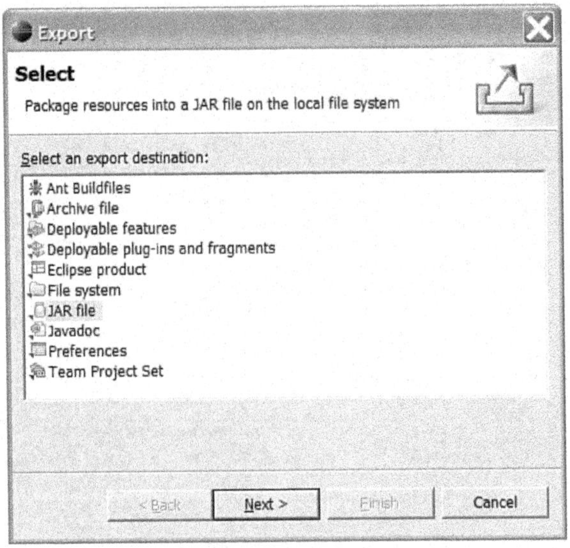

Figure 8.28   Export options.

The Java Scrapbook feature is a very handy feature to experiment with single lines of Java code, as shown in Figure 8.29. You can create a new Java scrapbook from the File, New, Other wizard (look for Java, Java Run/Debug, Scrapbook Page in the tree) and then execute it by highlighting your line of code and selecting Execute from the context (right-click) menu or the Run menu (or by pressing Ctrl+U on Microsoft Windows, for example).

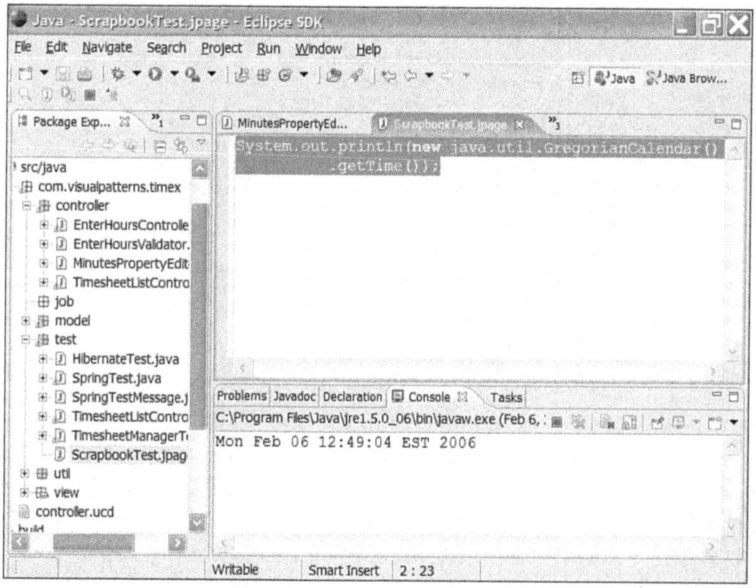

Figure 8.29   Java Scrapbook page.

The JDT provides extensive code refactoring options, although I must admit this is my weak area in that I have not used these features extensively. According to the Eclipse online help, "The refactoring tools support a number of transformations described in Martin Fowler's book *Refactoring: Improving the Design of Existing Code*, Addison Wesley 1999, such as Extract Method, Inline Local Variable, etc." The point behind refactoring is to improve the code without impacting the functionality it provides. Perhaps it's a personal preference for me to come up with my own refactoring ideas rather than trusting software to do it for me, although many of the refactoring options in Eclipse are simple and harmless to use.

Figure 8.30 shows the Refactor menu items. For example, we can *extract* (create) an interface class using the concrete methods of a concrete class. Other options provide the capability to pull up a method to a parent class, rename a package, class, or method, inline variables, add exceptions, and much more.

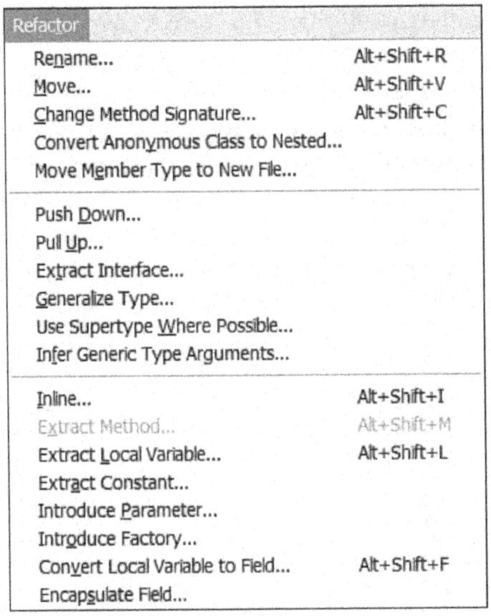

Figure 8.30   Refactor menu.

We just went through a lot of features provided by the combination of the Eclipse platform and the JDT plug-in, but as they say, *you ain't seen nothing yet!*

There is so much to Eclipse that it would take a few books to cover what's available on the eclipse.org website and elsewhere (and so much more under development, just waiting to surface). Nonetheless, I will cover a lot by the end of this chapter.

As I mentioned earlier, what makes Eclipse so powerful are the plug-ins available for this platform. So far, we have discussed only one plug-in, the JDT. I also mentioned earlier that hundreds of plug-ins are available out there—some small and simple, others more complex. Borland is one example; however, there is a very long list of companies developing plug-ins for Eclipse, including the Eclipse Foundation itself, as we will see in the next section.

Installing the Eclipse Web Tools Platform (WTP) Plug-ins

If you thought the JDT was a feature-loaded plug-in, you will be impressed by the variety of plug-ins provided as part of the Eclipse Web Tools Platform (WTP) Project.

According to the eclipse.org website, "The Eclipse Web Tools Platform (WTP) project extends the Eclipse platform with tools for developing J2EE Web applications. The WTP project includes the following tools: source editors for HTML, JavaScript, CSS, JSP, SQL, XML, DTD, XSD, and WSDL; graphical editors for XSD and WSDL; J2EE project natures, builders, and models and a J2EE navigator; a Web service wizard and explorer, and WS-I Test Tools; and database access and query tools and models." All of this is true and works as advertised. However, there is more than this because the brief description from eclipse.org does not mention support for managing various web/application servers, which we will use to start and stop Tomcat later in this chapter.

To install the WTP, follow the instructions provided on the http://www.eclipse.org website to install this plug-in. For example, I was able to install this using the Help, Software Updates, Find and Install menu option. Figure 8.31 shows how I essentially added a new Remote Site for the WTP, http://download.eclipse.org/webtools/updates/, and obtained all the plug-ins from there using this Eclipse software update feature. The process itself is very smooth; however, it is a big download, so it'll take some time to download and install. After the WTP is installed, we will be prompted to restart Eclipse. Also, after installing the WTP, Eclipse might take a bit longer to load at start, presumably because the additional plug-ins we installed require extra time to get verified and loaded.

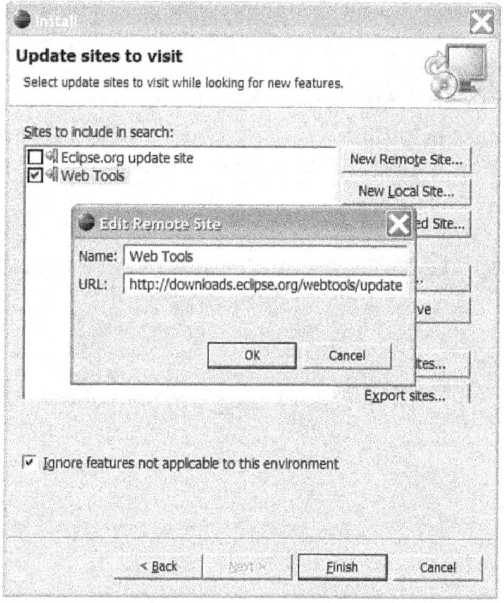

Figure 8.31   Eclipse software update (WTP install shown here).

After we have WTP installed successfully, we can select the J2EE perspective from the Window, Open Perspective menu option.

The WTP enables us to work with both static (such as HTML) or dynamic (such as EAR files) projects. For example, you will find editors for markup languages such as HTML, XML, as well as editors for JSP and JavaScript; you get the features you have probably come to expect from Eclipse by now—things such as code assist, templates, and more. However, the WTP is more than just a J2EE content editor. It also provides powerful data and server tools, as we will see later in this chapter, when we leverage these for HSQLDB and Tomcat.

Using Eclipse for Time Expression

Until now, we have used a variety of tools and technologies from the command line, so it would be nice to get the same or better functionality, given the toolbox paradigm I used to describe Eclipse earlier in this chapter.

You'll be glad to know that plug-ins are available for each of these technologies. The JDT already tightly integrates views for Ant and JUnit, so we just need to get the plug-ins for the other technologies. This is relatively simple using the Eclipse software update feature or by downloading the plug-in as an archive file (.zip and .tar.gz, for example) and installing.

Let's review the various plug-ins applicable to Time Expression.

Prebundled JDT Plug-ins

As I mentioned earlier, the JDT provides several plug-ins, such as a JSP editor, Ant view, and JUnit plug-ins. Also, we looked at a couple of Ant and JUnit plug-in related screenshots in Figures 8.26 and 8.27.

Figure 8.32 shows our view file for our Enter Hours screen, enterhours.jsp, being edited. Notice the context help (invoked using Ctrl+spacebar) for the spring:bind tag library and the integration with the Outline view (to display the JSP elements and attributes).

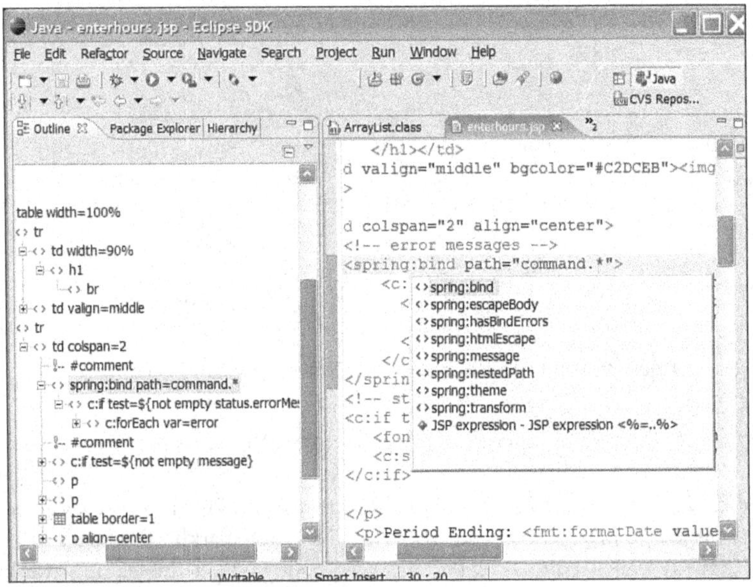

Figure 8.32   JSP Editor.

I use Ant within Eclipse only when I want to copy configuration files, build/deploy a distribution, or perform other special tasks I have defined in our `build.xml` file. However, for compilation of individual `.class` files, I rely on JDT's builder because it is so fast and transparent (that is, it compiles automatically every time I save my `.java` files). To begin using our `build.xml` file within Eclipse, we need to add it from the Ant view. Select Window, Show View, Ant to add the Ant view. From the Ant view, select the Add Buildfiles option and select the Time Expression `build.xml` file as shown in Figure 8.33.

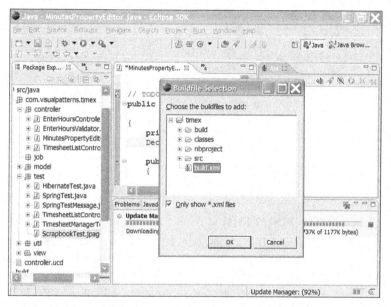

Figure 8.33   Adding the Time Expression build.xml.

When it comes to JUnit, I use the JDT integrated support for JUnit extensively. Let's start out by adding the JUnit view using the Window, Show View, Other menu item (look for Java, JUnit in the list of views). Figure 8.34 shows how we can run the TimesheetManagerTest class by selecting the Run, Run As, JUnit Test option (available on the Eclipse menu, source code context menu, or Package Explorer). The results of the test case run are shown in the JUnit view and the command output in the Console view.

Although I have discussed a single JUnit test class here, real-world projects typically contain lots of such JUnit test classes (potentially, in the tens to hundreds).

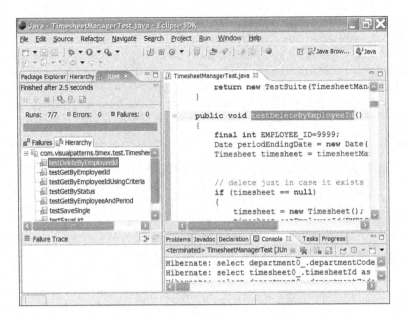

Figure 8.34   Sample JUnit test case run.

Data Plug-in (for HSQLDB)

Next we will set up the capability to work with HSQLDB within the Eclipse workbench. Ensure that the HSQLDB server is running as specified in Chapter 5, "Using Hibernate for Persistent Objects." Next, we will add the Data, Database Explorer view. From the Database Explorer view, either right-click the Connections icon or the corresponding button on the view's toolbar. Figure 8.35 shows my connection parameters. I couldn't find a database manager for HSQLDB, but I was able to fake it by using DB2 UDB V8.1, and everything seemed to work. There is probably at least one or more plug-ins out there for HSQLDB, but I wanted to use the standard plug-ins provided with the WTP.

Figure 8.36 shows a variety of things we can do with the Data related plug-ins. For example, as I'm browsing the database objects, I ran a query against the Employee table and can even generate a DDL script!

Servers Plug-in (for Tomcat)

Next, we will set up the capability to work with Tomcat from the Eclipse workbench. Let's begin by adding the Servers view. We can right-click in the Servers view (or open Server from the File, New, Other list of wizards). On the next screen, we will select Tomcat v5.5 for your setup; if you are using another server, you can choose it here as well (BEA, IBM, or JBoss, for example). On the screen shown in Figure 8.37 (part of the New Server Wizard), I noticed a little warning message indicating that Tomcat requires a JDK (versus a JRE), so I added a new JDK via the Installed JREs button, and after returning to the wizard screen, I selected it from the JRE drop-down list (yes, the JRE and JDK cross-referencing can get confusing).

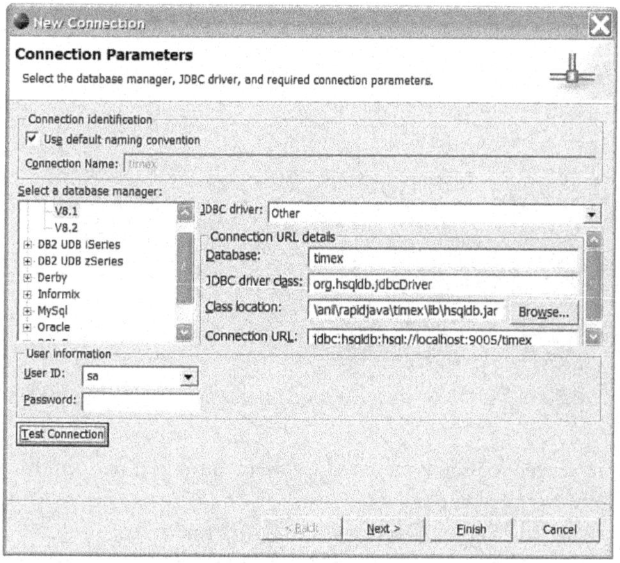

Figure 8.35   HSQLDB setup for Database Explorer.

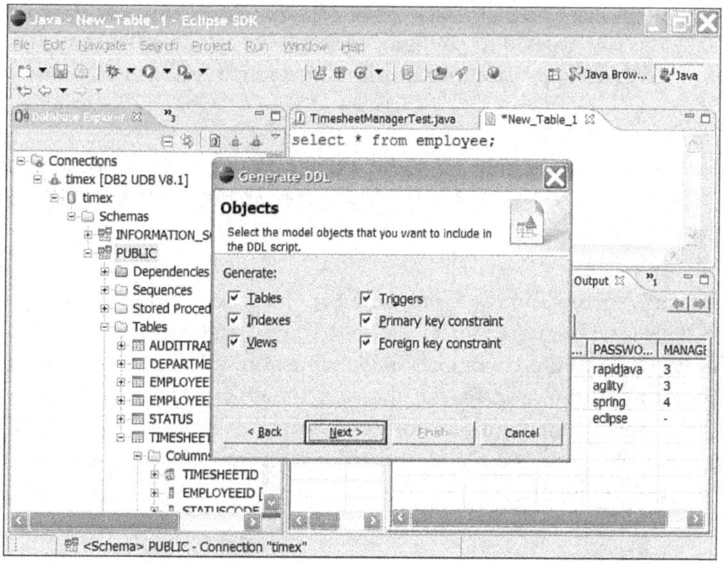

Figure 8.36   A variety of features provided by the Data plug-ins.

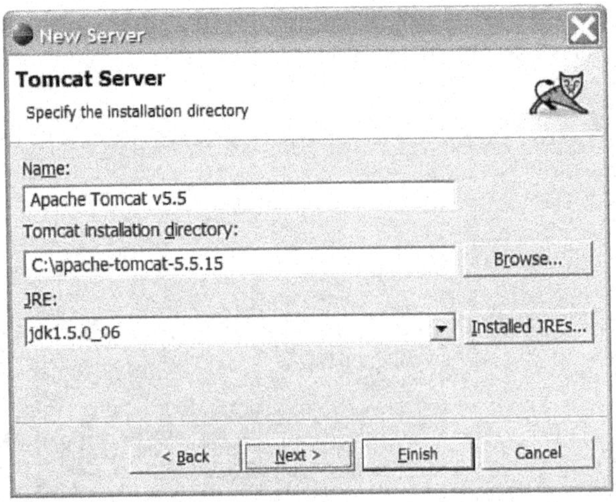

Figure 8.37   Add New Server Wizard screen (for adding Tomcat Server).

After our Tomcat Server is added, we need to tweak an entry. (It sounds easy now, but it took me a while to figure this out.)

Figure 8.38 shows the Server Overview configuration editor (yup, an editor; Eclipse can have any number of content editors and not just for text, but also for images and other types of content). Next, we will uncheck the Run Modules Directly Checkbox from Workspace option because we want to use the existing configuration so that our Ant can continue to function. Also, notice the Modules tab toward the bottom-left part of Figure 8.38; this can be used to configure external modules, both web archives (.war files) and exploded web application directories (for example, our build/timex directory).

> **Note**
>
> Deploying an exploded directory versus a .war file is a better idea during development (versus UAT, for example) because you can quickly test changes to files such as JSP, HTML, and images without the need to redeploy the entire application (.war file).

Now we are ready to run Tomcat. Notice the Servers view crammed at the bottom of Figure 8.38. This is where we can stop and start Tomcat; the status shows as Started and the changes we made to the configuration are Synchronized. We can start, stop, and monitor Tomcat from this view. We can also start Tomcat in Debug mode, which enables debugging of server-side applications (for example, using breakpoints, inspecting variables, and so on; debugging is covered in detail in Chapter 9, "Logging, Debugging, Monitoring, and Profiling").

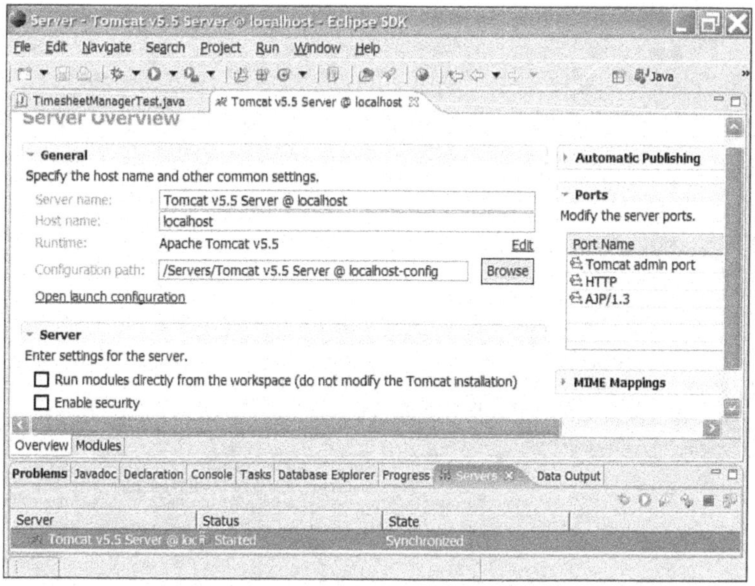

Figure 8.38   Tomcat Server configuration.

Hibernate Plug-in

Now that we have the plug-ins from eclipse.org installed and set up, we need to go out and get some third-party plug-ins. These can be installed in the same manner as the WTP plug-in—that is, from the Help, Software Updates, Find and Install menu item or by simply unpacking an archive into the /eclipse or /eclipse/plugins/ subdirectory (in case you are behind a firewall, for example), depending on how the archive is packaged by the vendor.

Hibernate provides a plug-in that eases the generation of the hibernate XML configuration and mapping files—a nice feature considering mapping is one of the tedious jobs of working with ORM technologies.

Hibernate plug-ins can be obtained as a direct archive download or via the Eclipse software update feature, which is my general preference. Follow the instructions on the Hibernate site (http://hibernate.org/) to obtain this plug-in. At the time of this writing, I was able to connect to http://download.jboss.org/jbosside/updates/development/ and download the latest plug-ins. After the installation, I had to restart Eclipse. Figure 8.39 shows some of the Hibernate views (organized inside a perspective named Hibernate Console). These views enable us to create a `hibernate.cfg.xml` file, mapping files, test run HQL scripts, and more.

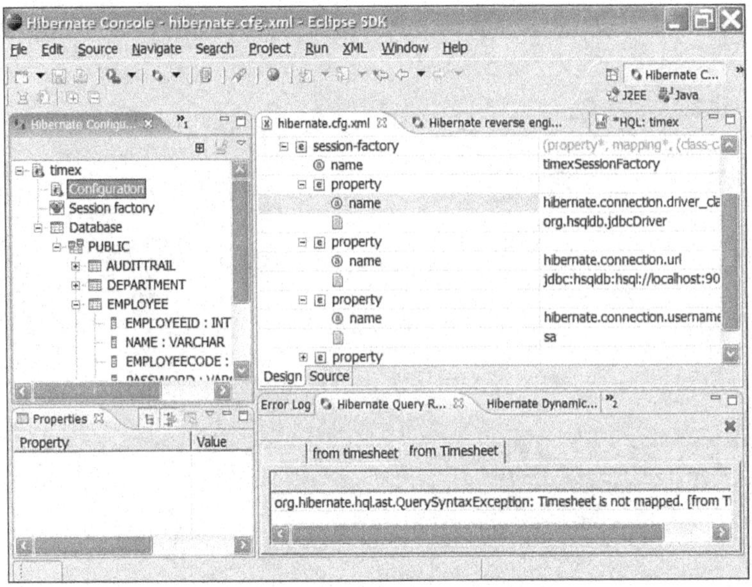

Figure 8.39   Hibernate plug-in views.

The Spring IDE Plug-in

Last, but not least, we will get a Spring plug-in known as the Spring IDE, a subproject of the Spring Framework. One of the fundamental problems of working with Spring is the heavy use of XML files for configuration. Before you know it, the XML grows and can become a cumbersome task to edit and maintain, even when you have it split into multiple application context XML files (as recommended by Spring).

According to the http://springide.org website, this plug-in should be downloaded using only the Eclipse software update feature. Sometime back, I personally tried this as a direct install (unzip of an archive file) and it corrupted my install, so beware! Follow the up-to-date instructions on the Spring IDE website to obtain this plug-in. At the time of this writing, I was able to download and install the plug-in from http://springide.org/updatesite/ within minutes. As expected, I had to restart Eclipse for this new plug-in to take effect.

> **Note**
> The Web Standard Tools (WST) project is required by the Spring IDE; luckily, we already installed it.

After this plug-in is successfully created, we need to right-click the timex project from the Package Explorer view and select the Add Spring Project Nature option (as shown in Figure 8.40). According to the following excerpt taken directly from the Eclipse help documentation:

"Project *natures* allow a plug-in to tag a project as a specific kind of project. For example, the Java development tools (JDT) uses a 'Java nature' to add Java-specific behavior to projects. Project natures are defined by plug-ins, and are typically added or removed per-project when the user performs some action defined by the plug-in."

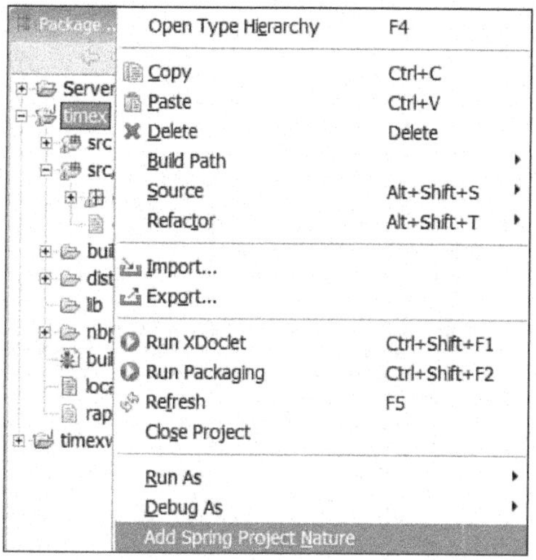

Figure 8.40   Add Spring Project Nature.

After we have tagged the `timex` project as a Spring nature, we need to do the following:

- Add the Spring Beans view.
- Use this view to add our application context, `timex-servlet.xml`, file (developed in Chapter 7, "The Spring Web MVC Framework") by right-clicking the project name (found at the top part of this view).
- Right-click an XML element in the Spring Beans view and select Show Graph; the result is shown in Figure 8.41.

We can now navigate using the graph or tree views to navigate our XML file! Beats using just a text-based editor. In addition, the Spring IDE integrates tightly with other Eclipse views, such as the Problems view, to display validation errors for the Spring application context files associated with Spring IDE. Also, notice the Outline view in Figure 8.41; it shows a scaled-down version of the diagram for easier navigation in case your diagrams become large and complex. The Spring IDE plug-in is bundled with online help, which can be accessed from Eclipse's Help, Help Contents menu.

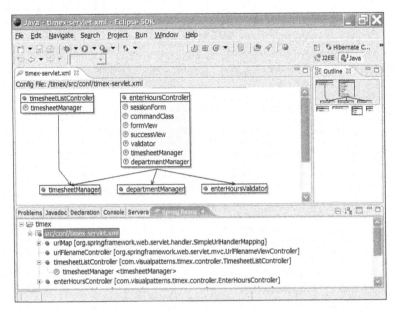

Figure 8.41   Spring Beans graph.

Other Notable WTP Plug-ins

We looked at a few plug-ins in this section that apply to Time Expression. However, the WTP project provides plug-ins, editors, views, and wizards for other aspects of JEE application development, such as support for EJB projects, application client projects, web services, connectors, and much more. These can all be conveniently accessed using the JEE perspective or related views.

More Eclipse? Yes, Plug-ins Galore!

As I mentioned at the beginning of this chapter, at the time of this writing, a query on google.com for the words "eclipse" and "plug-in" resulted in millions of hits! Although this isn't an exact indication of the number of plug-ins out there for Eclipse, it should give you an idea of how active the Eclipse community is.

Eclipse.org Projects

For starters, always look for new plug-ins from the source, as we did with the WTP plug-ins. Also, recall the list of Eclipse projects I provided toward the beginning of the chapter, in Table 8.1.

Plug-in Directories

There are many plug-ins available on the eclipse.org website for the various Eclipse projects I mentioned earlier in this chapter. In addition, the following are two Eclipse plug-in directories worth checking out, because they provide a large number of plug-ins, both free and commercial:

- http://www.eclipseplugincentral.com/
- http://eclipse-plugins.2y.net/eclipse/

For example, on the eclipseplugincentral.com website, hundreds of plug-ins are organized in the following categories: Application Management, Application Server, Code Management, Database, Deployment, Documentation, Editor, Entertainment, Graphics, IDE, J2EE Development Platform, J2ME, Languages, Modeling, Network, Other, Profiling, Rich Client Applications, SCM, Source Code Analyzer, Team Development, Testing, Tools, UI, UML, Web, Web Services, and XML.

The plugins.2y.net site has even more categories. For example, their categories include "Ant, AspectJ, Bug Tracker, Business Process Tools, Code Generation, Code Generation/Modeling, Code mngt, Com, CORBA/IDL, Database, Database Persistence, Decompiler, Deployment, Distribution Package, Documentation, Entertainment, J2EE development platform, Languages, LDAP, Logging, Misc, Mobile/PDA, Modelling, Network, Obsolete, Patterns, Profiling, Project management, Report, Rich Client, RSS, SAP, SCM, Source Code Analyzer, Source Code Formatter, Team, Testing, Tomcat, Tools, Tutorial, UI, UI components, UML, Web, Web Service, and XML."

MyEclipseIDE.com

You might have noticed that I haven't mentioned many commercial products in this book. This isn't because I'm an open source fanatic—I use many commercial products for my work. However, open source (and free) products are readily available for anyone to download; therefore, if you wanted to follow along an example in this book, it is easy to do without paying for a product. However, I have to point out one unique product and website found at http://myeclipseide.com. This is worth checking out, especially if you want a one-stop solution for plug-ins you will need for Java development, where everything under the sun (so to speak) can be found at one place.

The various categories on myeclipseide.com include "modeling and code generation (UML), web development tools (struts, spring, jsf, hibernate, DB, tapestry), productivity wizards (Web/EJB projects), application server integration (JBoss, WebLogic, Websphere, and more), packaging and installation (installer, and so on.)."

MyEclipseIDE.com is not a must-have, especially when projects such as Eclipse's Web Technologies Project (WTP) provide so much already. Furthermore, you could go out and get other plug-ins, such as the Hibernate plug-in from http://hibernate.org and the Spring IDE plug-in from http://springide.org. However, if you want one stop where you can find dozens of consistently organized plug-ins from one site (for a low price) along with support, myeclipseide.com might be for you.

Google.com

Of course, the largest directory in the world currently is google.com. You can find just about anything and everything using google.com searches. For example, I was able to locate EclipseUML (http://eclipseuml.com) by searching for the words "eclipse" and "uml".

Eclipse Team Support

The Eclipse workbench comes with a built-in Concurrent Versions System (CVS) client. If you have worked with CVS before, you are most likely familiar with the CVS servers and various commands. Eclipse provides two perspectives for working in teams: the CVS Repository Exploring and Team Synchronization perspectives. These perspectives contain a logical arrangement of a variety of views, such as CVS Repositories and Synchronize.

For example, based on the CVS instructions for the Spring Framework, I was able to connect to the Spring Framework's CVS repository and browse their CVS directory within seconds from Eclipse (as shown in Figure 8.42)!

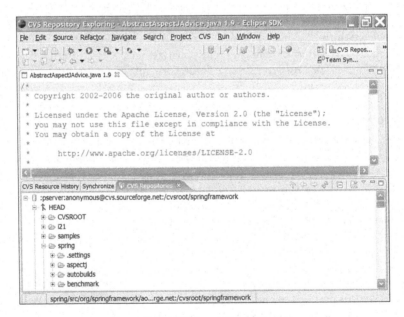

Figure 8.42   CVS repository browsing.

The Synchronize feature enables us to synchronize our local directory with CVS server. For example, I was able to create a new project and check out the entire Spring CVS directory using Eclipse's Synchronize Wizard. Subsequently, when I edited a sample

Spring .java file, I was able to right-click and get the Team context menu shown in Figure 8.43. Notice the variety of CVS options available here, such as Update, Commit, and so on.

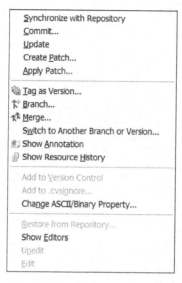

Figure 8.43   Team context menu.

Eclipse Help System

Eclipse provides an HTML-based help system that is completely searchable. Eclipse also comes bundled with help for the Workbench, JDT, JEE, and more. In fact, if you have been following along the examples in this chapter, you will see documentation on Spring (as shown in Figure 8.44), Hibernate, web tools, and more.

In addition, Eclipse provides Cheat Sheets, which walk you through an entire process. For example, Figure 8.45 shows how to build a Simple Java Application, end to end.

You can also use Eclipse to provide context-sensitive Javadocs, as shown in Figure 8.46. You obtain this help by hovering over a method to see the Javadoc for that given method. Subsequently, we can press F2 if we want to set focus to this window, perhaps to scroll through this mini help pop-up window. To activate this feature, you might have to attach to the API's source code (as I explain under Tips and Tricks later in this chapter).

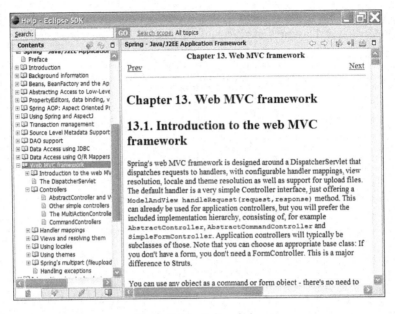

Figure 8.44   Eclipse help.

Figure 8.45   Eclipse cheat sheets.

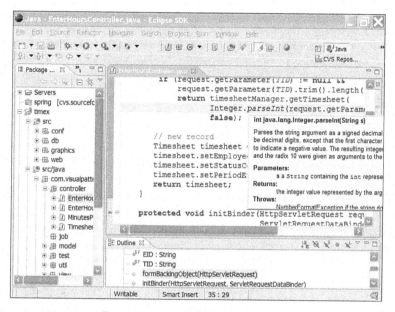

Figure 8.46   Context-specific Javadocs.

Personal Opinion: The GUI Development Tools Battle Has, Only Now, Begun!

Bear with me while I begin with a bit about my background, so you don't disregard this sidebar as uninformed babble talk.

In May of 2001, I wrote an article for JavaWorld.com titled "Does Sun Understand GUI Design?" This article was primarily referring to Java Swing's complexity, overengineered API, and slow performance (some of which are no longer true). However, I was also commenting on Sun Microsystem's Unix roots which, in my opinion, reflects on the state of Java tools prior to Eclipse SDK, NetBeans, and commercial products such as JetBrain's IntelliJ IDEA.

Before I offend Unix users, let me say that since 1990, I have worked on more than six flavors of Unix/Linux operating systems (Solaris, AIX, Irix, AT&T System V, SCO Unix, Red Hat, and others). In fact, I can safely say that almost 100% of the projects I have personally worked on have involved Unix servers (primarily Solaris) in some form. I've also been using Unix tools on Windows all along (MKS Tools or Cygwin, for example). Some of my colleagues occasionally comment about some of the regular expressions I like to use in the Vi editor and Unix shell scripts, which makes their head hurt when they try to decipher these. In other words, I love the flexibility and power of the Unix command-line tools, complex regular expressions, shell scripts, and other things that Unix offers (particularly for repetitive tasks that should be scripted so that they are reproducible). However, I have also been working with GUI platforms such as Microsoft Windows since version 2.1 (also known as Windows/286 and Windows/386 from the late 80s, Mac OS X, and X-Windows. So, I'm equally fond of GUI tools because when used properly, these can save enormous amounts of time by providing a consolidated environment; Eclipse is a perfect example of this. GUI tools also have their limitations at times, which is why all the earlier chapters in this book were based on the command line.

Given my mixed command-line and GUI background, I've always felt that Sun just does not understand GUI, or GUI tools for that matter, even though the Swing team was supposedly formed with some Apple and Nextstep engineers. Microsoft, on the other hand, always seems to be one step ahead when it comes to GUI tools, possibly because they literally invest billions of dollars in GUI-related R and D efforts being a GUI based operating system and applications company (versus Unix/Linux-based companies that have their roots in command-line interface-based operating systems).

I want to give you one more perspective on why I think Sun doesn't understand GUI, so bear with me a little longer. A few years ago, I had the distinct pleasure of having a brief, five-minute conversation with James Gosling at a JavaOne conference. He sat in a chair next to mine in a press room to check his email (we had a series of computers available for everyone to check email). So, naturally I had to say something to him (anything) given this rare opportunity of sitting right next to him. I suggested to him that Sun Microsystems should consider writing GUI (wrapper) tools around the most widely used Unix utilities on Solaris such as ls, cron, find, grep, and many others. I mentioned that GUI tools were one key reason Microsoft Windows NT (pre-Windows 200x days) was gaining so much ground. His response was that Sun's customers "prefer the command line" (Hmmm... how do you respond to such a comment coming from the father of Java, nonetheless).

Before Java came along, I was used to working on Unix, but also wrote quite a bit of code under Microsoft Windows using Microsoft Visual C++ and prior to that Borland C++. I could not understand why we had more stable products then and better debuggers, and not now with a better technology such as Java. Anyway, to end this long story, this is no longer true. Products such as Eclipse, NetBeans, and IntelliJ have come a long, long way.

To end a very long story (sorry), this is precisely why I'm glad to see the Eclipse Foundation focused on GUI tools. Finally, an Apache-like foundation focused on GUI tools and a community to write plug-ins, just imagine the possibilities!

The Eclipse phenomenon is something I haven't seen for a long time, and it comes somewhat close to the excitement I felt when I discovered Java and web programming more than a decade ago. The Eclipse platform levels the playing field by providing a consistent GUI platform with a variety of robust services, thereby enabling tools vendors to focus on providing advanced features. The possibilities are endless.

Also, rumor has it that the name Eclipse has a hidden agenda behind it, as in "the Eclipse of the Sun," so is this an attack on Sun Microsystems? Or is Eclipse competing with Microsoft Visual Studio? To make things more interesting, it has been a long time coming, but Swing and NetBeans finally look and perform great now!

Of course, JetBrain's IntelliJ is also a factor here...

In short, the battle of the IDEs has just begun!

Tips and Tricks

There are so many tips and tricks for the Eclipse platform that it would not be practical to list them all here! From bookmarks to drag-and-drop (on Microsoft Windows) to hotswap debugging to simply working effectively, the list goes on. I highly recommend checking out the Eclipse Help, Help Contents menu item for various tips and tricks, which are well documented.

Shortcut Keys

The following section provides shortcut key examples using Microsoft Windows. If you are using Eclipse on a Unix/Linux-based system or Mac OS X, these keys might be slightly different. For example, on the Mac OS X, the shortcut key to invoke the File, New, Other wizard dialog box is COMMAND+N but on Microsoft Windows, it is Ctrl+N. Also, note that the functionality provided by these shortcut keys is readily available from the main menu bar or context menus.

Two shortcut key combinations I have already mentioned earlier and will reemphasize here are Ctrl+spacebar and Ctrl+1. These work almost anywhere and everywhere and provide intelligent, context-specific assistance (automatically declaring variables, for example). Use these as often as you possibly can (in the right context, of course) because they will not only save you enormous typing but also making your coding almost error-free!

The other key combinations I tend to use include the following:

- Ctrl+M for minimizing and maximizing editors and views.
- Ctrl+N for creating something new using one of the 100 wizards available in Eclipse.
- Ctrl+Shift+spacebar provides hints on a method's parameters.
- Ctrl+Shift+M to insert a missing import.
- Ctrl+K to repeat the last find and Shift+Ctrl+K to find backward.
- Ctrl+Shift+X converts the selected text to uppercase and Ctrl+Shift+Y to lowercase.
- Ctrl+Shift+F formats the existing file (based on the preferences).
- Ctrl+/ comments a single line of code.
- Ctrl+F6, Ctrl+F7, and Ctrl+F8 enable me to cycle through editors, views, and perspectives, respectively (Ctrl+Shift+F6, Ctrl+Shift+F7, Ctrl+Shift+F8, go in the opposite direction).
- Tab and Shift+Tab indent and unindent blocks of code, respectively.
- F3 opens the declaration for selected item.
- F5 refreshes a view.

Last, but certainly not least, the mother of all keys is Ctrl+Shift+L, which is a shortcut key for the Help, Key Assist menu item; this feature provides a list of shortcut keys that can be executed right from the list shown in Figure 8.47.

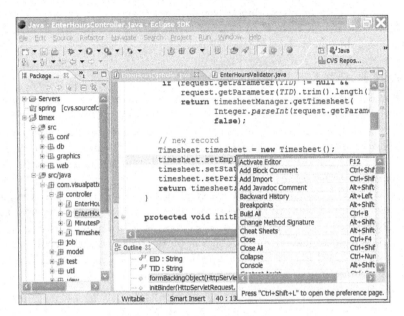

Figure 8.47   Help, Key Assist.

Preferences

Eclipse is a highly configurable tool. Figure 8.48 shows a screenshot of the Preferences dialog box accessible via the Windows, Preferences menu of the Eclipse workbench. There are almost too many configurable items (if that is possible); in fact, this is probably the reason there is a Filter option at the top of the Preferences window to narrow down the preference choices available.

Most views in the Eclipse SDK are also configurable via their own toolbars; some provide more configuration options than others. For example, the Package Explorer view allows us to change the layout and filter files out from the display (for example, if you want to filter out the JAR files from the listing or want to see a hierarchical view of the packages versus flat, both of which I personally like to do).

Bookmarks

Bookmarks are almost a must-have in any text editor used for development purposes. Eclipse is no different in this respect. The Edit, Add Bookmark menu item provides the capability to add bookmarks. The Basic, Bookmarks view allows us to view and go to bookmarks, as shown in Figure 8.49.

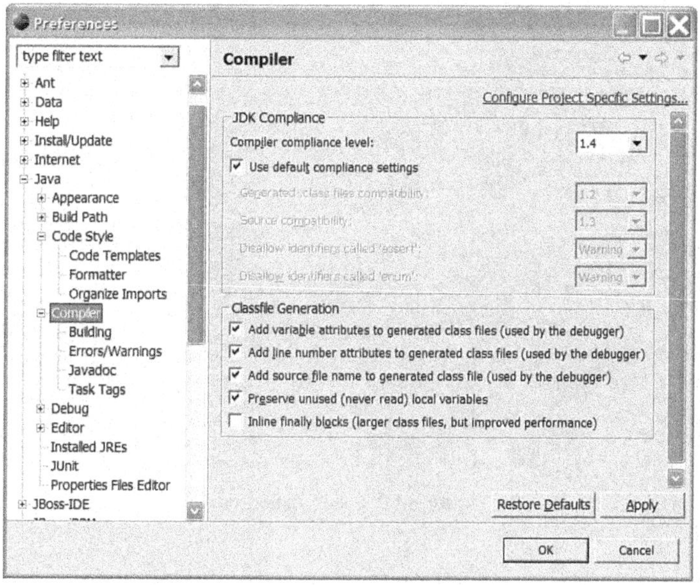

Figure 8.48   Windows, Preferences menu.

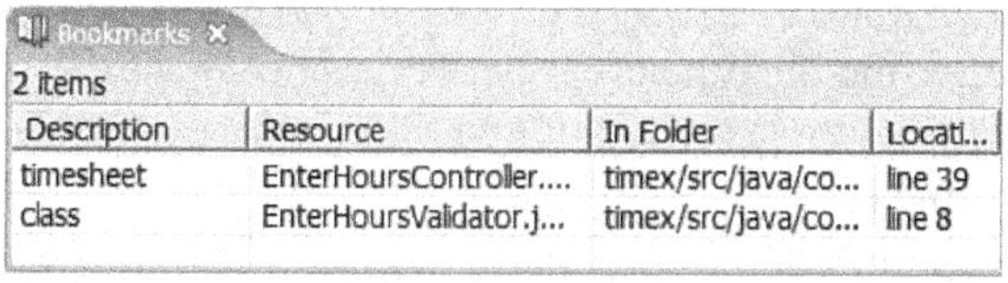

Figure 8.49   Bookmarks view.

Running External Tools and Web Browser

You can easily run external programs using the Run, External Tools menu item. You can also invoke a web browser of your choice from the Window, Web Browser menu item. For example, Figure 8.50 shows the Run dialog box; notice the various types of programs we can run and the various tabs to customize the program being run (command-line parameters, for example).

Local History

Local History allows us to compare and restore from other things from a history of this file. It can be accessed using the right-click context menu while editing a file.

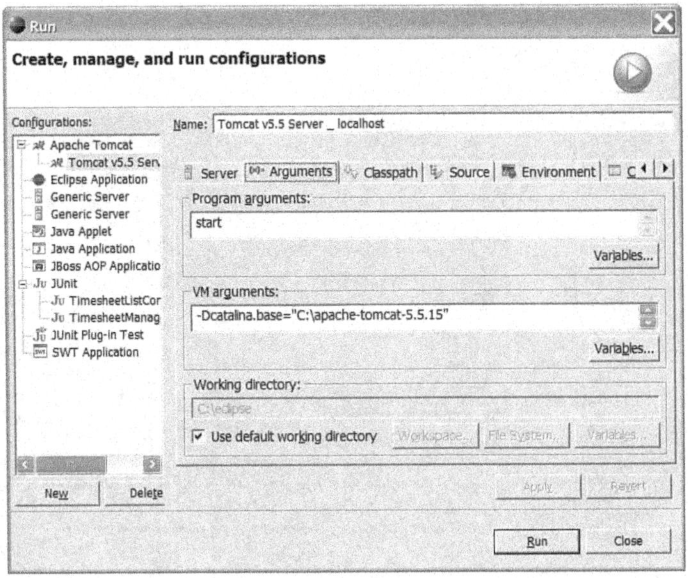

Figure 8.50   Run dialog box.

Reset Perspective

If you accidentally change a predefined perspective by closing windows you didn't want to or by moving stuff around, you can always get the original state of window sizes and positions back by selecting the Window, Reset Perspective option.

Copying Elements

When we copy a line of code from one file to another, the JDT automatically copies and pastes the necessary imports required for this code to the destination source file.

Project, Clean

If you think your compiled .class files are out of sync with Eclipse or you are seeing red errors when you shouldn't, you could try running a Clean option on the wizard from the Project, Clean menu item.

Convert Delimiters

If you are used to working with files on Microsoft Windows and other Unix/Linux-based systems, you might need to convert the line delimiters. This can easily be done using the File, Convert File Delimiters To menu item.

Eclipse/JVM Startup Parameters

One other thing worth mentioning is that most times Eclipse will be fine out of the box. However, if you run into out-of-memory errors (for very large projects), you can specify extra parameters to Eclipse and to the Java VM that is running Eclipse (to increase the heap size, for example). The following is a command-line example of running Eclipse on Microsoft Windows (refer to the help documentation for more details on the parameters):

```
\eclipse\eclipse.exe -vm "c:\Program Files\Java\jre1.5.0_06\bin\javaw.exe"
➡ -vmargs -Xmx512m
```

Refer to the Eclipse documentation for additional options; for example, the `-refresh` option, which performs a global refresh of the workspace on startup.

Browsing Through Third-Party Source Code

You can browse (and debug) the source code of JAR files by attaching them to the source code file or directory. One way to attach to the source is by double-clicking a `.class` file in a JAR file from the Package Explorer view and selecting the Attach Source Code button. For example, Figure 8.51 shows how I was able to browse the JDK code after attaching the JRE lib in my Package Explorer view to `C:/Program Files/Java/jdk1.5.0_06/src.zip`.

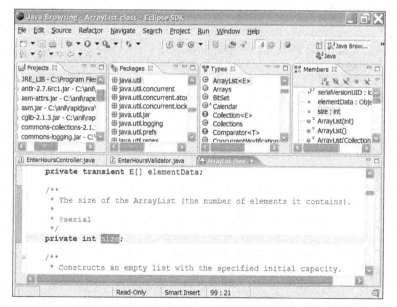

Figure 8.51   Browsing third-party source code.

Eclipse Hidden Files

If you experience some completely odd problems with your Eclipse project (which I have never encountered, by the way), you could try deleting the project from Eclipse and re-creating it. In addition, Eclipse creates some dot (hidden) files and directories created by Eclipse in the project directory—for example, .classpath, .project, and .metadata. You can try deleting these, in case there are some project-related remnants left over, and then re-create your project.

Uninstalling Eclipse

If you ever decide to uninstall Eclipse, you can simply delete the /eclipse directory. (There is no uninstaller, at least for version 3.1.2, which was used in this chapter.)

If you happen to use the default workspace (that is, you did not specify a workspace during Eclipse startup), you might want to back up your project files prior to deleting the /eclipse directory because project files belonging to the default workspace are stored under this /eclipse directory.

An Unfair Comparison to IntelliJ and NetBeans

The two other popular Java IDEs include JetBrain's IntelliJ and Sun Microsystem's NetBeans. I decided to install each and give them each about 30 minutes, just to see how quickly I could get up and running with these IDEs compared to Eclipse.

> **Note**
>
> Disclaimer: Let me state explicitly that my opinions here are extremely biased toward Eclipse, given everything I have mentioned so far in this chapter. So, I'm not entirely sure how much value this section adds because it is somewhat unfair to judge a product in 30 minutes or less. However, I was hoping to get some first impressions and also to see how I could re-create a project for Time Expression in other IDEs.

IntelliJ 5.0

First, I decided to try out JetBrain's IntelliJ 5.0 because I had heard so much from several people about IntelliJ being a wonderful product. The IntelliJ download was very quick and the installation went smoothly. However, the startup wasn't. For some reason, IntelliJ wanted to act as a server and my firewall program detects that. It took me a while to figure out how to set up a project. The setup of Tomcat was also not user friendly. Even the JDK setup was somewhat manual. Overall, I found IntelliJ's interface slick, but confusing and slower than Eclipse. Figure 8.52 shows a screenshot of the Time Expression files in IntelliJ. I did like the split window feature, which allows you see the same file in multiple windows, similar to Microsoft Word's Window, Split feature, but more powerful. Again, my opinions are extremely biased toward Eclipse and all I can give you here are first impressions.

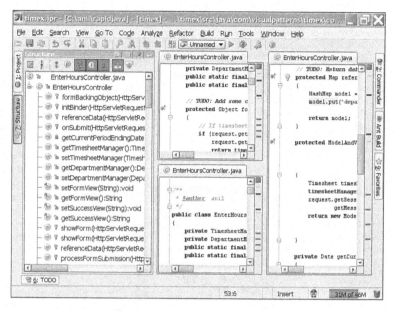

Figure 8.52   JetBrain's IntelliJ 5.0.

NetBeans 5.0

Next, I decided to install Sun Microsystem's NetBeans 5.0. The install was very straight-forward. I was also able to create a project for Time Expression from an existing build.xml file, just like Eclipse does. The integration with Tomcat was also very tight and smooth—in fact, slightly better than Eclipse. There was even a bundled version of Tomcat, but I added a server in NetBeans, which allowed me to point to the existing install. Given this, I was able to start up Tomcat immediately after configuring it and timex.war was deployed in NetBeans (see Figure 8.53). I was also able to test my JUnit code instantly with a single configuration.

I must say that NetBeans is also a very well done IDE and the overall download, install, build, unit test, and deploy app took under 30 minutes and without reading any online help! Overall, it was fun to use this IDE; there was something very enjoyable and elegant about it, possibly because everything worked the first time.

Even though NetBeans was set up faster and is a very well-designed IDE, the sheer number of plug-ins available for Eclipse and the community and marketplace behind it make Eclipse a clear winner and NetBeans a close second. At the time of this writing, there were more than 1,075 plug-ins on one of the Eclipse directories I mentioned earlier, whereas the NetBeans site listed 46 plug-ins. Also, when I did a search on google.com for the words "netbeans" and "plugin" (or "plug-in"), I got fewer than 500,000 hits; as I had mentioned in the beginning of this chapter, I got millions of hits for Eclipse!

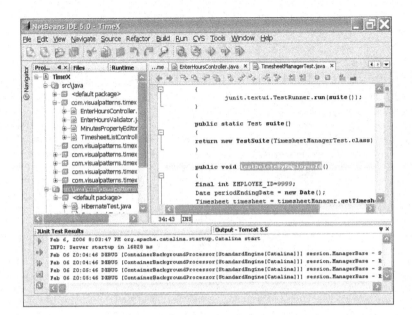

Figure 8.53   Sun Microsystem's NetBeans 5.0.

Startup Times

I could see that the Eclipse SDK startup time was faster, but I wanted to get some real test numbers on this—nothing too formal or extensive, just the number of seconds it took for each IDE to start and have the Time Expression project loaded and available.

I rebooted my PC to ensure that none of the IDE executables were cached in memory to give it a leg up on the others. The startup times for each IDE were as follows:

- Eclipse SDK—19 seconds
- IntelliJ—1 minute, 5 seconds
- NetBeans—42 seconds

Incidentally, I used an Intel Pentium M processor 750 based machine (1.86GHz/2MB Cache/533MHz FSB) with 1GB of shared memory (DDR2, 533MHZ) running Microsoft Windows XP Media Center Edition 2005. Also, the startup time shown for Eclipse here included all the plug-ins we covered in this chapter (without some or all of these plug-ins, the startup time would presumably have been faster).

Again, my views are biased; however, these numbers are not fudged. In fact, I rebooted my machine three times for various reasons to ensure that I was giving each IDE a fair trial. You may want to conduct similar tests if you are evaluating IDEs and have not made up your mind.

Summary

In this chapter, we learned about the following:

- The Eclipse Foundation
- The Eclipse platform and projects
- Eclipse SDK concepts
- Installing Eclipse
- Setting up Eclipse for Time Expression
- The Java Development Tools (JDT) plug-in
- Eclipse Web Tools Platform Project (for Tomcat support, JSP editing, and other JEE support)
- Using Eclipse for Time Expression (starting Tomcat and connecting to HSQLDB, for example)
- Eclipse team support using CVS
- Plug-in directories for both free and commercial plug-ins
- Eclipse tips and tricks
- Results of a 30-minute comparison to IntelliJ and NetBeans

In this chapter, we covered a lot of material about Eclipse. However, we aren't done with Eclipse just yet. In the next chapter, I will show you how to leverage Eclipse's debugging features. However, even then, we will have covered only a subset of the Eclipse SDK and the third-party plug-in market. For example, we will not be covering topics such as the UML2 project or even more importantly, the Visual Editor framework, which according to the eclipse.org website is a "vendor-neutral, open development platform supplying frameworks for creating GUI builders, and exemplary, extensible tool implementations for Swing/JFC and SWT/RCP." Swing and SWT, as you know, provide the capability to develop sophisticated GUI (thick client) applications. If what we have seen in this chapter is any indication of how powerful Eclipse is for web application development, you can only imagine how good the plug-ins for developing thick applications will be.

So much is going on in the Eclipse community that it is almost impossible to conceive of what types of products will come out of this rapidly growing community.

Recommended Resources

The following websites are relevant to or provide additional information on the topics discussed in this chapter.

Websites for competing technologies to ones discussed in this chapter:

- Eclipse Community   http://www.eclipse.org/community/
- Eclipse Directories   http://www.eclipseplugincentral.com/, http://eclipse-plugins.2y.net/eclipse/

- MyEclipseIDE.com   http://www.myeclipseide.com/
- Eclipse Technical Articles   http://www.eclipse.org/articles/
- Eclipse Platform Overview (white paper)   http://www.eclipse.org/whitepapers/eclipse-overview.pdf
- Blog about Ward Cunningham's departure from Microsoft   http://blogs.msdn.com/edjez/archive/2005/10/17/so_long_Ward.aspx
- Article:"Eclipse and HSQLDB: Embedding a Relational Database Server into Eclipse, Part 1"   http://www-128.ibm.com/developerworks/opensource/library/os-echsql/?ca=lnxw961HSQLDB
- EclipseCon conference   http://www.eclipsecon.org/

Alternative technology websites:

- Sun Microsystem's NetBeans   http://www.netbeans.org/
- JetBrain's IntellIJ   http://www.jetbrains.com/
- jEdit programmer's text editor   http://www.jedit.org/

III

Advanced Features

9

Logging, Debugging, Monitoring, and Profiling

Release 1, Week 7, Iteration 3

Ron: Hey, guys. How are things looking? I see you are pretty busy, so I won't bother you for too long. Don't work too hard, we want you guys to have a normal 40-hour schedule, so you can have a life outside of work, too.

Raj: Steve is refactoring the database and related code, because he found more efficient and cleaner techniques of handling persistence. I am debugging a nasty defect. I think we are almost there. Our velocity might drop a few points this iteration because of this defect caused by a 3rd party API. So, we might need to ask Susan to defer a user story or two or push the release date back.

Logging is an important issue that sometimes doesn't get the attention it deserves in various projects. Logging can be used for debugging, troubleshooting, tracing, or audit trail purposes. Logging can range from simple print statements to complex database or remote logging. Finding a good logging solution is key, preferably one that provides options such as control of output by severity level, formatting options, and the destination (for example, file or database).

Debugging, on the other hand, is necessary when bugs in a system are discovered, whether we like them or not. Bugs are software defects. Defects can surface for a variety of reasons, such as logic flaws in the code, wrong requirements, data problems, mismatch with an external interface (messaging service, for example), wrong versions of dependencies (for example, a third-party JAR file), invalid hardware/software combinations, and other reasons. The idea behind a defect is to locate the source of the defect and fix it! However, some defects can be harder to track down than others. Whereas one might take a couple of minutes to detect and fix, others can take days, typically, depending on the complexity of the system. The worst ones, in my opinion, are ones that are hard to reproduce or are intermittent in nature. (These drive me crazy!) Defects also vary in severity; some are minor UI aesthetics related and others are severe show-stoppers that can cause enormous amounts of financial damage to an organization, as a result of unavailable functionality. In short, a defect is something that fails to meet a customer requirement, and so, when defects surface, we need to find and fix them.

Debugging is typically the process of locating and fixing a defect, although it can sometimes be used to step through code to ensure the logic works correctly. Locating and fixing defects is perhaps one of the most difficult and frustrating tasks for a software developer. What can make this even worse is if you are debugging someone else's code.

Aside from logging and debugging, an application can have other design defects related to nonfunctional requirements (performance and scalability, for example). Monitoring and profiling an application can help meet such requirements by helping discover bottlenecks in an application related to memory consumption, CPU utilization, garbage collection, and so on. The Java Platform Standard Edition (JSE) 5.0 provides remote monitoring and management along with a nice GUI console that graphically displays information about the application being monitored.

In this chapter, I hope to provide you with some guidance on logging, debugging, monitoring, and also a bit on profiling.

What's Covered in This Chapter

In this chapter, we will cover the following logging and debugging techniques:

- Overview of logging concepts
- Logging with Jakarta Commons Logging (JCL)
- Debugging Java applications using Eclipse
- Debugging web user interfaces using Firefox
- JMX management and monitoring
- Java profilers
- Tips and tricks

By the end of this chapter, you should have enough information to apply effective logging and troubleshooting techniques for Java programs and web user interfaces in your software development project(s).

Logging Overview

I mentioned some uses of logging earlier, so I'll start by summarizing them here. This is sort of the "what" and "why" of logging; I'll provide the "how" right after.

Logging can be used for the following:

- Audit log—This is perhaps the most critical component of logging because it is generally used for record-keeping (auditing) purposes. For example, an organization might require all secure operations to be logged (for example, for compliance with Sarbanes-Oxley and Basel II regulations in the United States).

- Tracing—This involves generating information about what an application is doing at a given point. Tracing is typically sent either to System.out or a file, file being the better practice of the two. Tracing can be used for performance testing, seeing the flow of an application, and more.

- Error reporting—This is a common use for reporting errors and exceptions and is typically sent to System.err, although using System.err for error logging/reporting isn't a good practice. For errors, logging can highly effective for trouble-shooting the cause of a given problem.

Logging can also be saved in a file for later consumption, versus something like GUI-based debugging (discussed later in this chapter), which requires manual intervention. Also, at times a GUI debugger isn't even available—for example, when troubleshooting a problem on a server with *faceless* applications (that is, ones with no user interface). Also, logging is repeatable because the application can be rerun to generate fresh logging.

Although I've listed several benefits, following are some downsides to logging:

- Logging statements can clutter code and add extra work to development (that is, adding/removing print statements). Many developers put logging statements in their code but forget to either remove or maintain them, so sometimes the output messages are no longer valid or needed.

- Logging adds some overhead to the application's execution.

Now that we have reviewed some basics about logging, let's look at how we can implement logging in Java.

Jakarta Commons Logging (with Log4j and JDK Logging)

Many developers still use println statements in their Java programs for tracing and debugging purposes. However, logging frameworks can provide a nice alternative to this because they provide performance benefits and enable us to selectively turn on and off the messages generated by the logging; in addition, they provide various formatting options and the capability to send the messages to multiple devices without requiring us to add extra code in your application.

If you have been working in Java for some time now, you have likely heard of Apache's Log4j (logging.apache.org) and the logging built in to Java Platform Standard Edition Development Kit (JDK version 1.4 or later; java.sun.com). What you might not be aware of is Jakarta Commons Logging (JCL) API.

Instead of rephrasing the description provided on the commons-logging website (jakarta.apache.org/commons/logging/), I'll quote parts of it here because it is well written:

"The Logging package is an ultra-thin bridge between different logging implementations...using commons-logging does allow the application to change to a different logging implementation without recompiling code. Note that commons-logging does not attempt to initialise or terminate the underlying logging implementation that is used at runtime; that is the responsibility of the application. However many popular logging implementations do automatically initialise themselves; in this case an application may be able to avoid containing any code that is specific to the logging implementation used."

As you might guess from this description, JCL supports log4j and JDK logging, and we will use it here because it enables us to avoid coding to a concrete logging implementation. Also, JCL automatically detects which logging implementation is used underneath the covers—that is, log4j or JDK.

JCL can be downloaded from the http://jakarta.apache.org/commons/logging/. The only file we technically need out of this package is the commons-logging.jar file, which needs to be placed in your classpath. Beyond this, we either need JDK 1.4 (or later) or log4j-related files and configuration. I will demonstrate JDK 1.4-based logging here because it is built in to the JDK. For details on the log4j setup, refer to the http://logging.apache.org website.

How JCL Works

JCL is a simple API. The two key components are org.apache.commons.logging. LogFactory (a concrete factory class) and the instance it returns of an object that implements the org.apache.commons.logging.Log interface. What's really nice about JCL is that it requires a bare minimum of configuration. In most cases, if we have the commons-logging.jar (provided with JCL distribution) in the classpath, JCL will configure itself!

Furthermore, the default LogFactory provides a nice automatic discovery process of the underlying logging API. It first attempts to locate log4j.jar in the classpath; if this doesn't exist, it tries to drop back to JDK 1.4 (or later) logging. However, if we are using an old Java Virtual Machine (JVM), commons-logging will fall back on a default and rudimentary built-in logging wrapper.

Developing with JCL

After we have an instance of the org.apache.commons.logging.Log interface, we can call one of the following methods in it:

- fatal(Object message)
- error(Object message)

- warn(Object message)
- info(Object message)
- debug(Object message)
- trace(Object message)

These methods also have counterparts, which take a second parameter of type
`java.lang.Throwable`; for example, `log.fatal(Object message, Throwable t)`.

Let me demonstrate a simple example using JCL. The following code shows the simplest version of the program. I was able to get this programming running by having
`commons-logging.jar` in my classpath:

```
import org.apache.commons.logging.Log;
import org.apache.commons.logging.LogFactory;

public class CommonsLoggingTest
{
    private static Log log = LogFactory.getLog(CommonsLoggingTest.class);
    public static void main(String[] args)
    {
      log.fatal("This is a FATAL message.");
      log.error("This is an ERROR message.");
      log.warn("This is a WARN message.");
      log.info("This is an INFO message.");
      log.debug("This is a DEBUG message.");
    }
}
```

Message Logging Levels

One important thing to note about logging is the setting of a level for the types of messages we want printed. For example, as we see from the previous `CommonsLoggingTest` example, there are various methods for the level of logging we want (fatal, for example). The destination, formatting, and threshold of messages generated by your program can then be tweaked via log4j's `log4j.properties` file or JDK's `logging.properties` file (see the respective sites for details).

It is important to use the various log methods appropriately. For example, if we want to output only a debug message, we can use the .debug method versus .info or another method. This way, when the output level threshold is in property files set to WARN (in lo4j, for example), our debug messages won't be printed on the console. Similarly, use the fatal for serious errors because we wouldn't want our debug messages printing out when the application has been configured to be quiet versus noisy (discussed next).

An application's logging level is a design issue. In other words, you should decide whether you want your application to be noisy versus quiet; that is, will your application generate only true errors or spew out enormous amounts of trace messages (something I tend to discourage because I prefer quiet logging). Incidentally, the following are logging levels for log4j and JDK:

- log4j—DEBUG, INFO, WARN, ERROR, and FATAL (set in `log4j.properties`).
- JDK logging—FINEST, FINER, FINE, CONFIG, INFO, WARNING, and SEVERE (set in `logging.properties` under the JRE `lib/` directory or by passing the `-Djava.util.logging.config.file` parameter to the JVM).

The following lines show the output of `CommonsLoggingTest` class:

```
Feb 14, 2006 4:19:55 PM CommonsLoggingTest main
SEVERE: This is a FATAL message.
Feb 14, 2006 4:19:55 PM CommonsLoggingTest main
SEVERE: This is an ERROR message.
Feb 14, 2006 4:19:55 PM CommonsLoggingTest main
WARNING: This is a WARN message.
```

The reason you do not see the messages generated by the debug and info methods is that I tweaked the level in my `C:\Program Files\Java\jre1.5.0_06\lib\logging.properties` file by adjusting this line found in this file: `java.util.logging.ConsoleHandler.level = WARNING`.

I decided to do a quick test with log4J using Eclipse's Scrapbook feature discussed in Chapter 8, "The Eclipse Phenomenon!" (incidentally, this is a very useful feature).

First, I copied `log4j-1.2.11.jar` and `log4.properties` to my classpath. This is all we need to do to switch from JDK logging to log4j, using commons-logging. Then I evaluated the following single-line expression in a scrapbook page:

```
org.apache.commons.logging.LogFactory.getLog(CommonsLoggingTest.class)
    .fatal("This is a FATAL message.");
```

Notice that I'm still using the commons-logging API, not log4j or JDK logging calls, thus enabling me to decouple my code from the underlying logging framework. The output of the scrapbook page looked like this:

```
2006-02-17 10:25:50,654 FATAL [CommonsLoggingTest] - This is a FATAL message.
```

My `log4j.properties` (located in my classpath) looked like this (notice I'm using only the stdout appender, and not logfile):

```
log4j.rootLogger=WARN, stdout
# log4j.rootLogger=WARN, stdout, logfile
log4j.appender.stdout=org.apache.log4j.ConsoleAppender
log4j.appender.stdout.layout=org.apache.log4j.PatternLayout
log4j.appender.stdout.layout.ConversionPattern=%d %p [%c] - %m%n
log4j.appender.logfile=org.apache.log4j.FileAppender
log4j.appender.logfile.File=timex.log
log4j.appender.logfile.layout=org.apache.log4j.PatternLayout
log4j.appender.logfile.layout.ConversionPattern=%d %p [%c] - %m%n
```

Sample Logging in TimesheetListController

Let's try some sample logging in Time Expression. For example, let's slightly alter the code in the `TimesheetListControllerTest.handleRequest` method, as shown here:

```
List timesheets = timesheetManager.getTimesheets(employeeId);
Log log = LogFactory.getLog(TimesheetListController.class);
log.info("Returning " + timesheets.size() + " rows.");
return new ModelAndView(VIEW_NAME, MAP_KEY, timesheets);
```

Now let's also tweak the `log4j.properties` file we looked at previously, as follows:

```
log4j.rootLogger=INFO, stdout
```

The output of the log.info call shows something like the following:

```
2006-02-17 10:52:15,648 INFO [com.visualpatterns.timex.controller.TimesheetListC
➡ontroller] - Returning 4 rows.
```

A Note About Formatters

Both log4j and JDK logging provide formatters to output your message in a variety of formats, from simple text output to XML format logging (`java.util.logging.XMLFormatter`, for example) to custom pattern-based layout (`org.apache.log4j.PatternLayout`, for example).

We can also write custom formatters. This is a feature worth investigating further because you can customize the output to the way you need it and configure the new formatter in the respective configuration files without changing your code.

Using Logging for Spring and Hibernate

If you run into problems with Hibernate or Spring, you can turn the logging level up (that is, DEBUG for log4j and FINEST for JDK logging). This will probably produce more messages than you want to see; however, it can be very helpful, particularly with Hibernate, which shows you the database-specific SQL it generates (behind the scenes).

Debugging Java Applications Using Eclipse

GUI-based debuggers are excellent tools for detecting and fixing bugs because, among other things, they allow us to step through code and inspect variables. However, another feature often overlooked is that debuggers can also help you think about how your code is organized when you are stepping through the code; this can help you improve the stability of the code by allowing you to imagine the various ways your code could potentially break.

The Eclipse Java Development Tools (JDT) comes bundled with a debugger that provides stable and robust GUI-based Java debugging (it is quite impressive, really).

Java IDEs have indeed come a long way, in that they have robust features, a stable debugging environment, local as well as remote debugging capabilities, all the features of typical GUI debuggers, and some new and exciting ones such as Eclipse's Hotswap, which allows us to fix code on-the-fly (explained later).

I wrote my first-ever article about Symantec's Café (precursor to Visual Café) back in August of 1996 (for Dr. Dobb's Journal). Since then, I worked with Visual Café and Borland's JBuilder for a short while but found these IDEs to be clunky and their debuggers to be somewhat unstable. (What puzzles me the most is that I was using debuggers that enabled step-through-code style debugging almost 15 to 20 years ago with languages such as C/C++; so why it has taken so long for Java debuggers to get to this point is beyond my comprehension.)

The Eclipse JDT debugger is quite promising as far as its feature set and its consistency and stability are concerned. So let's take a look at some of its features here. If you have not read Chapter 8, I encourage you to do so prior to reading this section, because I'll assume that you have some understanding of the Eclipse platform and the JDT.

For starters, let's look at how we begin the debugging process in Eclipse. Eclipse enables us to debug various types of Java programs. Figure 9.1 shows some of the options available to us. Now let's look at the various concepts and features of the JDT debugger.

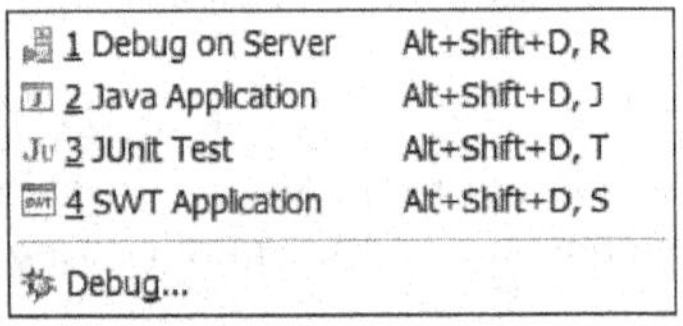

🔲 1 Debug on Server	Alt+Shift+D, R
🔲 2 Java Application	Alt+Shift+D, J
Ju 3 JUnit Test	Alt+Shift+D, T
🔲 4 SWT Application	Alt+Shift+D, S
✿ Debug...	

Figure 9.1   Eclipse's debug context menu.

JDT Debugging Concepts and Features

The JDT debugger enables us to detect, diagnose, and fix our bugs nicely. We can debug programs running locally or remotely (if remote debugging is supported by the remote JVM). The debug client runs inside Eclipse, whereas the remote debugger server (assuming you are doing remote debugging) runs inside the same JVM your server program is running in. I will demonstrate local debugging here but give you pointers for remote debugging as well, which is similar to local debugging, after you have the remote server configured (a relatively simple step). Let's review some basic JDT debugger concepts next.

The following is a list of debugging features provided by the JDT. Most of these features are available from the context menu (for the source code you are editing), Eclipse's Run menu, within one of the Debug views, or even by using shortcut keys. Hence, I will cover only the features and not point out where you can access them within Eclipse, because there are multiple ways of accessing them.

Debug Perspective and Views

For starters, Eclipse provides a Debug perspective that conveniently organizes a set of views for us. Also, when we begin debugging a program, Eclipse automatically switches to this perspective. Some of the related views include debug, expressions, variables, breakpoints, console, and a few others.

Breakpoints

Breakpoints are location(s) in your program where we want execution of the program to suspend, giving us time to inspect the variables or change your code. Breakpoints can be set at specific lines of code (I tend to use Ctrl+Shift+B on Windows XP to toggle a breakpoint; you can also do this by double-clicking or right-clicking on the left side of the editor window). This is all we need to do to set a breakpoint. However, there might be times when we want a breakpoint to be effective only under certain conditions, so let's look at that next.

After a breakpoint is set, we can set a *hit count* so that the program suspends at that breakpoint only after some number of *hits*—that is, the number of times that code has been executed. (This is done from the breakpoint's context menu.) We can also set conditional breakpoints (using the breakpoint's properties). For example, we might want the program to stop at the breakpoint only if a variable equals a certain value (as demonstrated in Figure 9.2). One thing I should point out is that I personally almost never use the *hit count* and conditional breakpoint features.

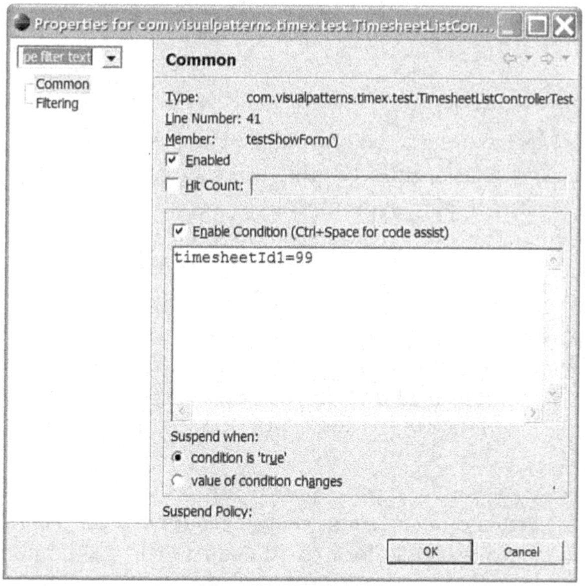

Figure 9.2   Setting conditional breakpoints.

One last type of breakpoint you can set is by catching exceptions, as shown in Figure 9.3. This is done using the little "J!" toolbar button in the Breakpoints view.

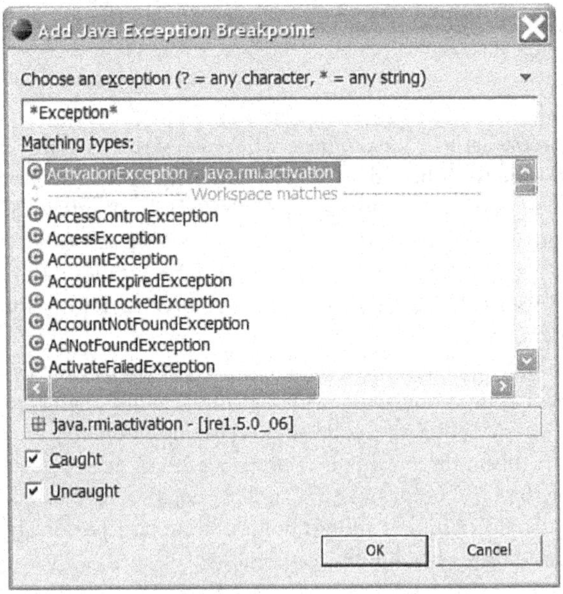

Figure 9.3 Java exception-based breakpoints.

Stepping Through Code

After we have our breakpoints set and our program launched (using the Run, Debug option, for example), we can begin debugging our code by stepping through it. When a breakpoint is hit—that is, the program suspends at a certain line of code—we can either step into a method call, step over it, or return out of the current method and back into the calling method (that is, one level up in the call stack). We can even use step filters (from Windows, Preferences, Java, Debug) to selectively step into methods.

Instead of stepping through every single line of code, we can set multiple breakpoints and resume execution of our program and have it automatically continue until the next breakpoint (effectively skipping all the steps between the two breakpoints).

Variables

Inspecting variables is one of the most important aspects of GUI-based debugging. After your program hits a breakpoint and suspends, you can look at the values of all the variables that are in scope (for example, local variables in a given method or class you are debugging). You can also watch expressions; for example, something like `"periodEndingDate != null"` can be added as an expression using the Watch view; this would appear as true in the Watch view if `periodEndingDate` does not equal to null.

The one very powerful feature of working with variables is that we can also change their values. By changing the value of a given variable at a specific line of code, we can alter the entire flow of the debugging session on-the-fly. This feature complements the Hotswap feature (discussed shortly), which provides the capability to change code on-the-fly and continue debugging.

One last feature worth pointing out is that you can display the value of a specific variable by selecting it in the source code and choosing Display from the context (right-click) menu.

Hotswap—Fixing Code On-the-Fly!

This is such a cool and powerful feature that it almost makes me drool (well, not quite—I do have a life outside of work).

Suppose we have stopped at a line of code triggered by a breakpoint and immediately realize the cause of the bug and want to fix it. Well, that's exactly what we should do! Immediately after we save the file (by pressing Ctrl+S, for example), Eclipse will recompile your class and reload the method in the same debugging session without the need for restarting the entire debugging session! How cool is that?

What excites me about this feature is that it is almost instantaneous and the debugger automatically positions your current line to the beginning of the method you are in, essentially restarting the debugging session but just from the beginning of the method, not the entire call stack.

Note that the Hotswap feature requires JRE 1.4 or later.

Remote Debugging

Eclipse enables us to debug remote programs as long as the remote server supports this feature. For example, I started Tomcat outside of Eclipse, on Windows XP, using the `catalina.bat` file using the following commands on the command line (notice the two environment variables that need to be set in advance):

```
set JPDA_ADDRESS=8000
set JPDA_TRANSPORT=dt_socket
catalina jpda start
```

Incidentally, JPDA stands for the Java Platform Debugger Architecture (architecture for remote debugging; java.sun.com). After starting Tomcat, I was able to connect to it using the Run, Debug, Remote Java Application (right-click New) option.

Other

You should browse through the various options available in the debug-related views. You will find several toolbar options in these views that might pleasantly surprise you. One feature is the copy stack option available in the Debug view via its context menu; this can help in various ways (emailing the stack to a colleague, for example). This feature essentially copies the call stack to the Clipboard as plain text, as shown in the sample excerpt.

```
TimesheetListControllerTest.testShowForm() line: 45
NativeMethodAccessorImpl.invoke0(Method, Object, Object[]) line:
➡not available [native method]
NativeMethodAccessorImpl.invoke(Object, Object[]) line: not available
DelegatingMethodAccessorImpl.invoke(Object, Object[]) line: not available
Method.invoke(Object, Object...) line: not available
TimesheetListControllerTest(TestCase).runTest() line: 154
TimesheetListControllerTest(TestCase).runBare() line: 127
TestResult$1.protect() line: 106
TestResult.runProtected(Test, Protectable) line: 124
TestResult.run(TestCase) line: 109
TimesheetListControllerTest(TestCase).run(TestResult) line: 118
TestSuite.runTest(Test, TestResult) line: 208
TestSuite.run(TestResult) line: 203
RemoteTestRunner.runTests(String[], String) line: 478
RemoteTestRunner.run() line: 344
    RemoteTestRunner.main(String[]) line: 196
```

Debugging Web User Interfaces Using Firefox

There are plenty of tools available in the market to debug Java applications. However, debugging a client-side JavaScript application isn't all that easy. Mozilla's Firefox browser aims to change some of this. For example, I have used the following two highly rated extensions (available from addons.mozilla.org or via Firefox's Tools, Extensions menu).

JavaScript Debugger

This extension (code name Venkman) is extremely useful for debugging JavaScript (in web-based user interfaces). This provides many of the features you would expect from a GUI debugger, such as stepping through code, inspecting variables, and more. Figure 9.4 shows a screenshot of this debugger.

Web Developer

The Firefox Web Developer extension is loaded with 50 or more utilities and is probably one of the best-written extensions I have seen for developers; it is no wonder this extension consistently gets a 5 out of 5-star rating on the Firefox extensions site.

I mainly use the Form and Resize menus only because I haven't gotten around to trying the others, which include features for working with CSS, validating links, showing comments, displaying information about every single element on the page, and much more!

For example, I use the resize menu to resize my screen to 800×600 resolution to ensure that my UI is usable in this resolution. The indispensable Form menu shows information about form fields and much more.

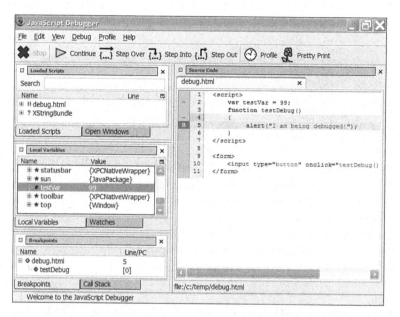

Figure 9.4   Firefox JavaScript debugger extension.

Other Firefox Extensions

Although I have demonstrated a couple of Firefox extensions here, there are many more where these came from. For example, at the time of this writing, there were more than 1,000 extensions on the Firefox website. Figure 9.5 shows one more example of such extensions, called Tamper Data. This extension allows us to change (tamper with) header and POST requests of a given page. This can be great for security testing, for instance. Visit the addons.mozilla.org website to see other extensions.

JavaScript Console

One other useful feature in Firefox worth mentioning is its JavaScript console (accessible from the Tools menu). This has helped me catch several errors with my user interfaces. It even also allows us to evaluate single-line JavaScript expressions.

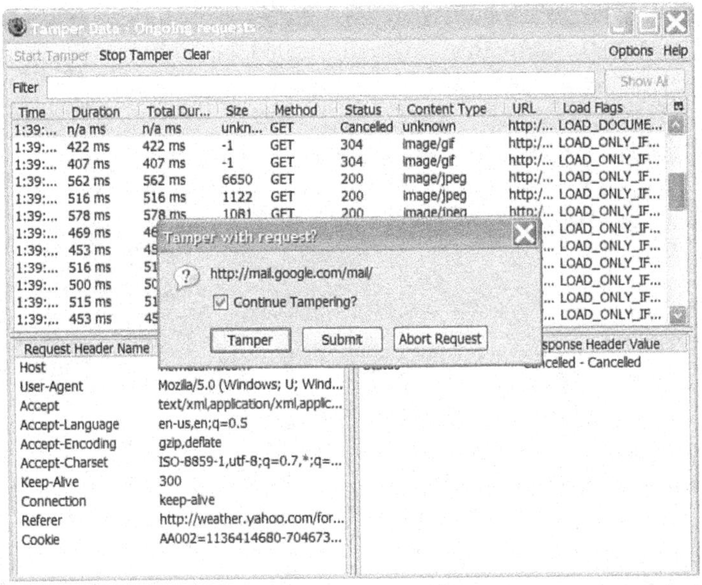

Figure 9.5   Firefox Tamper Data extension.

Debugging TimesheetManagerTest End-to-End (Browser to Database)

As I mentioned earlier, debugging can be a painful experience at times. It would be nice if we could simply tell the computer what the problem is and have it fix the bug for us. Considering that's not possible today, we have to find ways to make this experience slightly more pleasant, and Eclipse does a good job.

Being able to completely debug my server-side code (web and database, for example) is perhaps my favorite feature related to debugging in Eclipse. As we discussed Chapter 8, Eclipse has plug-ins galore. One of these is the Data related plug-in that is part of the Web Tools Platform (WTP) Eclipse project. Combining this with the built-in server-side debugging features makes for a very powerful concept! Let's look at an example of what I'm referring to.

Figure 9.6 shows a screenshot of Eclipse. Here I'm stepping through `TimesheetManagerTest.java`, inspecting the various memory variables, viewing the output in the Console view, viewing the test results in the JUnit view, and—are you ready?—watching the data in the database change (by manually refreshing it) right in front of my eyes (as I step over the `timesheetManager.deleteTimesheet` method) using the Data Output view. Now, that's cool!

On the client side, I like using some of the extensions I mentioned earlier, such as the JavaScript debugger, JavaScript console, and Web Developer. For example, Figure 9.7 shows a screenshot of our Enter Hours form with the field names, sizes, and other information displayed. This extension has helped me find field truncation errors because my HTML input text filed was too small, for example.

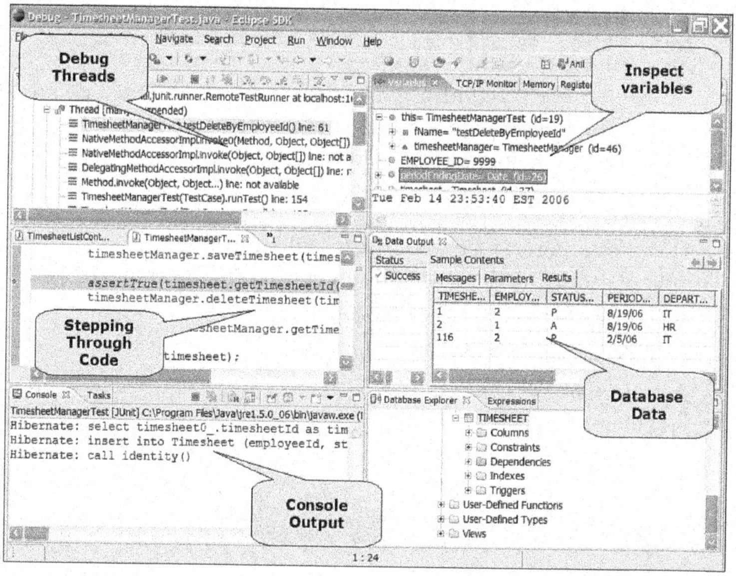

Figure 9.6   Consolidated debugging of Time Expression in Eclipse.

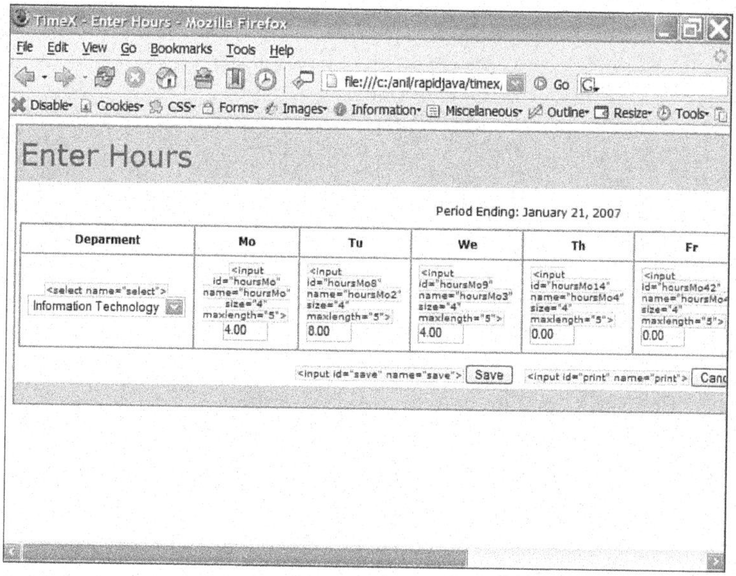

Figure 9.7   Firefox Web Developer extension.

JMX Management and Monitoring

Java Platform Standard Edition (JSE) 5.0 provides built-in remote monitoring, management, and a console to monitor applications that run using JSE 5.0 or later versions. These tools can be used to view the resource utilization of Java applications. For example, this can help with detecting memory issues, class loading and garbage collection, controlling JDK logging levels, and managing an application's Managed Beans (MBeans).

I decided to monitor Tomcat with Time Expression deployed in it. First, I had to set the CATALINA_OPTS environment variable as follows:

```
set CATALINA_OPTS=-Dcom.sun.management.jmxremote
```

After setting this environment variable, I started Tomcat from the command line. We could just as easily do this with Tomcat, within Eclipse. After starting Tomcat, I launched the JConsole utility provided with the JDK, as follows:

```
c:\program files\java\jdk1.5.0_06\bin\jconsole
```

Figures 9.8 and 9.9 show monitoring of a local instance of Tomcat using JConsole. For details on JMX-based management and monitoring, refer to the java.sun.com website.

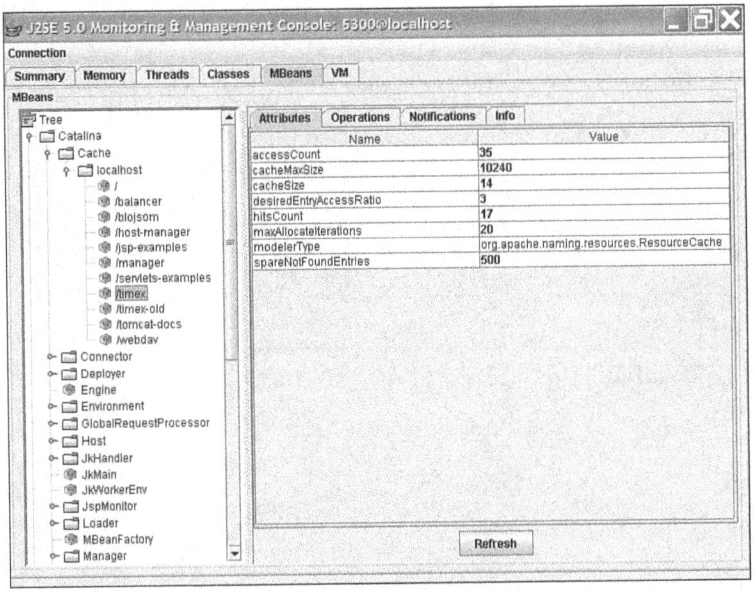

Figure 9.8   JSE 5.0's JConsole application (monitoring local
Apache Tomcat and timex.war).

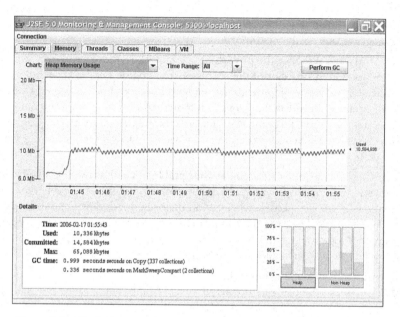

Figure 9.9   JSE 5.0's JConsole application (monitoring local Apache Tomcat).

In the next chapter, we will develop our own JMX bean (with the help of the Spring Framework) and monitor it using the JConsole application.

Java Profilers

Java profilers have been around for almost as long as Java has. Among other things, profilers allow us to analyze the heap for memory usage and leaks, CPU utilization, trace objects and methods, determine performance bottlenecks, and much more. A variety of open source profilers are available out there, as well as commercial ones (for example, YourKit profiler at yourkit.com and Quest JProbe Suite). Some run as standalone Java programs, others can be deployed to a servlet container, and yet others are available as Eclipse plug-ins.

The JMX monitoring I discussed previously is robust; however, it requires JSE 5.0 and might not provide the type of application-specific coverage and profiling you are looking for. So, if you are looking for an open source profiler, the following website lists a dozen or so open source Java profilers: http://www.manageability.org/blog/stuff/open-source-profilers-for-java/view/.

Debugging Tips

The following are some soft tips, some more obvious than others, but you might find one or more useful, so I'll list them here:

- If you have a bug you just cannot track down, walk away from the problem and return to it later or the next morning.

- Always try to reproduce the problem. For example, I often request that my customers provide a snapshot of the data they are using in a test environment so I can re-create it in the development environment. This snapshot can easily be obtained using database tools that allow you to import/export data (Aqua Data Studio is one such tool; aquafold.com). Also, ask the customer to re-create the problem for you—that is, what action was taken and what state was the application in when the problem occurred.

- Get a second pair of eyes to look at your problem. There is nothing like having someone walk up to you and tell you the problem within a second because of bringing a fresh perspective, whereas you might be heads down and too close to the problem (the can't-see-the-forest-for-the-trees syndrome). If you are using Extreme Programming, this is one of the side benefits you get from pair programming (details at extremeprogramming.org).

- Use a process-of-elimination technique. That is, in your mind, separate the code that works and the part that doesn't. If possible, physically separate the code that works from the code that does not. Debugging smaller snippets of code is much easier than a complex system.

- Determine whether any of your dependencies are causing the problems. For example, has an external API or interface changed? Is the data bad? Has the application server or database version changed? Is it a hardware problem?

- Program defensively by checking for valid input values. A nice way to do this is by using assertions introduced in J2SE 1.4 (details available at java.sun.com/j2se/ 1.4.2/docs/guide/lang/assert.html). Another option is to check for valid values manually and throw a `java.lang.IllegalArgumentException` exception for invalid values.

- Use new `Exception().printStackTrace()` in your code to print the stack without actually throwing an exception. This can be helpful if you want to know where something came from.

- Try to always write simple `toString()` methods in your classes. This can help significantly when you are printing objects.

Personal Opinion: Bug Prevention Techniques

Bugs are a normal part of our lives as software developers. Here are a couple of suggestions to help you prevent bugs.

For starters, there is no substitute for printing out your own code and walking through it on paper, away from the computer. This is perhaps one of most effective practices, but requires a bit of patience. Many organizations take this one step further by doing code walkthroughs. Extreme Programming handles this via its pair programming.

Another good option is to walk through your code using a GUI debugger. You don't have to use a debugger just for debugging; you can also use it to verify that your code is working as you expect it to.

However, in my opinion, one of the best ways to reduce bugs is by developing software in smaller chunks. In other words, for each iteration, two weeks in length, we have minimal requirements up front in the form of high-level and low-level requirements. For the high-level requirements, you could do some initial UI sketches (for a user interface application), domain modeling, user stories, and so on. These are typically done at the beginning of a release. At the beginning of each iteration, you get detailed requirements in the form of acceptance tests. Given this approach, there is a lot less that can go wrong. Furthermore, when you factor in the test-first approach (recall the "Writing Unit Test and Actual Code in Same Sitting" sidebar from Chapter 7, "The Spring Web MVC Framework") combined with refactoring as and when needed, your code is bound to be more solid at the end.

Iterative development using short and fixed cycles (two fixed-week iterations, for example) combined with active stakeholder participation can help reduce some of the pressures of time-sensitive software delivery; this is possible because the customer sees progress on a regular basis and is likely to be more flexible and understanding when it comes time for missed deliverables. This reduction of time-sensitive pressure can also help you write more stable code and not just something you throw over the wall, so to speak.

Finding bugs is no fun. I sometimes feel like it is similar to looking for a real-life tiny bug that is hiding in a big room filled with lots of stuff.

By doing true iterative development (from requirements through deployment) and having smaller-size fixed-iteration lengths (two weeks being ideal), you are likely to prevent bugs and enjoy coding a lot more!

Summary

In this chapter, we covered the following:

- Overview of logging concepts
- Logging with Jakarta Commons Logging
- Debugging Java Applications using Eclipse
- Debugging web user interfaces using Firefox
- JMX management and monitoring
- Java profilers
- Tips and tricks

We are just about done with this book. However, we have some advanced features to cover in the next chapter. So, let's move forward with that.

Recommended Resources

The following websites are relevant to or provide additional information on the topics discussed in this chapter:

- Java open source profilers   http://www.manageability.org/blog/stuff/open-source-profilers-for-java/view/
- Eclipse SDK   http://www.eclipse.org/
- Extreme Programming   http://extremeprogramming.org/
- Firefox extensions   https://addons.mozilla.org/
- Jakarta Commons Logging (JCL)   http://jakarta.apache.org/commons/logging/
- JDK logging   http://java.sun.com
- JMX monitoring and management   http://java.sun.com
- Log4J   http://logging.apache.org/
- Simple Logging Facade for Java (SLF4J)   http://slf4j.org/
- Software debugging, testing, and verification (article)   http://www.research.ibm.com/journal/sj/411/hailpern.html
- Eclipse TPTP   http://www.eclipse.org/tptp/home/downloads/quicktour/v41/quick_tour.html
- YourKit Java Profiler   http://www.yourkit.com/

10

Beyond the Basics

Release 1, Week 8, Iteration 4

Raj: Mindy, this data center is impressive. Amazing that the application Steve and I built will be running on one of these servers.

Mindy: It sure is. I hear your application is well built since it takes into consideration failover, security, reliability, and so on. Now, if the operations staff maintains 99% uptime for the hardware and network they signed-up for in the contract, then Susan and her group should be happy overall.

W E HAVE COVERED A LOT OF foundational material and now it is time to go beyond the basics in this chapter. This is the last chapter with code examples; the next chapter will provide some ideas for further research and reading.

So let's look at a few new, advanced, and cool features in this book to begin wrapping things up.

What's Covered in This Chapter

In this chapter, we will look at some beyond-the-basics type features of the various technologies we covered earlier in the book. I have decided to follow the same order that I introduced these technologies in the earlier chapters. In this chapter, we will cover the following material:

- Recently added Java features
- Additional built-in and external Ant tasks
- JUnit custom suites
- Additional Hibernate features
- Other Spring Framework features
- Integrating Hibernate with Spring
- The Displaytag tag library and writing custom tag libraries
- Sample refactoring of our sample application
- Other important considerations such as transaction management, security, exception handling, clustering, and several others
- A simple Ajax example

Note

The complete code for the examples used in this chapter can be found within this book's code zip file (available on the book's website).

Note that this chapter provides very brief descriptions of the features mentioned here. I have taken the approach to demonstrate more by using code over detailed explanations. Also, many of the features mentioned here are covered in detail by their corresponding reference documentation, which I have provided links to.

Recently Added Java Features

Let's begin with the Java Platform Standard Edition (JSE) Development Kit (JDK), because this is where we began our hands-on work back in Chapter 4, "Environment Setup: JDK, Ant, and JUnit."

JDK 1.5 (also known as JSE 5.0) introduced some new features that aim to enhance the Java languages. Let's look at some of these features here; if you are already familiar with these features, you can skip this section.

Backward Compatibility with JDK 1.4 for Time Expression

I intentionally did not use any of these new features in our sample application, Time Expression, because I wanted it to provide backward compatibility with JDK 1.4 in case your organization has not adopted JDK 1.5 yet. Also note that I used Eclipse's Window, Preferences, Java, Compiler option to maintain compatibility with JDK 1.4. This is a very handy feature, which I encourage you to investigate if you aren't already familiar with it.

The complete code for the features discussed next can be found in a file named `DemoNewJavaFeatures.java` in this book's code zip file. I will provide only brief descriptions here because the examples are simple, and ample documentation is available for these on the java.sun.com website.

Static Import

Since JSE 5.0, it is possible to use static members directly. For example, something like `Integer.MAX_VALUE` can be used as follows:

```
import static java.lang.Integer.*;
System.out.println(MAX_VALUE);
```

Generics

In previous releases, we could insert any type of object in a class from the Collections framework; then we had to cast objects retrieved from the Collections framework. This provided somewhat unsafe operations because the compiler couldn't check for type safety. Now we can avoid this by doing something similar to what's shown next—notice how I can simply use the `get` method without the need for casting:

```
ArrayList<String> arrayList = new ArrayList<String>();
arrayList.add("Testing");
System.out.println(arrayList.get(0));
```

Furthermore, we add only objects of type `String` to this ArrayList. For example, the following code would cause a compilation error:

```
arrayList.add(new Integer(1));
```

Enhanced for Loop

The for loop has been greatly simplified since JSE 5.0. To iterate through a collection class, instead of using the old style, `for (int i=0; i < c.size; i++)`, we can do the following:

```
public static void demoForLoop(Collection<Integer> c)
{
  // using new style for loop
  for (Integer i : c)
    System.out.println(i);
}
```

This not only unclutters the code slightly but can also help reduce common errors caused by invalid checking of index variables (for example, the variable i in this example).

Autoboxing

This is a nice feature and in my opinion should have been supported in Java all along. As you might know, we cannot put primitive data types (for example, int) in collections classes. With this new feature, we can add a number into something like an `ArrayList`, as shown here, without the need to use new `Integer(1)`:

```
ArrayList<Integer>list = new ArrayList<Integer>();
list.add(1);
```

Enums

The simple example provided next does not demonstrate the power of enums in Java:

```
enum BookName { RAPID, JAVA, DEVELOPMENT };
for (BookName bookName : BookName.values())
  System.out.println(bookName);
```

The following description taken directly from the java.sun.com website does more justice to this feature:

"Java programming language enums are far more powerful than their counterparts in other languages, which are little more than glorified integers. The new enum declaration defines a full-fledged class (dubbed an enum type)... it allows us to add arbitrary methods and fields to an enum type, to implement arbitrary interfaces, and more. Enum types provide high-quality implementations of all the Object methods. They are Comparable and Serializable, and the serial form is designed to withstand arbitrary changes in the enum type."

Varargs

Varargs provide the capability to pass variable arguments in methods. Before, we had to do this using something like an Object array. Now, we can use ellipses(...)to do this, as shown here:

```
public static void demoVarargs(Object... args)
MessageFormat.format(
    "I''m working on {0}"
    + " on {1}"
    + " at {2} hours.", args);
```

The code that calls our `demoVarargs` method looks as follows:

```
demoVarargs("Rapid Java Development", new Date(), 1800 );
```

Furthermore, JDK classes such as MessageFormat also accept variable arguments, as demonstrated in this example.

Other Features

There are other features (annotations, for example) and enhancements to the API and JVM that I have not covered here; however, details and tutorials on these can readily be found on the java.sun.com website. Furthermore, my simple examples do the new features justice. As we can see from Figure 10.1, Java is a huge platform; it is no wonder there are hundreds of books on Java and entire books on single subjects such as Java Security APIs, JDBC, and others.

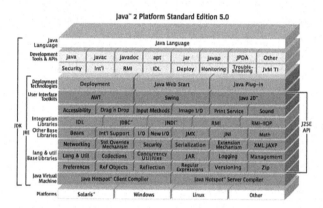

Figure 10.1   Java Platform Standard Edition 5.0 (source: java.sun.com).

Also, at the time of this writing, J2SE 6 beta was announced, which provides new/ enhanced security features, integrated web services, enhanced JMX support, improved GUI, and more. Visit the java.sun.com website for details.

Ant Tasks

We used Ant throughout the book, including within Eclipse. Although we have already looked at some very useful and robust features of Ant, let's explore a few more Ant tasks here, demonstrated in our `antextras.xml` file. Some of these are built-in tasks, others are considered external tasks in that they require you to place one or more JAR files (libraries) in the `<ant-home>/lib` directory (ant-home implies the Ant's install directory; for example, `C:\apache-ant-1.6.5`).

As you will see from some of these tasks, Ant is one of those beautifully designed tools because of its simplicity; yet it has enormous power. It is much more than a build tool, as I will demonstrate next.

For additional information on these and other tasks not mentioned here, visit the ant.apache.org website. This site also provides information about writing your own custom Ant tasks.

CVS

As the name implies, this task enables us to work with CVS. This does require you to have the CVS executable in your path. For example, I downloaded TortoiseCVS from the tortoisecvs.org website and was able to use the `cvs.exe` found in this program's directory (on Linux, Unix, and Mac OS X systems, you might already have CVS preinstalled). The following XML demonstrates how this task works; here I was able to download the Spring framework spring module using Ant:

```
<cvs cvsRoot=":pserver:anonymous@cvs.sourceforge.net:/cvsroot/springframework"
   package="spring"
     dest="/temp"
/>
```

Exec

This task enables us to run external programs; for example, the following code runs the date command:

```
<exec command="date"/>
```

Get

The Get task enables us to fetch a file using HTTP GET as demonstrated here:

```
<get src="http://visualpatterns.com/comics/funny.gif"
   dest="funny.gif"
   verbose="true"/>
```

Sleep

As you might guess, this task allows us to pause processing by a specified amount of time, as demonstrated here using 2 seconds:

```
<sleep seconds="2"/>
```

FTP

This is a very powerful task because it enables us to use FTP directly from the Ant XML file. For example, while working on this book, I used it to back up my book-related files and Time Expression files to an FTP server, automatically using the Microsoft Windows Scheduled Tasks feature!

```
<ftp server="mirrors.kernel.org"
    action="get"
    remotedir="/gnu/chess"
    userid="anonymous"
    password="guest@guest.com"
    verbose="yes"
    binary="yes">
  <fileset file="README.gnuchess"/>
</ftp>
```

FTP is an external task and requires the following files to be present in the `<ant-home>/lib` directory:

- Jakarta Commons Net (http://jakarta.apache.org/commons/net/; commons-net `<version>`.jar)

- Jakarta-ORO (http://jakarta.apache.org/oro/; jakarta-oro`<version>`.jar)

Mail

This task enables us to send mail using SMTP. It also allows us to attach files using the `<fileset>` element. This makes for a very powerful combination because we could use this to send emails after a build is complete, for example (particularly useful in a auto-mated continuous build/integration environment). The following is a simple example of how this task can be used:

```
<mail tolist="friend@somehost.com"
    subject="Hello!"
    from="me@myhost.com"
    mailhost="myhost.com"
    user="myuserid"
    password="mypassword"/>
```

This feature requires `mail.jar` (part of the JavaMail API) and `activation.jar` (part of the JavaBeans Activation Framework) present in the `<ant-home>/lib` directory. Both of these can be found on the java.sun.com website.

Tasks Galore!

I've mentioned only a few Ant tasks that I thought you might find useful. There are lit-erally hundreds of Ant tasks available, everything from vendor-specific tasks to general ones such as Gzip, Tar, and many more. Visit the ant.apache.org website to learn about some of these tasks and how to write your own custom tasks.

JUnit

Up to this point in the book, we have been using single test suites to test just the methods that begin with the word "test." We also looked at how to run all test classes in a batch from a particular directory using Ant. Now let's take a look at how to create custom test suites and reuse *fixture* code.

Custom Test Suites

JUnit allows us to build our own test suites. Furthermore, suites can contain other suites, which makes for a powerful concept despite JUnit's simplicity. The following code excerpt from our `AllTests.java` file (in the `timex/` directory) demonstrates how to build custom suites.

```
TestSuite modelTestSuite = new TestSuite("Model Tests");
modelTestSuite.addTestSuite(TimesheetManagerTest.class);
TestSuite controllerTestSuite = new TestSuite("Controller Tests");
controllerTestSuite.addTestSuite(TimesheetListControllerTest.class);
TestSuite fullSuite = new TestSuite("All Tests");
fullSuite.addTest(modelTestSuite);
fullSuite.addTest(controllerTestSuite);
return fullSuite;
```

Test Fixture Code

When we write unit test classes, it is a good idea to move test "fixture" code to a parent class, which in turn can extend the `junit.framework.TestCase` class.

A *fixture* is a set of objects (for example, test data) that might be used by one or more test cases. The benefit of a fixture is that it helps us avoid redundant setup and teardown code. For example, on past projects, I have moved the JDBC connection code, the Spring application context-loading code, and various other common code to a parent class. See junit.sourceforge.net/doc/cookbook/cookbook.htm for details on fixture code.

For our sample application, our fixture code has been moved up to the constructor of a parent class named `TimexTestCase`, as shown here:

```
protected TimexTestCase()
{
  FileSystemResource res =
          new FileSystemResource("src/conf/timex2-servlet.xml");
  springFactory = new XmlBeanFactory(res);

  departmentManager = (DepartmentManager)
          springFactory.getBean("departmentManagerProxy");
  employeeManager = (EmployeeManager)
          springFactory.getBean("employeeManagerProxy");
  timesheetManager = (TimesheetManager)
```

```
        springFactory.getBean("timesheetManagerProxy");
    applicationSecurityManager = (ApplicationSecurityManager)
        springFactory.getBean("applicationSecurityManager");
}
```

Note that I have set up the fixture code in a constructor. You could also set this up in the JUnit setUp method. Alternatively, if you are using JDK 1.5 or later, you can use annotations to initialize your fixtures (visit the junit.org website for details on this feature).

Now, classes such as TimesheetManagerTest can extend our new TimexTestCase class instead of directly inheriting TestCase, as shown in this example:

```
public class TimesheetManagerTest extends TimexTestCase
```

By having common fixture code in the TimexTestCase parent class, all subclasses can have instant access to precreated and fully set up objects (thanks to Spring's dependency injection). This enables the subclasses to focus on implementing the unit tests to pass user acceptance tests, versus spending time setting up fixtures for each test case.

For additional details on unit testing, test fixtures, test suites, and related topics, visit the junit.org website.

Hibernate

Although we covered a lot of ground on Hibernate in Chapter 5, "Using Hibernate for Persistent Objects," there is a lot more to Hibernate, which is the very reason there are entire books written on this technology. However, a couple of other features you might find useful are discussed next.

Native SQL Queries

Most relational databases provide ANSI-SQL–compliant features; however, they also tend to go further by providing their own custom extensions, which might not be supported by HQL. To take advantage of such native SQL features, we can use Hibernate's Session.createSQLQuery method as demonstrated by the following code, which uses HSQLDB's datediff built-in function:

```
String sql = "select datediff('dd', NOW, ?) AS daysleft"
    + " from timesheet";
Integer valueObject = (Integer)session.createSQLQuery(sql)
        .addScalar("daysleft", Hibernate.INTEGER)
        .setDate(0, DateUtil.getCurrentPeriodEndingDate())
        .uniqueResult();
if (valueObject != null)
    daysLeft = valueObject.intValue();
```

Interceptors

Interceptors, as you might guess, intercept a request. Perhaps the following description from the Hibernate reference documentation best describes the use of Hibernate interceptors: "The Interceptor interface provides callbacks from the session to the application allowing the application to inspect and/or manipulate properties of a persistent object before it is saved, updated, deleted or loaded. One possible use for this is to track auditing information."

To use Hibernate interceptor, we must either implement all the methods defined in the org.hibernate.Interceptor interface or alternatively, subclass the convenient org.hibernate.EmptyInterceptor concrete class and override only the methods we need to, as demonstrated by the following code excerpt.

```
public class AuditInterceptor extends EmptyInterceptor
{
  public void afterTransactionCompletion(Transaction tx)
```

After we have written an interceptor class, we can either activate it for a given session using the `Session.openSession(Interceptor interceptor)` method or activate it at the Configuration level, as shown here:

```
sessionFactory = new Configuration()
        .setInterceptor(new AuditInterceptor())
        .configure().buildSessionFactory();
```

The Spring Framework

On one hand, we dedicated two chapters to the Spring Framework, so you might be wondering why more Spring? The short and simple answer is that although technologies such as Hibernate are robust, they also have a single focus (object-relational mapping, for example). However, the Spring Framework is such a large framework and is loaded with so many features that it is difficult to cover everything about Spring even in a small book. So, let's look at some more examples of using Spring here.

Scheduling Jobs

It is not uncommon for many applications to have requirements for scheduled jobs to run, perhaps for batch processing, to send data to downstream applications or generate CPU-intensive reports at the end of the day. To facilitate the scheduling of jobs, many companies use schedulers such as Unix/Linux CRON, Computer Associate's Unicenter AutoSys, Microsoft's Scheduled Tasks feature, and so on.

Open Symphony's Quartz system (opensymphony.com) provides the capability to schedule jobs within Java programs, and the Spring Framework provides support for this product (and JDK timers). The Quartz API is much more robust than JDK timers because it provides powerful scheduling features such as CRON-like expressions (discussed next).

You might recall from Chapter 2, "The Sample Application: An Online Timesheet System," that the business requirements for our sample application, Time Expression, require a reminder email to be sent on Fridays at 2 p.m. Our two files— `ReminderEmail.java` and `timex-servlet.xml`–combined provide this functionality. `ReminderEmail.java` will be discussed in the next section. However, let's look at the code excerpt from `timex-servlet.xml` that schedules the job.

```
<!-- Spring job scheduling -->
<bean id="reminderEmailJobDetail"
      class=
    "org.springframework.scheduling.quartz.MethodInvokingJobDetailFactoryBean">
    <property name="targetObject" ref="reminderEmail" />
    <property name="targetMethod" value="sendMail" />
</bean>
<bean id="reminderEmailJobTrigger"
      class="org.springframework.scheduling.quartz.CronTriggerBean">
    <property name="jobDetail" ref="reminderEmailJobDetail" />h
    <property name="cronExpression" value="0 0 14 ? * 6" />
</bean>
<bean
      class="org.springframework.scheduling.quartz.SchedulerFactoryBean">
    <property name="triggers">
        <list>
            <ref bean="reminderEmailJobTrigger" />
        </list>
    </property>
</bean>
```

Notice the `0 0 14 ? * 6` value; this is a CRON-like expression that indicates that the job should be run at 14:00 hours (or 2 p.m.) on Fridays (6 for the sixth day of the week). Also, visit quartz.sourceforge.net for detailed documentation on the Quartz API.

Another notable configuration item is how we tell Spring which target method in which target object to invoke for us, as shown next:

```
<property name="targetObject" ref="reminderEmail" />
<property name="targetMethod" value="sendMail" />
```

This feature requires Open Symphony's `quartz.jar`, available on the opensymphony.com website. In the case of Time Expression, we would need this to be installed in the `timex/lib` directory.

The one issue we face with running jobs inside a web or application server is if the server is *clustered*—that is, there is more than one instance of the server. (Clustering is discussed later in the chapter.) As you might guess, the job will run on all instances (servers) in the clustered environment. To get around this problem, in the past, I have used a database technique to manage this job concurrency issue. This technique uses a table named ObjectLock with a column name isLocked. The isLocked column can be used to simulate a job lock; this can then be checked by the jobs to determine if the job is already running (that is, locked).

Spring Mail Support

As I mentioned earlier, our business requirements dictate that a reminder email be sent out to all employees who have not submitted a weekly timesheet. To implement this feature, we will use a simple mail-sending API provided by the Spring Framework, instead of using something like JavaMail directly. Note that Spring uses JavaMail for this mail support.

Our two files, `ReminderEmail.java` and `timex-servlet.xml`, combined provide this functionality. The following is the excerpt from the `timex-servlet.xml` file:

```
<bean id="mailSender"
    class="org.springframework.mail.javamail.JavaMailSenderImpl">
    <property name="host" value="acme.com" />
    <property name="username" value="myuserid" />
    <property name="password" value="mypassword" />
</bean>

<bean id="reminderEmailMessage"
    class="org.springframework.mail.SimpleMailMessage">
    <property name="from" value="me@me.com" />
    <property name="subject" value="Reminder: Submit Timesheet" />
    <property name="text"
        value="Please don't forget to submit your timesheet. Thank you!" />
</bean>

<bean id="reminderEmail"
    class="com.visualpatterns.timex.job.ReminderEmail">
    <property name="employeeManager">
        <ref bean="employeeManager" />
    </property>
    <property name="mailSender">
        <ref bean="mailSender" />
    </property>
    <property name="message">
        <ref bean="reminderEmailMessage" />
    </property>
</bean>
```

The following method from `ReminderEmail.java` shows the actual code, which demonstrates how a list of emails is retrieved from the database (using one of our model classes from Chapter 5) for sending the email to various employees:

```
public void sendMail()
{
    List list = employeeManager.getHourlyEmployees();
```

```
  if (list == null || list.size()< 1)
    return;
  String emailAddresses[] = new String[list.size()];
  Employee employee;
  for (int i=0; i < list.size(); i++)
  {
    employee = (Employee)list.get(i);
    emailAddresses[i] = employee.getEmail();
  }
  message.setTo(emailAddresses);
  SimpleMailMessage threadSafeMailMessage =
    new SimpleMailMessage(message);
  mailSender.send(threadSafeMailMessage);
}
```

This feature requires `mail.jar` (part of the JavaMail API) and `activation.jar` (part of the JavaBeans Activation Framework) are present in the `timex/lib` directory. Both of these can be found on the java.sun.com website.

JMX Support

We looked at the Java Management Extensions (JMX) technology in the previous chapter. Although this technology is primarily used for managing servers currently, in my opinion it can easily be used to monitor business aspects of an application. For example, we could monitor how many users have logged on to the system for a given day, how many invoices were processed for an accounting system, how many claims were processed for an insurance system, and so on. This can be used not only to monitor the health of the application, but also to provide a comfort level that everything is operating in a business-as-usual fashion.

Spring's JMX support enables us to automatically register plain JavaBean objects. In our case, this is accomplished via two files: one is `timex-servlet.xml` and the other is a simple JavaBean class (`TimexJmxBean.java`) that tracks how many users signed into Time Expression and how many timesheets records were fetched.

The following is a code excerpt from `timex-servlet.xml`:

```
<bean id="timexJmxBean"
    class="com.visualpatterns.timex.util.TimexJmxBean" />
<bean id="exporter"
    class="org.springframework.jmx.export.MBeanExporter">
    <property name="registrationBehaviorName"
        value="REGISTRATION_IGNORE_EXISTING" />
    <property name="beans">
        <map>
            <entry key="Time Expression:name=timex-stats"
                value-ref="timexJmxBean" />
        </map>
    </property>
</bean>
```

The following code excerpt shows an excerpt from the `TimexJmxBean.java`:

```
public class TimexJmxBean
{
  private static int signInCount;
  private static int timesheetsFetched;
  public int getSignInCount()
  {
    return signInCount;
```

Figure 10.2 shows our JMX Bean in the JConsole application (bundled with JSE 5.0). Again, this is a great way to monitor, right from your desktop, the health and status of applications running on a remote server! In my opinion, this provides a great view for developers versus larger and much more robust tools, such as HP's OpenView or Computer Associate's Unicenter related products, which are intended for use by operations departments.

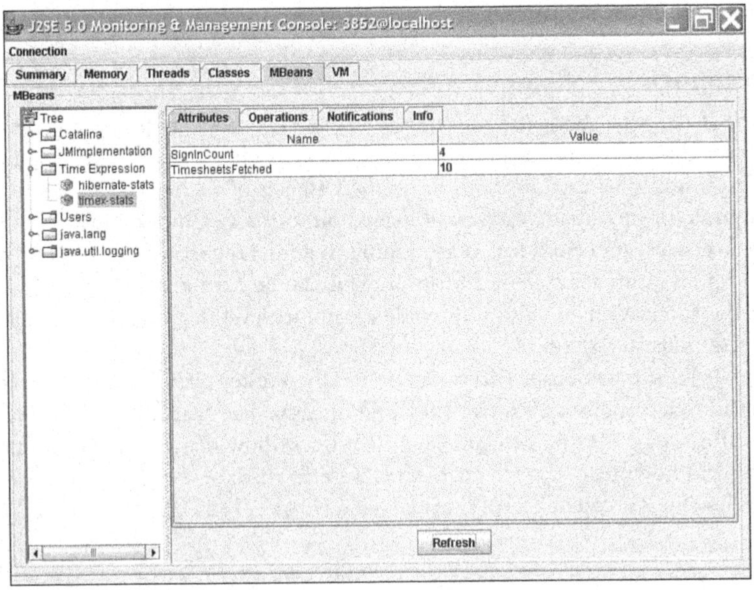

Figure 10.2   JConsole with TimexJmxBean.

More Spring

Again, Spring is such a large framework and so loaded with features that I could cover only the ones applicable to our sample application.

New Tag Libraries

At the time of this writing, the most current version of the upcoming Spring Framework was M4 (or RC1). This version introduced several new tag libraries to ease working in JSP. Some of the new tags include form:form, form:input, form:password, form:hidden, form:select, form:option, form:radiobutton, form:checkbox, form:textarea, and form:errors.

The tag libraries mentioned here were still unstable and I was requested by the Spring Framework team to not cover these in detail until they became stable.

Visit the springframework.org website for the latest documentation and downloads.

Support for Web Services, JMS, JTA, EJB, DAO, RMI, JDBC

Spring also provides support for remoting protocols such as the Java Remote Method Invocation (RMI), Web Services (using JAX-RPC), Java Connector Architecture (JCA), DAO (Data Access Object) support for various object-relational mapping (ORM) products other than Hibernate (JDO and iBATIS, for example), and Java Database Connectivity (JDBC), EJB, Java Message Service (JMS), Java Transaction API (JTA), and more.

Startup Classes

You might be familiar with the concept of startup classes or servlets in web and application servers. Spring doesn't explicitly have the notion of startup classes. But this is easily done using the depends-on attribute for the bean element. Most of the objects are automatically created in the correct order because Spring resolves the dependencies.

However, if you have independent classes such as the HibernateUtil class, the depends-on attribute can come in handy for ensuring that those objects get instantiated beforehand, so they are prepared to be used by the objects that need them.

Other

Another notable feature is Spring's capability to load an external properties file, as shown in this example:

```
<bean id="placeholderConfig"
      class=
"org.springframework.beans.factory.config.PropertyPlaceholderConfigurer">
   <property name="location" value="WEB-INF/classes/pas-servlet.properties"/>
</bean>
```

After the properties file is loaded, it can be used to replace bean-related attribute values, as shown here:

```
<property name="url" value="${db.url}" />
```

The Spring and Hibernate Harmony

The Spring Framework provides first class integration with Hibernate. Some of the benefits of integrating these two technologies include ease of testing, consistent data exceptions (for example, `DataIntegrityViolationException`), and one key benefit for our specific needs, declarative transaction management in light-weight containers! (For details on the benefits of the Spring and Hibernate integration, refer to the Spring Reference Documentation on the springframework.org website.)

Now let's look at how we can leverage Spring to provide us declarative transaction management features, thereby shifting the burden to the Spring container and allowing us to focus on business logic (declarative transaction management is discussed in detail later in the chapter).

We will also see how using declarative transaction management will cut down the lines of code in some of our `model` package classes to almost half!

Configuring Transaction Management in Spring

Until now, we have been looking at the Time Expression under the `timex/` directory. However, this book's code zip file also contains a refactored version of this application under a `timex2/` directory; incidentally, this is also the code base that demonstrates the Spring and Hibernate integration, so we will analyze some of the files under this directory next.

The Java code refactoring is discussed in Appendix B, "Refactoring Done to Sample Application." Here, we will walk through the changes we made to our `timex-servlet.xml file`, now renamed to `timex2-servlet.xml` (found under the `timex2/` directory).

Reconfiguring Our Sample Application

Figure 10.3 shows how our controller classes (in `timex/`) use the manager classes directly; for example, notice how our `EnterHoursController` class uses `DepartmentManager` directly. This direct approach is further demonstrated in the following XML configuration from our original `timex-servlet.xml` file:

```
<bean name="enterHoursController"
    class="com.visualpatterns.timex.controller.EnterHoursController">
    <property name="departmentManager">
        <ref bean="departmentManager" />
    </property>
```

By using the manager classes directly, we had to implement our own transaction management—in other words, programmatic transaction management.

Now, let's look at how we will work with our manager classes *indirectly*; that is, via transaction proxy bean classes.

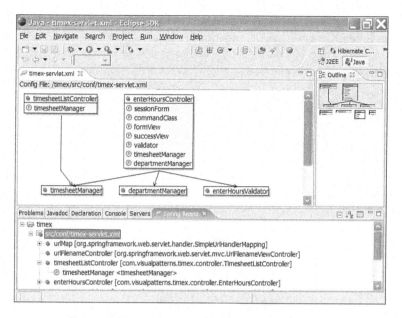

Figure 10.3   Graphical view of `timex-servlet.xml`.

Figure 10.4 shows a Spring IDE graph for the `EnterHoursController` and related beans as they are defined in our refactored `timex2-servlet.xml` file. Notice how the `EnterHoursController` class now goes through a proxy bean named `departmentManagerProxy` (a Spring `TransactionProxyFactoryBean` class). This proxy bean provides us two primary benefits:

- Management of Hibernate sessions so we don't have to worry about closing the Hibernate session manually.

- Declarative transaction management inside light-weight containers with the capability to scale down to single database transactions or scale up to global Java Transaction API (JTA) based transactions. Spring even provides special transaction manager support classes (for example, `WebLogicJtaTransactionManager`) for products such as ObjectWeb's Java Open Transaction Manager (JOTM; jotm.objectweb.org), BEA's WebLogic application server (bea.com), and IBM's WebSphere application server (ibm.com).

Now let's review the code behind the graph shown in Figure 10.4.

Less and Cleaner Java Code!

One of the key benefits of declarative transaction management I mentioned earlier is that the burden of transaction management is shifted to the container. This also translates into reduced code, which in turn enables us to focus on business logic more than low-level plumbing-type coding such as transaction management. This feature has been available in Enterprise JavaBeans for sometime now, but as I mentioned earlier, by using Spring, we get the same facilities of enterprise transaction management in light-weight containers such as Apache Tomcat.

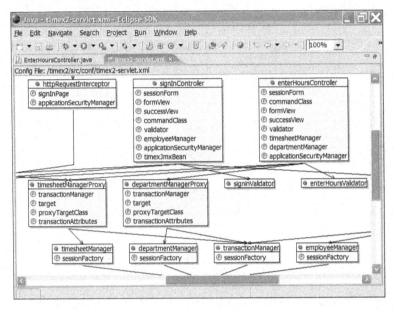

Figure 10.4   Graphical view of `timex2-servlet.xml`.

The following original code excerpt shows our `saveTimesheet(Timesheet timesheet)` method from the existing Time Expression's `TimesheetManager` class (found under the `timex/` directory). This uses Hibernate's programmatic transaction management.

```
Session session = HibernateUtil.getSessionFactory()
        .getCurrentSession();
session.beginTransaction();
try
{
    session.saveOrUpdate(timesheet);
    session.getTransaction().commit();
}
catch (HibernateException e)
{
    session.getTransaction().rollback();
    throw e;
}
```

Note
Appendix B demonstrates the code changes discussed in this section.

The same code can be reduced to the following single line of code using Spring (demonstrated in the `TimesheetManagerImpl1` class under the `springhibernate/` directory):

```
this.sessionFactory.getCurrentSession().merge(timesheet);
```

Alternatively, we can extend Spring's `HibernateDaoSupport` support class, which enables us to reduce our Java code even further by eliminating the `getSessionFactory` and `setSessionFactory` methods. Furthermore, the Hibernate exceptions are automatically translated into a consistent data exception hierarchy.

`HibernateDaoSupport` provides a method named `getHibernateTemplate` that provides methods typically found in Hibernate's Session interface, as shown here:

```
getHibernateTemplate().merge(timesheet);
```

Our three manager classes, `DepartmentManager`, `EmployeeManager`, and `TimesheetManager`, have now been refactored (in the `timex2/` directory) to extend the `HibernateDaoSupport` class. As a result, these classes combined have 126 fewer lines of code now! Table 10.1 shows the comparison of the number of lines of code in these three class files using both types of transaction management.

Table 10.1 **Lines of Code for Programmatic Versus Declarative Transaction Management**

File	Programmatic	Declarative
DepartmentManager.java	39	22
EmployeeManager.java	66	36
TimesheetManager.java	166	87
TOTAL	**271**	**145**

If only three simple classes can cut down so much code, imagine how many fewer lines of code we would have in a typical real-world enterprise Java application with many more classes in this category (that is, service layer).

Although `HibernateDaoSupport` provides some benefits, there are also some minor drawbacks to consider, including the following:

- It tightly couples Hibernate and Spring, so if Hibernate provides an upgrade that Spring doesn't support, we would have to wait for the Spring Framework to be updated.

- Because Java supports only single inheritance, after we extend `HibernateDaoSupport`, our only shot at extending another class is lost; of course, we could extend our own custom class, which in turn could extend `HibernateDaoSupport` to get around this limitation.

Nevertheless, the benefits discussed earlier would appear to outweigh the minor drawbacks.

Unit Testing Our Integrated Code

Now that we are using a new style of transaction management in the `timex2/` related refactored code, we also need to use these classes differently in our unit tests. For example, to use one of our manager classes, we must now load the proxy bean instead, as demonstrated in this code excerpt from our `TimexTestCase` class:

```
FileSystemResource res =
    new FileSystemResource("src/conf/timex2-servlet.xml");
springFactory = new XmlBeanFactory(res);
departmentManager =
    (DepartmentManager)springFactory.getBean("departmentManagerProxy");
```

Interface-Based Approach

Incidentally, there is another project bundled in this book's code zip file, under the `springhibernate/` directory (see filenames in Appendix A, "Downloadable Code for This Book"). This project demonstrates two things:

- How to configure and code using interfaces with implementation classes.
- How to force a `org.springframework.dao.DataIntegrityViolationException` exception to see how Spring's consistent data exception works and also how the Spring Web Framework can redirect the user to a view (`dberror.jsp`, in our case) for a given mapped exception.

One thing to note about this demo: Because it uses an interface-based approach (versus the class-based approach used in Time Expression), we do not need to use the `proxyTargetClass` attribute, as we do in our `timex2-servlet.xml` file.

```
<bean id="departmentManagerProxy"
    class=
    "org.springframework.transaction.interceptor.TransactionProxyFactoryBean">
    <property name="proxyTargetClass" value="true"/>
```

Figure 10.5 shows a graphical view of the Spring application context file, `springhibernate-servlet.xml`, used in this demo. Notice that the `proxyTargetClass` attribute is not used in the proxy classes.

> **Note**
> There is one feature of Eclipse worth pointing out here. Notice on the left side of Figure 10.5 how Eclipse enables us to work with multiple projects in the same workspace; in this case, we are working with our three projects: `springhibernate`, `timex`, and `timex2`.

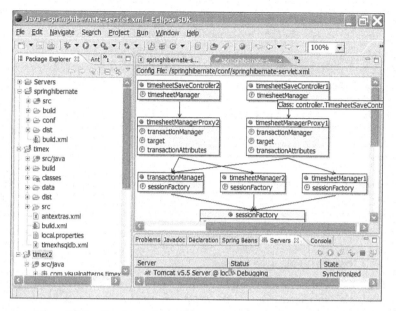

Figure 10.5   Graphical view of `springhibernate-servlet.xml`.

JSP Tag Libraries

We have already used several tag libraries in this book, primarily in Chapter 7, "The Spring Web MVC Framework," where we discussed the Spring Web MVC Framework. These tag libraries include the spring:bind library, JSTL, and others. One of my favorite tag libraries is Displaytag, so let's look at that next.

Displaytag

Displaytag, according to its website (displaytag.sourceforge.net), "is an open source suite of custom tags that provide high-level web presentation patterns which will work in an MVC model. The library provides a significant amount of functionality while still being easy to use."

I've used this tag library before and love its simplicity and robustness. For example, in fewer than 20 lines of JSP code, we could generate a sophisticated HTML table using data from a database via JDBC. We will use it to convert the HTML table on our Timesheet List screen, which we originally generated using a combination of JSTL's c:forEach and c:out tags. The key benefit for our sample application is the capability to sort the list and also export it to a PDF file, CSV file, or other formats, if needed.

The following code excerpt from our refactored `timesheetlist.jsp` file (found under `timex2/`) shows how the Displaytag library works:

```
<%@ taglib prefix="display" uri="http://displaytag.sf.net/el" %>
<display:table name="timesheets" id="timesheet" defaultsort="1"
        requestURI="timesheetlist.htm"
        cellpadding="5" cellspacing="0"
        export="false" class="tableborder">
<display:column property="department.name" sortable="true"
           title="Department"/>
</display:column>
```

This tag library can be downloaded from displaytag.sourceforge.net along with documentation on additional features of Displaytag. As explained on the web, this has several dependencies. Follow the instructions on the website to install it for our sample application.

Writing Custom Tag Libraries

Although many tag libraries are available on the web, at times you will need to write a custom tag library that is specific to your project. In the past, I have had to write a custom tag library to hide certain buttons on a screen based on the authorization level of the user.

Our `PayPeriodCheckTag.java` file shows a complete and functional custom tag library used for Time Expression. This tag library is a simple demonstration of what tag libraries can be used for. This particular tag library checks the current date against the period starting and ending dates. If the current date is outside this start and end date range, the Save button is not displayed on the screen because the user is only allowed to update the current pay period's timesheet.

The following snippet from `PayPeriodCheckTag.java` shows how we extend the `javax.servlet.jsp.tagext.TagSupport` class and provide a custom tag library.

```
public class PayPeriodCheckTag
    extends TagSupport
{
  private Date checkDate;
  public int doStartTag() throws JspException
  {
    boolean includeText = (DateUtil.isInCurrentPayPeriod(checkDate));
    if (includeText)
      return TagSupport.EVAL_BODY_INCLUDE;

    return TagSupport.SKIP_BODY;
  }
```

The following code shows an excerpt from the supporting tag library descriptor (TLD) file, `timex.tld`.

```
<shortname>timex</shortname>
<tag>
  <name>periodcheck</name>
  <tagclass>com.visualpatterns.timex.util.PayPeriodCheckTag</tagclass>
  <attribute>
    <name>checkDate</name>
    <required>true</required>
    <rtexprvalue>true</rtexprvalue>
```

This code excerpt from our `enterhours.jsp` file shows how the `timex:periodcheck` tag is used to either show or hide the Save button.

```
<%@ taglib prefix="timex" uri="/WEB-INF/timex.tld"%>
<timex:periodcheck checkDate="${command.periodEndingDate}">
  <input name="save"  type="submit" value="Save">
</timex:periodcheck>
```

Refactoring

Throughout this book, I have stressed refactoring, so it would only make sense that I practice what I preach. Indeed, a lot of the code has been refactored between Chapter 5 and this chapter.

As I mentioned earlier, refactoring is not a new concept; what is relatively new is the term itself, which was coined by Martin Fowler (refactoring.com). *Refactoring* is the process of improving the internal implementation of a code without impacting (or minimally impacting) the external interface. This is something developers do daily and have been doing for years; now we just have a common term to express this practice.

Appendix B shows some of the code that was refactored over the course of Chapters 5, 7, and this chapter. This reflects how things work in real life! In other words, we refactor code over a period of time as we discover better ways to improve it.

Examples of Refactoring in Our Sample Application

The following are a few examples of the type of refactoring I did to the Java and JSP code of Time Expression. Allow me to reemphasize that refactoring is not rocket science or an earth-shattering technique, so some of these might seem simple or obvious ways of improving code, but they demonstrate the very nature of refactoring—that is, improving code.

Note

Appendix B demonstrates many of the refactoring-related code changes mentioned next.

Java Refactoring Examples

The following are a few Java code-related refactoring examples for Time Expression:

- Programmatic to declarative transaction management—As we discussed previously, integrating Hibernate with Spring required significant refactoring to our three manager classes.

- Extract superclass—The refactoring.com website lists "Extract Superclass" as a refactoring type; the definition is as follows: "You have two classes with similar features. Create a superclass and move the common features to the superclass." We did just this for our JUnit parent test case class named TimexTestCase (discussed earlier).

- Move method—I moved the getCurrentPeriodEndingDate from TimesheetListController to DateUtil because I needed this method in multiple places and it made sense to put it in a common utility class. This is referred to as Move Method on refactoring.com.

- Move class—I originally placed ReminderEmail in the util package; however, I ended up moving it to the job package because that was a more appropriate place for this class.

- Removed unused variables—Thanks to Eclipse's warning about unused Java elements, when we got to Chapter 8, "The Eclipse Phenomenon!" I realized I had some unused variables and import statements. I removed many of these without impacting the external interface of these classes or methods.

JSP Refactoring

The following list describes some JSP-related refactoring I had to do.

- Moved error message for JSP in a common include file—Because I was duplicating the display of error and status messages, I moved it to a common file named includemessages.jsp and included it in the files that required it (for example, enterhours.jsp, timesheetlist.jsp, and signin.jsp).

- Changed to displaytag—Upon discovering a better way to display and sort HTML tables, I moved all the code to the Displaytag library instead of using JSTL. This also demonstrates a key benefit of the MVC design pattern—that is, we were able to change the view without impacting the model.

Refactor Mercilessly but...Save a Code Snapshot

You might have heard the term *refactor mercilessly*; this is one of the principles of extreme programming (extremeprogramming.org). I tend to agree with this but would also caution you to save a snapshot of your code either in a source code repository such as CVS or keep a copy of your working code in a separate directory. This enables you to roll back to your working code if your refactoring doesn't work out as you had hoped. For example, there was a point in this book where I extensively refactored some code to give something new a try. However, it didn't work out as I planned, so I was able to quickly revert to the previously saved snapshot of code. Eclipse's Local History option (discussed in Chapter 8) can also be used to restore your previous code.

Online Refactoring Catalogs (refactoring.com and agiledata.org)

Refactoring doesn't just happen with code, it can also be done at the database level.

For code-related refactoring, visit refactoring.com; it has a growing catalog of refactoring techniques (almost 100 at the time of this writing).

For database-refactoring techniques, check out agiledata.org. This, too, boasts a long list of common database-refactoring techniques (almost 70 at the time of this writing).

You might find that you are already using many of these refactoring techniques.

A Note About Refactoring in Eclipse

As we discussed briefly in Chapter 8, Eclipse provides several Java code refactoring options.

For example, for the Spring and Hibernate integration demo (in the `springhibernate/` directory) we discussed earlier in the chapter, I used Eclipse's Extract Interface refactoring menu option and was able to have Eclipse automatically create an interface file for me and have the concrete classes implement this interface.

Other Considerations

We have covered a lot of ground in this book and in this specific chapter, but it is practically impossible to cover everything about developing robust and secure applications in one book. However, the following sections provide a brief overview of additional items to consider when designing and developing solid applications. Note that I have covered most of these considerations at a conceptual level here.

Transaction Management

A transaction is series of operations that must be successful or the system should be placed back to its original state. The simplest example of this is perhaps two tables in the same database: one parent and one child. If we delete records from the parent table, we must also delete the children records. However, if the child record delete fails, we must roll back the transaction and restore the database to its original state. Although this is a single database example, the same concept applies across databases.

Ensuring transactional integrity is a vital part of any enterprise application. Typically, transaction management is handled in two ways: programmatically or declaratively. Whereas programmatic transaction management provides control to the developer in the code, declarative transaction management allows us to control the transaction demarcation points and isolation levels by manipulating XML (configuration) files. Also, whereas programmatic transaction management is static in nature (because it needs to be coded in), declarative transaction management is more dynamic in nature because it can be postponed to the time of deployment.

Declarative transaction management plays a large role in enterprise distributed computing these days because transaction management no longer applies only to single databases (local transaction) because organizations tend to store information across databases (global transaction).

Note

We already saw examples of programmatic transaction management using Hibernate in Chapter 5 and declarative transaction management using Spring earlier in this chapter. This book's code zip file contains demonstrations of both types of transaction management.

The programmatic transaction management code and configuration can be found under the `timex/` directory (the declarative transaction management code using Spring can be found under `timex2/`).

Declarative transaction management shifts the burden of transaction management to the container (an EJB container, for example) and enables the developer to focus on the business logic. Furthermore, it can unclutter code a bit because there is no transaction management code mixed in with the business logic. As we discussed earlier in this chapter, the Spring Framework provides support for declarative transaction management without requiring your applications to run in an EJB container; in other words, your application can run inside a servlet container such as Apache Tomcat. To understand how declarative transaction management works, let's look at some related concepts next.

Enterprise transactions typically conform to the ACID properties; that is, *atomicity, consistency, isolation,* and *durability.* ACID transactions ensure that a series of operations are either successful or are left in a pretransaction state—in essence, an all-or-nothing proposition. Atomicity ensures that all operations in a transaction are successful or the system is restored to its original state. Consistency ensures that all transactions transition data from one state to the other consistently. Isolation means that transactions are isolated from other transactions until transactions are committed. Durability indicates that after all transactions have been successfully committed, the changes are permitted.

The following are some additional terms related to enterprise transaction management.

- Demarcation—This is a way of marking the boundaries for a given transaction. It also enables grouping of transactions, which can participate in a broader global transaction. In a distributed environment, you could contain transactions within transactions (known as *nested* transactions).

- Transaction isolation level—This is the level of separation of one transaction from others. In other words, it specifies how much work one transaction can see of another transaction. Although different technologies use different terms for isolation levels, some of the Spring Framework contains the following levels: ISOLATION_READ_COMMITTED, ISOLATION_READ_UNCOMMITTED, ISOLATION_REPEATABLE_READ, and ISOLATION_SERIALIZABLE. Note that ISOLATION_READ_UNCOMMITTED is the lowest isolation form, because dirty read/writes can occur, but it provides faster performance. ISOLATION_SERIALIZABLE, on the other hand, is the highest and safest form and accordingly impacts performance because of the extra safeguards.

- Transaction propagation—This implies whether a group of code should run within its own transaction or participate in an existing transaction, which might have already begun prior to reaching that code. For example, Spring supports the following transaction propagation types: PROPAGATION_MANDATORY, PROPAGATION_NESTED, PROPAGATION_NEVER, PROPAGATION_NOT_SUPPORTED, PROPAGATION_REQUIRED, PROPAGATION_REQUIRES_NEW, and PROPAGATION_SUPPORTS.

Again, declarative transaction has been supported by EJBs for some time now; however, the Spring Framework makes it possible to get this enterprise-level transaction management even in a servlet container and not force us to use an EJB container. So, if we wanted to unclutter the code in Time Expression, we could convert to using Spring's declarative transaction management support and remove all Hibernate programmatic transaction management code. For additional information on Spring's declarative transaction management code, refer to the springframework.org website.

Application Security

Application security is a huge topic in itself that can take several books to cover. However, let's review some application security concepts in the context of our sample application, which would include the following: authentication, authorization, and encryption (see Figure 10.6).

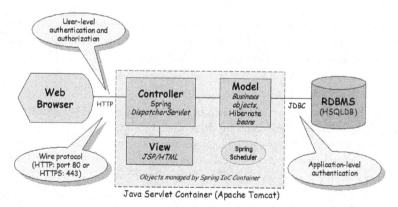

Figure 10.6 Application security concepts (authentication, authorization, encryption).

Authentication

This includes user-level authentication and application-level authentication. Authentication is a process of verifying user credentials to ensure that users are who they claim they are. In Time Expression, user-level authentication is a simple sign-in screen where the user provides credentials (for example, id and password). Application-level authentication is the credentials required for the application to connection to the database. In real-world projects, this can also include connections to an LDAP server and Java Message Service (JMS) server, for example.

Authorization

Authorization controls access to features based on the user's role (or type). For example, in Chapter 2 we defined various types of roles in our user stories, such as Employee, Manager, Executive, and Accounting. Each of these roles would have different types of access; for example, employees could not pay themselves.

Encryption

Encryption in the context of our sample application could occur in two places: the wire protocol and the configuration files. For the wire protocol, using HTTPS (port 443) is typically enough to protect the data being transferred over the wire, and even if the data was being hijacked over the wire, it would be encrypted. Encryption can also happen in configuration files. If you do not want the application-level passwords (for example, application-level database user id and password) stored in clear text—you could use an algorithm such as SHA or MD5 to store passwords as encrypted strings in your configuration files. By the way, this can be done using the Java Cryptography Extension (JCE). Visit the java.sun.com website for details.

Other

As I mentioned previously, security is a big topic and there are many types of books dedicated to this subject. However, I have provided a concise list on how to secure web applications in Appendix D, "Securing Web Applications."

Exception Handling

Exceptions come in two flavors: unchecked or checked. Unchecked exceptions (for example, java.lang.NullPointerException) do not need to be caught by the code, whereas checked exceptions (for example, java.io.IOException) do require the code to either catch the exception or throw it up the call chain using the throws statement. There are also errors (for example, OutOfMemoryError) that are generally difficult to recover from.

Deciding when to have your application's exception-handling code as one or the other requires some careful thought. I recently read the following line in Sun's Java Tutorial (at http://java.sun.com/docs/books/tutorial/):

"If a client can reasonably be expected to recover from an exception, make it a checked exception. If a client cannot do anything to recover from the exception, make it an unchecked exception."

Another reason to catch an exception and rethrow it, as either itself or repackaged as a new exception, is in case you want to do some central logging or send out alert notifications (for example, email or pager).

A Hypothetical Exception-Handling Scheme

Given the preceding considerations, we can see that the application exception-handling approach might vary from application to application. Figure 10.7 portrays how our sample application could use handling exceptions:

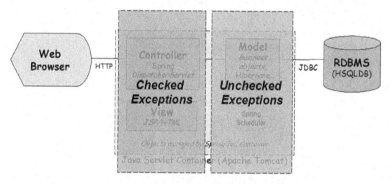

Figure 10.7   Sample exception handling for Time Expression.

- com.visualpatterns.timex.model—Any exceptions that occur in the model package (for example, database errors) could be repackaged as class ModelException and rethrown as an unchecked exception. Similarly, the job package could contain a JobException class and the util package a UtilException class. If we wanted to, we could even define more specific exceptions such as IllegalTimesheetHoursException, but I typically use one exception class per package (just a personal preference).

- com.visualpatterns.timex.controller—Any exception occurring in the controller package could be checked and a user-friendly error message displayed to the UI. For instance, this might include UI data validation parsing related exceptions (for example, caused by Integer.parseInt).

One last note about exceptions is that many projects tend to hide exceptions using the following type of code; this typically is not a recommended approach, but there might be times where this approach is valid if the exception truly can be ignored:

```
try { // some code that causes an exception … }
catch (Exception e) { e.printStackTrace(); }
```

Handling Exceptions Using the Spring Web MVC Framework

The Spring Web MVC Framework provides a convenient and practical exception-handling scheme. More specifically, Spring allows us to configure exception class names to views; this enables us to handle unexpected exceptions somewhat gracefully by displaying a formatted web page.

The following code excerpt from our `springhibernate-servlet.xml` file (under the `springhibernate/` directory) demonstrates how the `org.springframework.dao.DataIntegrityViolationException` exception can be mapped to our view file, `dberror.jsp` (discussed earlier in this chapter).

```
<bean id="exceptionResolver"
class="org.springframework.web.servlet.handler.SimpleMappingExceptionResolver">
    <property name="exceptionMappings">
        <props>
            <prop key="org.springframework.dao.DataIntegrityViolationException">
                dberror
```

The following code excerpt from our `dberror.jsp` view file demonstrates how Spring passes the exception object via the request's session attribute named `exception` and we print its stacktrace:

```
<%
  Exception ex = (Exception)request.getAttribute("exception");
  if (ex != null)
      ex.printStackTrace(new java.io.PrintWriter(out));
%>
```

Clustering

According to webopidia.com, clustering is defined as "two or more computers together in such a way that they behave like a single computer. Clustering is used for parallel processing, load balancing and fault tolerance."

Clustering can apply to everything from application servers to databases to networking devices and more. In the world of Java, clustering is typically used to achieve stability and reliability in enterprise applications. For example, on the scalability front, this can mean HTTP session and component failover.

Entire articles have been written on this subject, but let me provide some minimal guidelines here for clustering your Java applications:

- Serialize the objects that we want to provide failover for (for example, a user object established after a login session). Clustering can be done only for Java primitive types and Serializable objects.

- Do not use static variables to hold information, because this will not get replicated or will be applicable to only one instance of the server. For example, using singleton on one server won't get us the same information on another server. This is perhaps one reason the Spring Framework doesn't advocate the use of Singleton objects and instead recommends having Spring handle singletons for us.

- Limit the quantity of data in components that need to be failed over. This can impact performance of the application server, for example, because it needs to replicate this information across multiple instances.

- Clustering in application (and web) servers is done for in-memory persistent data. For example, your data that is persistent in the database but not in memory won't get replicated by a web/application server.

- In general, strive for simplicity when designing the classes you want clustered.

Multithreading

In the Java Platform Enterprise Edition (JEE) world, multithreading is typically not recommended because the application server is the only program that is supposed to have control over the threads within the JVM to ensure a stable application server environment. However, at times you may need multithreading in your JEE application. Isolating this multithreading to a single class where we can control the threading is a better design than, for example, multiple classes implementing their own threading. Regardless of how multithreading is designed/used for an application, careful thought should be given to synchronization, blocking, and other related issues.

JSE 5.0 introduced the `java.util.concurrent` package, previously developed by Doug Lea (note for pre-J2SE 5.0: use Doug Lea's backward-compatible distribution, which can be found at http://gee.cs.oswego.edu/dl/). This is a clean way to use multithreading in your enterprise applications.

A Note About Java GUI (Thick Client) Applications

We did not look at building thick client applications at all in this book because our application had a web user interface. Currently, there is an implicit war going on between Java's Swing and IBM's SWT (Standard Widget Toolkit). Swing is the reference GUI toolkit for JSE, and SWT is a graphics library available with the Eclipse platform. Both of these technologies are cross-platform technologies.

SWT is a thin wrapper around the native operating system's GUI widgets, and it has a higher-level interface named JFace. In contrast, Swing renders its own look-and-feel and tries to closely match it with the native operating system's look-and-feel.

Both of these technologies have their pros and cons. For example, if you read online articles on this subject or browse through messages in various online discussion forums, you will get the sense Swing is over-engineered and slower than SWT. On the other hand, by choosing SWT, you are committing to the Eclipse platform—something certainly worth considering. My personal general impression tends to be that if you are developing a GUI application only for Microsoft Windows, SWT appears to be a better choice. However, if you sell or distribute your application to external customers, Swing might be a better choice. Again, this is my personal opinion. You should investigate these technologies further if you have a need for this type of functionality.

Another factor to consider for GUI applications is the Java Web Start technology from Sun, which allows applications to be launched with a single click, independently of a web browser. The application can also be launched through desktop shortcuts, making launching the web-deployed application similar to launching a native application. The application itself is cached locally, so if there are no updates to the application, it is run instantly. Otherwise, an updated version can be downloaded from the network (this is made possible by Java's Network Launching Protocol specification—JNLP for short).

For details on SWT, visit the eclipse.org website. For Java Swing and Web Start technologies, visit the java.sun.com website.

Configuration Management (CM) Environments

You might have noticed the following lines in our Ant `build.xml` file.

```
<property name="env" value="local"/>
<property file="local.properties"/>
```

Although `local.properties` is our default properties file, this can easily be substituted with another file—for example, test.properties—using a command such as the following (on the command line):

```
ant -Denv=test
```

This provides the capability to use different files for different deployment environments. For example, Figure 10.8 demonstrates how we could have the same architecture across different environments, from development through production and everything in between, using unique host/server names for our web server and database server in each environment.

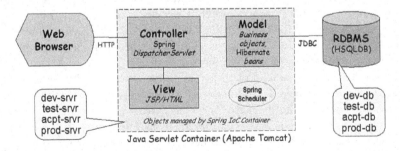

Figure 10.8 Our sample application in different environments.

Using external files versus embedding everything in the Ant build file provides us the advantage of saving password and other information in a separate, presumably smaller and simpler, properties file versus a big `build.xml` file. For example, I have come across the following environments in many companies.

- Local—Individual development on a personal computer
- Dev—Integrated team-based development on a server
- Test—Used for functional testing (also known as quality assurance, or QA)
- User-acceptance testing (UAT)—Also known as staging area and used for user testing
- Production—Live deployment of the application

For smaller projects, one or two of the preceding environments can be eliminated. For example, if the project uses smaller iterations (two-week fixed cycles, for example) or has a small team (two to four developers), the integrated development environment can be used for functional testing. Alternatively, the UAT and Test environments could be combined into one. So pick and choose the environments that best suit your needs. In short, our Ant file can accommodate various environments by having different property files and using the –Denv parameter I demonstrated.

Asynchronous JavaScript and XML (AJaX)

Ajax is a web technology that enables us to make pages interactive. Ajax is a powerful concept for two reasons. First, it provides a richer experience to the user because the entire page does not need to be reloaded. Second, it shifts some of the burden to the client because the browser requests only a subset of the screen (for example, updated stock quotes or alerts) instead of reloading the entire page.

I have provided an extremely simple example in this book's code zip file (files `rapidjava-ajax.html` and `rapidjava-ajax.jsp`). Although this example doesn't truly demonstrate the power of Ajax, it should give you ideas on what we can achieve with this technology. Ajax essentially uses the JavaScript `XMLHttpRequest` object combined with the `<div>` HTML tag to provide dynamic updates to only a section of the page.

For introductory information on AJaX, http://en.wikipedia.org/wiki/AJAX might be a good website to start with. However, many books and articles are available on this subject and online search engines such as Google can also turn up many links on this subject.

Also, check out DWR (Direct Web Remoting), an open source framework available at http://getahead.ltd.uk/dwr/. According to the website, "DWR is Easy Ajax for Java." The website further explains that DWR "is a way of calling Java code on the server directly from Javascript in the browser." Note, I have not worked with DWR personally.

One last note about AJaX. What I have demonstrated in my examples is extremely basic. The power of AJaX comes in when little portions of the web UI can make requests to individual services from a collection of services on the backend, in other words, Service-oriented architecture (SOA)[md]this makes for a very powerful concept!

Javadoc and Comments

Considering how much emphasis I placed on the code (and physical database structure and data) being the long-lasting artifacts, it is important to add documentation to our code! Developers need to be able to understand other developers' code, and having Javadoc and comments for complex code is a big help. Always think from the perspective of someone else; imagine in your mind other persons working with your code and how you can make their job easier. However, you also need to find the right balance in the amount of documentation you provide; I tend to do minimal Javadoc in my code—just enough to give them information about given classes, methods, variables, and most important of all, complex logic.

In light of this, you will notice that all our code has comments in them. Also, you will notice it has minimal comments, again everything in moderation, not too much and not too little. By having these comments, I can run the JDK javadoc command against my Java code to generate comprehensive documentation on the code for our sample application.

Entire System in One WAR File!

One last and cool thing to note is that the Time Expression deployable web application archive files (`timex.war` and `timex2.war`) contain 100% of the Time Expression system (as depicted in Figure 10.9). Recall that these WAR files can be built using our Ant `build.xml` script or Eclipse's export feature (see Chapter 8 for details).

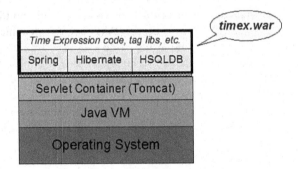

Figure 10.9 `timex.war`—a fully self-contained system.

The cool aspect is that this war contains all our Java source code and compiled classes, static and dynamic web files, the dependencies (third-party libraries), job scheduling capabilities, and even a relational database!

The point I'm trying to make is that this is the power of Java. There are very few languages that you can do this in.

Summary

In this chapter, we covered the following topics:

- Recently added Java features
- Additional Ant built-in and external tasks
- JUnit custom suites
- Additional Hibernate features
- Other Spring Framework features
- Integrated Hibernate with Spring
- The Displaytag tag library and writing custom tag libraries
- Sample refactoring of our sample application
- Other important considerations such as transaction management, security, exception handling, clustering, and several others
- A simple Ajax example

Well, this just about wraps up this book! In the next chapter, I will provide you with some guidelines on what you can look for next.

Recommended Resources

The following websites are relevant to or provide additional information on the topics discussed in this chapter:

- Agile data (database refactoring and more)   http://agiledata.org/
- Apache Ant   http://ant.apache.org/
- Displaytag tag library   http://displaytag.sourceforge.net/
- JUnit Fixture Code   http://junit.sourceforge.net/doc/cookbook/cookbook.htm
- Hibernate   http://hibernate.org/
- JUnit testing framework   http://junit.org
- Martin Fowler's refactoring website   http://refactoring.com/
- Spring framework   http://springframework.org/
- Sun's Java website   http://java.sun.com/

11

What Next?

Week 9 - Release 1 Complete!

Susan: Hey, guys. I just want to congratulate you on a job well done. This is perhaps one of the best applications I have worked on. I love the software process you guys used; I like the fact that I was involved the whole way through, it was nice to see iterations every 2 weeks, as well! I can't wait to get this application in front of the users, I think they will love it! By the way, Ron and I are meeting next week to discuss release 2, so expect a meeting to discuss initial user stories for that. Again, great job, guys!

W E HAVE COVERED A SIGNIFICANT AMOUNT of material up to this point in the book—enough to build complete, robust, and enterprise-ready Java applications. However, hundreds of books are available on Java technology, primarily because there are lots of Java-related technologies out there to learn about. Given this fact, it was practically impossible to cover everything, so let's look at potential areas you might want to investigate further.

What's Covered in This Chapter

In this chapter, I will give you some suggestions on areas to investigate further, including the following:

- Complete the Time Expression application
- XP and AMDD-based software development
- Java platform
- Ant
- JUnit
- Hibernate
- The Spring Framework
- Eclipse SDK
- Logging, debugging, monitoring, and profiling
- Getting help

Complete the Time Expression Application

If you have read this book end-to-end, you have invariably realized that we finished only a subset of the functionality defined in our fictional business requirements from Chapter 2, "The Sample Application: An Online Timesheet System." The user stories I picked were based on following two reasons:

- Being able to enter hours electronically seemed like a good start and something real world users would want in the first couple of iterations.
- These user stories worked nicely from a demonstration perspective, in that I was able to show how to build both, form and no-form, screens.

A great way to learn more about the various technologies covered in this book is to work with the code presented here and to complete the remainder of the application. For example, we finished the first five user stories from Table 2.2 in Chapter 2. You could try completing the remaining user stories. If you decide to do this and come up with innovative ideas, I would love to hear about them. (My contact information can be obtained on visualpatterns.com.)

XP and AMDD-Based Software Development

In Chapters 2 and 3, we discussed Extreme Programming (XP) and Agile Model Driven Development (AMDD) methods. If this style of working appeals to you, you could try incorporating it in your projects. For details on these, visit agilemodeling.com and extremeprogramming.org. Also, I have provided cheat sheets on these methods in the appendixes section.

Another related website I mentioned earlier is refactoring.com, which contains a growing catalog of code-related refactoring techniques. Also, agiledata.org has a list of database techniques including both database refactoring and agile data modeling. This is an area that is gaining momentum.

Java Platform

Java technology is constantly evolving and you frequently see new releases being introduced by Sun Microsystems on the java.sun.com website. I covered only a few of the newer features, but considering that Java is an entire platform, there is a lot more to learn there. You could spend some time learning about the new language features and APIs.

Ant

As I mentioned in earlier chapters, Ant is a wonderful tool that comes loaded with built-in tasks. However, there are lots of external tasks available on the Net and you can also write your own. I would highly encourage you to explore Ant a bit further. Visit http://ant.apache.org/ for more details.

Also, look into *continuous integration* (martinfowler.com). This is a concept that is quickly becoming popular, and tools such as CruiseControl (cruisecontrol.sourceforge.net) are facilitating this concept.

One other notable product is Apache's Maven (maven.apache.org). This aims to automate and simplify the build process and has been gaining a lot of momentum recently.

JUnit

JUnit is a pretty straightforward framework, so on one hand, I have provided you more than enough information to do unit testing. On the other hand, several other tools and utilities available on the junit.org website might be worth checking, such as various mock objects, JSystem, JUnit PDF Report, and many others.

I would also encourage you to explore the Test-Driven Development (TDD) approach, which advocates writing tests first. This method of working takes some getting used to, but after you do, you will probably want to continue working only in this fashion. Again, give this approach some time because initially you might feel that you are spending more time writing tests; but if you factor in the amount of time you spend unit testing your code and fixing defects reported by your testers or users, you will begin to see why this approach can actually save you time. Also, this technique works best if you write small chunks of code (for example, smaller methods and classes versus big and complex ones).

Hibernate

We looked at some of the core functionality provided by Hibernate, enough to help you build a complex application using Hibernate. However, as I indicated earlier, entire books have been written on this subject. Also, for legacy or complex applications, you probably want to include the more complex techniques provided by Hibernate. For example, you could investigate the following features of Hibernate a bit further:

- Component mapping
- Bidirectional associations
- Inheritance mapping
- Performance improvements
- Stored procedures
- Caching

For details on these and other Hibernate features, visit the hibernate.org website.

The Spring Framework

Even after dedicating Chapters 6, 7, and part of Chapter 10 to the Spring Framework, I have probably covered only half of the Spring Framework (if that). There is a lot more to Spring. Here are some features of Spring you might want to investigate further:

- Aspect-Oriented Programming (AOP) features
- Remoting support for the following technologies: Java Remote Method Invocation (RMI), Web Services (using JAX-RPC), Java Connector Architecture (JCA), Enterprise JavaBean (EJB), and Java Message Service (JMS)
- Database-related support for Data Access Object (DAO) objects, ORM support (for Hibernate, JDO, iBATIS), and Java Database Connectivity (JDBC)
- Transaction support for Java Transaction API (JTA)
- Spring Portlet MVC framework (support for JSR-168 Portlet API)
- Integration of the Spring Web MVC Framework with a site composition technology such as Apache Tiles (struts.apache.org/struts-tiles/) or decoration technology such as OpenSymphony's SiteMesh (opensymphony.com)
- Spring subprojects (including Web Flow, Acegi security, BeanDoc, and Rich Client support)

- New tag libraries introduced in Spring
- Other (Spring's support for JEE such as JMS, EJB, and more)

Eclipse SDK

As I mentioned in Chapter 8, "The Eclipse Phenomenon!" the Eclipse platform is growing at a marvelous pace! So there is certainly a lot to check out in this area. For example, new or enhanced plug-ins are being introduced literally every week from various sources. Be sure to visit the eclipse.org website often and also visit the various plug-in directories if you are looking for specific plug-ins.

As for the core Eclipse SDK platform (including the bundled Java Development Tools), here are some suggestions on what to investigate next:

- Code style formatting—This feature in Eclipse provides extensive customization for the way you like your code formatted. This option is available from the Windows, Preferences menu item.

- Tips and tricks—Be sure to view the online help for the various plug-ins (for example, JDT). You will find a long list of tips and tricks in here that can save you some time and enhance your user experience when working in Eclipse.

- Refactoring support—Eclipse's refactoring is already robust but it is likely to continue improving. Also, these refactoring techniques are based on some of the concepts available on refactoring.com, which has a growing catalog of refactoring techniques, so Eclipse is bound to increase its support for some of the newer refactoring methods.

Writing Eclipse plug-ins isn't exactly rocket science, so you might want to investigate this option. Custom plug-ins do not have to be for technical or development needs only. I personally know of a project related to computer forensics that was developed using the Eclipse Standard Widget Toolkit (SWT) and deployed as Eclipse plug-ins.

Logging, Debugging, Monitoring, and Profiling

We looked at logging, debugging, monitoring, and profiling techniques in Chapter 9, "Logging, Debugging, Monitoring, and Profiling." However, I merely scratched the surface with the material I covered:

Logging can be used minimally for simple tracing and debugging, or it can be used for security-related audit-trail logging locally. Writing your own custom logging extensions using JDK logging or log4j logging is relatively simple, so you could write logging classes for various types of tasks. Also, logging can be done at a local level or remotely, which opens up some interesting opportunities.

Debugging is somewhat of an art because developers like to approach this in different ways. Whereas some developers debug using print statements, others enjoy GUI debugging. If you like GUI-based debugging, investigate the Eclipse debugger further. We covered a lot of the basics of Chapter 8—enough to get you debugging in Eclipse effectively. However, when you begin working with the Eclipse debugger (if you don't already), you will likely find unique ways of debugging using watch expressions, conditional breakpoints, and more.

We looked at extremely basic monitoring techniques in Chapters 9 and 10. This is a whole world in its own and requires an in-depth look into the Java Management Extensions (JMX) technology. Visit java.sun.com for details on this technology.

I briefly discussed profiling Java applications in Chapter 9. Profiling requires much more investigation if your application has a need for performance tuning. For example, Sun's NetBeans IDE has a wonderful profiler and the Eclipse SDK has profiler plug-ins available for it. As I mentioned in Chapter 9, a lot of open source Java profilers are also worth a look.

Getting Help

When working with any technology, you will invariably run into technical difficulties. This can be frustrating, so any assistance you can get to help with troubleshooting the problem is welcome. Here are a couple of suggestions on where to get help for the technologies we covered.

Online Discussion Forums

The Spring Framework discussions forums (forum.springframework.org) have come in handy for me personally when I was stuck on a problem and needed help. In fact, the core Spring developers frequently answer questions in these forums. I have even had Rod Johnson (founder of Spring) answer my questions personally!

The Hibernate discussion forums (forum.hibernate.org) have been equally helpful, although from time to time, I have found that you get terse responses from the founders of Hibernate. (I wish this wasn't the case, but it is.) Nevertheless, there are plenty of other Hibernate users willing to help.

Also, Eclipse had public newsgroups accessible via the eclipse.org website.

Javadoc and Source Code

Although both Spring and Hibernate have good reference manuals, there are times when you need information about these frameworks. As I stressed at the end of the previous chapter, adding Javadoc is very important because the code is one of the artifacts that lasts and is always current, considering that is what the users are typically working with. The Spring Framework and Hibernate seem to follow this logic, hence you will find lots of documentation in their Javadocs—more than you might expect. If you cannot locate the information in the reference documentation, there is a good chance you will find it in the Javadocs for these APIs.

One additional source of documentation, although not an optimal one, is to browse through the source of open source technologies such as Spring and Hibernate. Most open source technologies either bundle the source with their distribution or provide a separate download for it. This can also come in handy with tools such as Eclipse, which allows you to attach to a source code folder when you are debugging through your code. Debugging isn't the only reason you might want to attach to their source code in Eclipse; at times, you might want to browse the source code behind these APIs to understand how they work behind the scenes.

A Quick Note About Code "Quality" Tools

One other area that I personally have not worked extensively with, but am beginning to look into, can be best described as *code quality tools* (or *static code analysis* tools). These tools help you verify the quality of your code—for example, code adherence to standards, dead code, unit test coverage of code, and so on. Some tools in this area worth checking include the following:

- Checkstyle (checkstyle.sourceforge.net)
- Clover (www.cenqua.com)
- Cobertura (cobertura.sourceforge.net)
- PMD (pmd.sourceforge.net)

Summary

In this chapter, we looked at areas to investigate further for the following topics:

- Complete the Time Expression application
- XP and AMDD-based software development
- Java platform
- Ant
- JUnit
- Hibernate
- The Spring Framework
- Eclipse SDK
- Logging, debugging, monitoring, and profiling
- Getting help

Well, this pretty much wraps up this book! Be sure to investigate the appendixes section, which contains refactored code examples, cheat sheets, cool tools, and more!

Recommended Resources

The following websites are relevant to or provide additional information on the topics discussed in this chapter:

- Agile Data   http://www.agiledata.org/
- Agile Modeling   http://www.agilemodeling.com
- Ant   http://ant.apache.org/
- Apache Tiles   http://struts.apache.org/struts-tiles/
- Checkstyle   checkstyle.sourceforge.net
- Clover   www.cenqua.com
- Continuous Integration   http://www.martinfowler.com/articles/continuousIntegration.html
- Cobertura   cobertura.sourceforge.net
- Eclipse SDK   http://eclipse.org
- Extreme Programming   http://extremeprogramming.org
- Hibernate Framework   http://hibernate.org
- Hibernate discussion forums   http://forum.hibernate.org/
- HSQLDB database engine   http://hsqldb.org/
- Hub for Spring Framework resources   http://www.springhub.com/
- Java Technology   http://java.sun.com
- JUnit   http://junit.org
- Maven   http://maven.apache.org/
- OpenSymphony Sitemes   http://www.opensymphony.com/sitemesh/
- PMD   http://pmd.sourceforge.net/
- Spring Framework   http://springframework.org
- Spring Discussion Forums   http://forum.springframework.org/
- NetBeans IDE   http://netbeans.org
- Visual Patterns   http://visualpatterns.com

12

Parting Thoughts

Week 10 - Post Release 1 Training

Susan: Welcome to this training class, everyone. I think you will find that this application is well designed and contains the features we will need and requested, nothing more, nothing less.

So, let me begin with an overview ...

(c) Visual Patterns, Inc.

I HOPE YOU ENJOYED THIS BOOK and found it useful. Given the intended size of the book, I couldn't cover everything I wanted to. However, my intention was to show you enough to build a completely functional application along with a good knowledge of advanced features.

> **1,400 Hours in 4 Months!**
> A lot of blood and sweat went into this book (mine and others who helped me). You might be interested in knowing that this book was written over approximately 1,400 hours in less than 4 months! (No exaggeration. I averaged 14- to 15-hour days, nonstop for weeks.) That's more hours than some people work in 9 months of normal work weeks. It was a crazy schedule but we did it to have the book out by the 2006 JavaOne conference (Moscone Center–San Francisco, California).

My Near Future Plans

This book was both a happy and a sad event for me because this will most likely be my last significant publication about Java after exactly a decade of writing about this wonderful technology (28 articles and 2 chapters in a Java book). Although I plan to continue consulting around Java technologies for a long time to come, I'm shifting my writing and speaking focus toward modeling techniques using agile methods. I also hope to collaborate with others on special projects, particularly with some innovative people I have the distinct pleasure of knowing.

In the upcoming months, I will be researching visual ways of improving the use of software methodologies and various diagramming methods. I'm convinced there is a better way to model than UML. I'm also convinced that there are visual ways to teach (us) developers bare-bones software processes that provide some structure that makes managers and executives happy, yet allows us to do what we enjoy most—code! I hope to present this balanced approach in the near future.

> **Note**
> In the coming months, I will be building a global virtual community composed of people from various parts of the world–this process has already begun. Our objective will be to research better modeling and unique visual process techniques (see Appendix I, "Visual Patterns Research," for more details).
>
> If you are interested in joining this virtual community, contact me via visualpatterns.com.

The Future, Agile Methods, Java Technology

I have recently embraced the Extreme Programming (XP) and Agile Modeling (AM) methods (as you probably sensed in this book). After years of using big requirements up front (BRUF) and big design up front (BDUF), I'm thoroughly enjoying this new and natural-feeling style of working, probably because they help me no longer feel guilty about not doing enough documentation or keeping it up-to-date throughout the project life cycle!

As for Java, it is thriving and still a dominant technology! I definitely see it remaining that way for at least a few more years because Java runs on everything from mobile phones to electronics to appliances to desktops to small and large servers (with a long list of supported operating systems). Remember, Java is a platform and not merely a language!

Cheers!

In summary, I hope you found my personal opinions throughout the book bearable and the objective material valuable enough to adopt some of the techniques I demonstrated. If you are interested in staying in touch, please visit my site, visualpatterns.com. Once again, thank you from the bottom of my heart for reading this book. Best of luck!

Anil Hemrajani
2006

IV

Appendices

Downloadable Code
for This Book

THIS SECTION CONTAINS A PARTIAL LIST of files found in this book's downloadable code zip file, `bookcode.zip`, available at the book's website. Many of these files (`.java` and `.xml`, for example) are referenced throughout this book.

> **Note**
> The `bookcode.zip` contains three project directories within it: `timex/`, `timex2/`, and `springhibernate/`; these are described in detail in this appendix.

The remainder of this appendix provides a list of files found in the `bookcode.zip` file. At the top-level directory, you will find the following file, which provides further instructions on the three web applications in `bookcode.zip`:

`rapidjava/README.txt`

> **Note**
> The complete sample code described throughout this book is available on the Sams website. For convenient access to the book's page, register your book at www.samspublishing.com/register, enter this book's ISBN (without the hyphens), and then click SUBMIT. When the book's title is displayed, click the title to go to a page where you can download the code.

Third-Party Libraries Shared Directory

The following third-party JAR files are used by the three web applications described in this appendix. These are picked up by the Ant `build.xml` scripts for each of these three projects and bundled in their respective deployable WAR file.

> **Note**
> I typically have the `lib/` directory underneath the specific project (for example, `rapidjava/timex/lib/`); however, to reduce the size of the `bookcode.zip` file, I had the three projects share this one `lib/` directory because each of these projects required almost the same set of external JAR files.

```
rapidjava/lib/activation.jar
rapidjava/lib/antlr-2.7.6rc1.jar
rapidjava/lib/asm-attrs.jar
rapidjava/lib/asm.jar
rapidjava/lib/cglib-2.1.3.jar
rapidjava/lib/commons-beanutils-1.7.0.jar
rapidjava/lib/commons-collections-2.1.1.jar
rapidjava/lib/commons-lang-2.1.jar
rapidjava/lib/commons-logging-1.0.4.jar
rapidjava/lib/displaytag-1.1.jar
rapidjava/lib/displaytag-export-poi-1.1.jar
rapidjava/lib/dom4j-1.6.1.jar
rapidjava/lib/ehcache-1.1.jar
rapidjava/lib/hibernate3.jar
rapidjava/lib/hsqldb.jar
rapidjava/lib/itext-1.3.jar
rapidjava/lib/javax.servlet.jar
rapidjava/lib/jstl.jar
rapidjava/lib/jta.jar
rapidjava/lib/junit.jar
rapidjava/lib/log4j-1.2.11.jar
rapidjava/lib/mail.jar
rapidjava/lib/quartz-1.5.1.jar
rapidjava/lib/spring-hibernate3.jar
rapidjava/lib/spring-mock.jar
rapidjava/lib/spring.jar
rapidjava/lib/standard.jar
```

Sample Application Directory
(`rapidjava/timex/`)

The following files are related to the sample application named Time Expression, introduced in Chapter 2, "The Sample Application: An Online Timesheet System." These files can be found under the `rapidjava/timex/` directory.

Ant Files

```
antextras.xml
build.xml
local.properties
timexhsqldb.xml
```

HSQLDB Database Files

```
data/timexdb.lck
data/timexdb.log
data/timexdb.properties
data/timexdb.script
```

Configuration/Java Source

```
src/conf/log4j.properties
src/conf/messages.properties
src/conf/springtest-applicationcontext.xml
src/conf/timex-servlet.xml
src/conf/timex.tld
src/conf/web.xml
src/java/com/visualpatterns/timex/controller/EnterHoursController.java
src/java/com/visualpatterns/timex/controller/EnterHoursValidator.java
src/java/com/visualpatterns/timex/controller/HttpRequestInterceptor.java
src/java/com/visualpatterns/timex/controller/MinutesPropertyEditor.java
src/java/com/visualpatterns/timex/controller/SignInController.java
src/java/com/visualpatterns/timex/controller/SignInValidator.java
src/java/com/visualpatterns/timex/controller/SignOutController.java
src/java/com/visualpatterns/timex/controller/TimesheetListController.java
src/java/com/visualpatterns/timex/job/ReminderEmail.java
src/java/com/visualpatterns/timex/model/AuditInterceptor.java
src/java/com/visualpatterns/timex/model/Department.hbm.xml
src/java/com/visualpatterns/timex/model/Department.java
src/java/com/visualpatterns/timex/model/DepartmentManager.java
src/java/com/visualpatterns/timex/model/Employee.hbm.xml
src/java/com/visualpatterns/timex/model/Employee.java
src/java/com/visualpatterns/timex/model/EmployeeManager.java
src/java/com/visualpatterns/timex/model/hibernate.cfg.xml
src/java/com/visualpatterns/timex/model/Timesheet.hbm.xml
src/java/com/visualpatterns/timex/model/Timesheet.java
src/java/com/visualpatterns/timex/model/TimesheetManager.java
src/java/com/visualpatterns/timex/test/AllTests.java
src/java/com/visualpatterns/timex/test/DemoNewJavaFeatures.java
```

```
src/java/com/visualpatterns/timex/test/HibernateTest.java
src/java/com/visualpatterns/timex/test/SimpleTest.java
src/java/com/visualpatterns/timex/test/SpringTest.java
src/java/com/visualpatterns/timex/test/SpringTestMessage.java
src/java/com/visualpatterns/timex/test/TimesheetListControllerTest.java
src/java/com/visualpatterns/timex/test/TimesheetManagerExtras.java
src/java/com/visualpatterns/timex/test/TimesheetManagerTest.java
src/java/com/visualpatterns/timex/util/ApplicationSecurityManager.java
src/java/com/visualpatterns/timex/util/DateUtil.java
src/java/com/visualpatterns/timex/util/HibernateUtil.java
src/java/com/visualpatterns/timex/util/PayPeriodCheckTag.java
src/java/com/visualpatterns/timex/util/TimexJmxBean.java
src/java/com/visualpatterns/timex/view/enterhours.jsp
src/java/com/visualpatterns/timex/view/signin.jsp
src/java/com/visualpatterns/timex/view/timesheetlist.jsp
src/web/index.jsp
src/web/rapidjava-ajax.html
src/web/rapidjava-ajax.jsp
src/web/includes/timex.css
```

Refactored Sample Application Directory (`rapidjava/timex2/`)

The following files are related to the material discussed in Chapter 10, "Beyond the Basics." These files can be found under the `rapidjava/timex2/` directory.

This listing provided next lists only files impacted as a result of refactoring done to the sample application (see Appendix B, "Refactoring Done to Sample Application," for details); the other files found under `timex2/` are similar to the files described for `timex/` in this section.

```
antextras.xml
build.xml
local.properties
timexhsqldb.xml
src/conf/timex2-servlet.xml
src/java/com/visualpatterns/timex/model/DepartmentManager.java
src/java/com/visualpatterns/timex/model/EmployeeManager.java
src/java/com/visualpatterns/timex/model/hibernate.cfg.xml
src/java/com/visualpatterns/timex/model/TimesheetManager.java
src/java/com/visualpatterns/timex/test/TimesheetManagerTest.java
src/java/com/visualpatterns/timex/view/dberror.jsp
src/java/com/visualpatterns/timex/view/enterhours.jsp
```

```
src/java/com/visualpatterns/timex/view/includemessages.jsp
src/java/com/visualpatterns/timex/view/signin.jsp
src/java/com/visualpatterns/timex/view/timesheetlist.jsp
```

Spring-Hibernate Integration Demo Directory (rapidjava/springhibernate/)

The following files are related to the Spring and Hibernate integration section in Chapter 10. These demonstrate two styles of using Spring's support API for Hibernate (for example, to leverage Spring's declarative transaction management support).

```
conf/springhibernate-servlet.xml
conf/web.xml
build.xml
src/controller/TimesheetSaveController.java
src/model/Timesheet.hbm.xml
src/model/Timesheet.java
src/model/TimesheetManager.java
src/model/TimesheetManagerImpl1.java
src/model/TimesheetManagerImpl2.java
src/view/dberror.jsp
src/view/timesheetsave.jsp
```

B

Refactoring Done to Sample Application

THE FOLLOWING CODE, CONFIGURATION, AND SCRIPT excerpts show a few simple examples of how the sample application in this book was *refactored* as it was being built incrementally.

> **Note**
>
> The book's code zip file contains two project directories for our sample application: `timex/` and `timex2/`. The latter contains much of the refactored code discussed next.
>
> Because you have both versions, you can compare the two code bases to see how refactoring works in the real world. Remember, it isn't about being perfect the first time—just good enough. Get everything working first; then optimize your code later. This is what refactoring is all about—continuous design and redesign, by improving code as necessary, versus trying to perfect everything up front.
>
> For details on the concepts and types of refactoring, visit refactoring.com.

SignInController.java: JMX Monitoring

The following lines of code were added for JMX monitoring purposes:

```
import com.visualpatterns.timex.util.TimexJmxBean;
    private TimexJmxBean timexJmxBean;
...
    timexJmxBean.setSignInCount(timexJmxBean.getSignInCount() + 1);
...
    public TimexJmxBean getTimexJmxBean()
    {
        return timexJmxBean;
    }
```

```
public void setTimexJmxBean(TimexJmxBean timexJmxBean)
{
    this.timexJmxBean = timexJmxBean;
}
```

TimesheetListController.java: JMX Monitoring

The following lines of code were added for JMX monitoring purposes:

```
import com.visualpatterns.timex.util.TimexJmxBean;
...
private TimexJmxBean timexJmxBean;
...
    timexJmxBean.setTimesheetsFetched(timexJmxBean.getTimesheetsFetched()
            + timesheets.size());
...
public TimexJmxBean getTimexJmxBean()
{
    return timexJmxBean;
}

public void setTimexJmxBean(TimexJmxBean timexJmxBean)
{
    this.timexJmxBean = timexJmxBean;
}
```

Manager Classes: Spring-Hibernate Integration

In Chapter 10, "Beyond the Basics," we discussed the Spring and Hibernate integration. By leveraging and using Spring's declarative transaction management support, we were able to reduce the lines of code in our Manager classes significantly. The refactored code can be found under the rapidjava/timex2/ directory.

For example, the following is the original method in our TimesheetManager class (found in timex/) to save a Timesheet object:

```
public void saveTimesheet(Timesheet timesheet)
{
    Session session = HibernateUtil.getSessionFactory()
            .getCurrentSession();
    session.beginTransaction();
    try
    {
        session.saveOrUpdate(timesheet);
        session.getTransaction().commit();
    }
    catch (HibernateException e)
```

```
    {
        session.getTransaction().rollback();
        throw e;
    }
}
```

This code was reduced to just one line! The new `saveTimesheet` method can be found under `timex2/` and looks like this:

```
public void saveTimesheet(Timesheet timesheet)
{
    getHibernateTemplate().merge(timesheet);
}
```

timesheetlist.jsp: Switch to Include File and Displaytag

To centralize the JSP code that displays error and status messages, we moved it to `includemessage.jsp`:

```
<%@ taglib prefix="display" uri="http://displaytag.sf.net/el" %>
...
<%@ include file="/WEB-INF/jsp/includemessages.jsp" %>
...
```

Furthermore, to gain sorting capabilities in our web user interface, we switched from JSTL's `C:forEach` to `Displaytag` tag library. This not only demonstrates refactoring, but also the benefit of the Model-View-Controller (MVC) design pattern—that is, our view code changed but the model was not affected:

```
<display:table name="timesheets" id="timesheet" defaultsort="1"
               requestURI="timesheetlist.htm"
               cellpadding="5" cellspacing="0"
               export="false" class="tableborder">
<display:column sortable="true" title="Period Ending"
               href="enterhours.htm"
               sortProperty="periodEndingDate"
               paramId="tid" paramProperty="timesheetId"
               class="tdcenter">
    <fmt:formatDate value="${timesheet.periodEndingDate}"
                type="date" pattern="MM/dd/yyyy"/>
</display:column>
<display:column sortable="true" title="Hours"
               sortProperty="totalMinutes" class="tdright">
    <fmt:formatNumber value="${timesheet.totalMinutes / 60.0}"
                pattern="0.00"/>
</display:column>
...
```

enterhours.jsp: Swith to Include File and Timex Tag Library

Added `timex` taglib to check for current period. Also moved status and error messages to `includemessage.jsp`.

```
<%@ taglib prefix="timex"  uri="/WEB-INF/timex.tld" %>
<timex:periodcheck checkDate="${command.periodEndingDate}">
<input name="save"  type="submit" value="Save">
</timex:periodcheck>
...
<%@ include file="/WEB-INF/jsp/includemessages.jsp" %>
```

★Test Classes and TimexTestCase

Most of our earlier ★Test classes looked something like the following code snippet from our original `TimesheetManagerTest` class:

```
public class TimesheetManagerTest extends TestCase
{
    TimesheetManager timesheetManager = new TimesheetManager();
    public static void main(String args[])
```

Now, instead of extending the `JUnit TestCase` class directly, we extend the `TimexTestCase` class (in the `timex2/` directory), as shown next:

```
public class TimesheetManagerTest extends TimexTestCase
{
    public static void main(String args[])
```

The benefit of this approach is that we can put all the fixture code in a parent class (such as `TimexTestCase`), so the test subclasses can focus on the unit tests versus fixture code (visit junit.org for details on fixture code).

DateUtil.java: New Method

Added new method for use with timex tag library.

```
public static boolean isInCurrentPayPeriod(Date checkDate)
{
    Date weekStartDate = getDateWithZeroTime(getCurrentPeriodStartingDate());
    Date weekEndDate = getDateWithMaxTime(getCurrentPeriodEndingDate());

    return (!checkDate.before(weekStartDate) && !checkDate
        .after(weekEndDate));
}
```

timex.css: New Styles

Added some new styles.

```
thead { background-color: #D0D6EA;}
.tableborder { border: thin; }
.tdright { text-align: right; }
.tdcenter {    text-align: center;}
.even { background-color: #F1F8FE}
```

timexhsqldb.xml: Bad Data Defect Fix

Fixed passwords in SQL INSERTS because of a discovered defect in test data (not code). Chapter 3, "XP and AMDD-Based Architecture and Design Modeling," has an acceptance test that indicates "The password must be between 8 and 10 characters." The original passwords were fewer than 8 characters, thereby not allowing a user to log in.

```
INSERT INTO Employee (employeeId, name, employeeCode,
                   password, email, managerEmployeeId)
      VALUES (2, 'Ajay Kumar', 'H', 'visualpatterns', 'akumar@acme.com', 3);
INSERT INTO Employee (employeeId, name, employeeCode,
                   password, email, managerEmployeeId)
      VALUES (3, 'Teresa Walker', 'M', 'agilestuff', 'twalker@acme.com', 4);
INSERT INTO Employee (employeeId, name, employeeCode,
                   password, email)
      VALUES (4, 'Tom Brady', 'E', 'superbowl', 'tbrady@acme.com');
```

It is important to note that defects are not always code related; they can also be related to bad data.

C

Java Code Conventions

THE FOLLOWING ARE SOME OF THE GUIDELINES I like and use from the Code Conventions for the Java Programming Language prescribed by Sun on the java.sun.com website. (Note: There are many more conventions recommended by Sun, so be sure to visit this website.)

- All source files will have a beginning Javadoc comment.
- The first line of code in the source file will be the package statement followed by any import statements.
- Package names should begin with a lowercase top-level domain name (for example, com. or edu.).
- Class and interface names should be nouns and should use a mixed case with each word being capitalized (for example, EmployeeHours).
- All class files should have the following in the order listed here:
    - Have a Javadoc for the class.
    - List variables as follows: static variables, instance variables (public, protected, no access specified, and then private).
    - List methods as follows: constructors and then methods (methods should be grouped by functionality, not scope).
- Method names should be verbs and should use a mixed case with each word being capitalized, except that the first letter is lowercase (for example, getHoursWorked).
- Variable names should be verbs and should use a mixed case with each word being capitalized, except that the first letter is lowercase (for example, hoursWorked). Variables should start with alphabets. One-character variables (for example, i, j, or k) should be avoided and used only for temporary variables (for example, in a for statement).
- Try to make all class variables nonpublic and accessible only via methods.

- Constants should be all uppercase, with words separated by an underscore (for example MAX_WORK_HOURS).

- Try to use numeric values as constants (for example, int MAX_WORK_HOURS=24;).

- Try to initialize local variables where they are declared.

- Avoid lines longer than 80 characters.

- Each line should contain only one statement.

- If-else, for, while, do, and switch statements should always use braces.

D

Securing Web Applications

THE FOLLOWING ARE A FEW GUIDELINES on how to secure web applications. For further reading on this subject, visit the owasp.org website.

- Validate browser input (parameters, special characters, SQL injections) on the server side, not just the client side (that is, JavaScript). If you are working directly with JDBC, consider using `java.sql.PreparedStatement` versus a `java.sql.Statement`.
- Don't use a shell (Runtime.exec) in your web-related code; this is almost certainly an open invitation to hackers.
- Do not store sensitive data anywhere (databases, files, and so on). If you absolutely must store this information, store it in encrypted form.
- Don't allow direct access to any system resource—for example, files, databases, classes, or programs. Turn off directory browsing on all web servers. Don't use real filenames and/or directories (for example, hide JSP files under WEB-INF).
- Use HTTPS versus HTTP for sensitive data such as username, password, financial data, health information, and secure government information.
- Require strong user ids and passwords (for example, six- to eight-character minimum, special characters in password, and so on).
- Hidden HTML fields are not hidden; anyone can view the HTML code in the browser, so keep this mind.
- Disable accounts, either temporarily or permanently, after three failed attempts.
- Do not store clear-text passwords (for example, app id/password in config files).
- Log all or only suspicious activity.
- Use industry standard, well-tested security protocols over a custom, home-grown solution.

- POST is slightly better than GET to hide sensitive data (for example, the browser's address bar, access logs). Suggestion: Conduct security testing with Firefox Tamper Data extension.

- Have source code reviews. Your colleagues might be able to see something you have missed.

- Beware of cross-site scripting (XSS); a hacker can use this technique to hijack personal information about your users.

- Last, but not least, be paranoid! There really are people out there trying to guess passwords, hack, and so on; always remain vigilant about security! Think like a hacker; assume the hacker knows as much or more than you, and have regular security audits. Remember, you cannot entirely avoid security threats; however, you can manage and control them. More importantly, there are automated crawlers looking for security holes. When a hole is found, a human can move in for the kill.

E

Sample Development Process Cheat Sheet

THIS FOLLOWING IS A SAMPLE (and simple) development process cheat sheet. For details, you can either refer to Chapter 2, "The Sample Application: An Online Timesheet System," or Chapter 3, "XP and AMDD-Based Architecture and Design Modeling," in this book, or review the extensive material provided on the extremeprogramming.org or agilemodeling.com websites.

Project Initiation

- Informal business need/problem discussions
- Project kickoff
- Define problem statement (for example, essential use cases or shall statements)

Exploration Phase

- Explore business domain concepts (develop domain model).
- Develop basic prototypes and storyboard (for user interface applications).
- Define scope (what's included/deferred in next release).
- Define user stories for next release.
- Do informal whiteboarding of architecture and so on.

Planning

- Develop release plan for next release/version of system.
- Define glossary of common business terms.
- Develop iteration plan for next iteration.
- Define system conventions (naming, code check-in/integration, and more).

Incrementally Build Software in Iterations

- Develop software in increments using 2-week iterations; use iteration 0 (or cycle 0) for environment setup and proof-of-concept.
- Have an iteration planning meeting before each iteration to pick the user stories that will be developed in the next iteration.
- Get best-guess estimates from developers, based on chosen stories for iteration.
- Users provide acceptance tests as detailed requirements; developers implement these as unit tests.
- Let developers design and develop the system with user available for Q&A, as needed.
- Deploy production-ready code every two weeks after it has passed the user acceptance tests.

Agile Modeling Values, Practices, and Principles Cheat Sheet

Source of information on this page: www.agilemodeling.com

Values

Communication, simplicity, feedback, courage and humility.

Practices	Principles

Practices

CORE PRACTICES:

Active Stakeholder Participation
Model with Others
Apply the Right Artifact(s)
Iterate to Another Artifact
Prove It with Code
Use the Simplest Tools
Model in Small Increments
Single Source Information
Collective Ownership
Create Several Models in Parallel
Create Simple Content
Depict Models Simply
Display Models Publicly

SUPPLEMENTARY PRACTICES:

Apply Modeling Standards
Apply Patterns Gently
Discard Temporary Models
Formalize Contract Models
Update Only When It Hurts

REALLY GOOD IDEAS:

Refactoring
Test-First Design

Principles

CORE PRINCIPLES:

Model with a Purpose
Maximize Stakeholder Investment
Travel Light
Multiple Models
Rapid Feedback
Assume Simplicity
Embrace Change
Incremental Change
Quality Work
Software Is Your Primary Goal
Enabling the Next Effort Is Your Secondary Goal

SUPPLEMENTARY PRINCIPLES:

Content Is More Important Than Representation
Open and Honest Communication

Extreme Programming (XP) Cheat Sheet

Source of information on this page: extremeprogramming.org

Overview

- Customer lists the features that the software must provide.
- Programmers break the features into standalone tasks and estimate the work needed to complete each task.
- Customer chooses the most important tasks that can be completed by the next release.
- Programmers choose tasks and work in pairs.
- Programmers write unit tests.
- Programmers add features to pass unit tests.
- Programmers fix features and tests as necessary, until all tests pass.
- Programmers integrate code.
- Programmers produce a released version.
- Customer runs acceptance tests.
- Version goes into production.
- Programmers update their estimates based on the amount of work they've done in release cycle.

Rules and Practices

Planning

User stories are written.

Release planning creates the schedule.

Make frequent small releases.

The Project Velocity is measured.

The project is divided into iterations.

Iteration planning starts each iteration.

Move people around.

A stand-up meeting starts each day.

Fix XP when it breaks.

Coding

The customer is always available.

Code must be written to agreed standards.

Code the unit test first.

All production code is pair programmed.

Only one pair integrates code at a time.

Integrate often.

Use collective code ownership.

Leave optimization until last.

No overtime.

Designing

Simplicity.

Choose a system metaphor.

Use CRC cards for design sessions.

Create spike solutions to reduce risk.

No functionality is added early.

Refactor whenever and wherever possible.

Testing

All code must have unit tests.

All code must pass all unit tests before it can be released.

When a bug is found, tests are created.

Acceptance tests are run often and the score is published.

H

Cool Tools

W E ALL HAVE OUR FAVORITE TOOLS and utilities we like to use to work *rapidly*.
   Listed next are ones that either I have used personally or that were recommended by various friends and colleagues. These were all free (at the time of this writing), unless otherwise noted here. Of course, all the products covered in this book (for example, Eclipse) qualify for cool tools, as well.
   Like all free software, use at your own risk!

Cross-Platform Tools

- 7-Zip   File archiver with high compression ratio
- http://www.7-zip.org/
- Aqua Data Studio (Java)   Slow, but good for data import/export—http://aquafold.com/
- ArgoUML   UML design tool—http://argouml.tigris.org/
- CruiseControl   Framework for a continuous build process—http://cruisecontrol.sourceforge.net
- CVS   Source configuration management—http://www.nongnu.org/cvs/
- DbVisualizer   Database tool—http://www.minq.se
- FreeMind   Mind-mapping software—http://freemind.sourceforge.net/
- Gaim   Multi-protocol instant messaging (IM) client—http://gaim.sourceforge.net/
- Image Manipulation Program   http://gimp.org/
- JAR Class Finder   Eclipse plug-in utility for finding JAR files containing a given class—http://www.alphaworks.ibm.com/tech/jarclassfinder
- J text editor (Java)   http://armedbear-j.sourceforge.net/

- KDiff3   Compare/merge two or three text input files or directories—http://kdiff3.sourceforge.net/
- Mozilla Firefox plug-ins   Hundreds of useful plug-ins for Firefox browser—https://addons.mozilla.org/extensions/
- Netbeans   Fully featured Integrated Development Environment (IDE)—http://www.netbeans.org/
- Nvu   Web Authoring System—http://nvu.com/
- OpenOffice   Complete office applications, comparable to Microsoft Office—http://www.openoffice.org/
- Poseidon (community edition)   UML design tool—http://gentleware.com
- SQuirreL SQL Client   Manage JDBC compliant databases—http://squirrel-sql.sourceforge.net/
- Sun Java Studio Enterprise   IDE with integrated UML tool—http://developers.sun.com/prodtech/javatools/jsenterprise/
- TkCVS (includes TkDiff)   Graphical interface for CVS and Subversion configuration management systems—http://www.twobarleycorns.net/tkcvs.html
- Vim   GUI text editor mimics Unix 'Vi'—http://www.vim.org/
- vnc2swf   Screen recording tool—http://www.unixuser.org/%7Eeuske/vnc2swf/
- XEmacs   Text editor and application development system—http://www.xemacs.org/
- Yahoo widgets   http://widgets.yahoo.com/

Microsoft Windows-Based Tools

- AppRocket keyboard launchpad (for Windows)   http://www.candylabs.com/approcket/ (trial version, but too cool not to mention here)
- ReplaceEm   Windows text search-and-replace program (Probably the easiest, fasted installing, and the most intuitive program of its kind I have come across.)—http://www.orbit.org/replace/
- MWSnap   Snapping (capturing) images from selected parts of the screen—http://www.mirekw.com/winfreeware/mwsnap.html
- Textpad   Powerful, general purpose editor for plain-text files—http://www.textpad.com/
- FileZilla   FTP client and server—http://filezilla.sourceforge.net/
- PrimoPDF   Convert to PDF from any application via printing—http://www.primopdf.com/
- Cygwin   Linux-like environment for Windows—http://www.cygwin.com/

- Sysinternals   Advanced system utilities for Windows—http://www.sysinternals.com/

- WinMerge   Visual text file differencing and merging tool—http://winmerge.sourceforge.net/

- Whiteboard Photo (limited version)   Image capturing software—http://www.polyvision.com/

- ExamDiff   Visual File Comparison Tool—http://www.prestosoft.com/ps.asp?page=edp_examdiff

- TortoiseCVS   CVS client integrated with Windows Explorer—http://www.tortoisecvs.org/

Mac OS X-Based Tools

- Vim (Vi IMproved) for Mac OSX   http://macvim.org/OSX/

- Adium   Instant messaging application; can connect to AIM, MSN, Jabber, Yahoo, and more—http://www.adiumx.com/

- Grab It   Build part of Mac OS X

- Quicksilver (for Mac OS X)   http://quicksilver.blacktree.com/

Linux-Based Tools (KDE)

It is difficult to recommend a few cool tools for a platform that comes loaded with so many cool utilities. Furthermore, some of the cross-platform tools recommended in this section also run on Linux. Nevertheless, here are a few recommended to me by colleagues.

Some K Development Environment (KDE) utilities that you might want to check out—Konsole, Klipper, KEdit, KPrinter, Kate, Kompare, KFind, KSnapshot, KRuler, K3B, KAlarm, KTimer, KInfoCenter, KWiFiManager, and KSayIt.

Pollix Live CD (based on Knoppix, which boots directly from the CD; no install!)—Pollix is loaded with programming tools such as Eclipse, NetBeans, Python, and others; http://moe.tnc.edu.tw/%7Ekendrew/pollix/.

Other Linux utilities include locate, expect, and wish.

I

Visual Patterns Research

MANY ORGANIZATIONS, LARGE AND SMALL, need custom software applications built for their business because off-the-shelf software often doesn't meet their needs. These custom software applications are built in-house, off-site, or using a combination of the two. This appendix discusses some of the problems our industry currently faces with custom software development. The research and development project I have recently launched on my website, visualpatterns.com, addresses some of these problems (described next).

The Problem

Because building software isn't the core business of many of these organizations, they end up facing issues and challenges associated with building complex software.

The Past: How We Have Been Kidding Ourselves

In the past, many projects have approached software development in a serial fashion—that is, completing each phase of a software development life cycle (for example, requirements, architecture, design, coding, testing) in its entirety before moving on to the next phase. Furthermore, many of these projects estimate the time frames to complete a project based on these big, up-front efforts, which is similar to looking into a "crystal ball." To make matters worst, most organizations attempt to keep the big documentation (produced up front) up-to-date throughout the life cycle but are almost never able to keep it current as the project progresses. This method of working results in failed or challenged projects, as reflected in Figure I.1.

The Standish Group further claims that the larger a project gets, the higher it is at risk of failing, as reflected in the numbers shown in Figure I.2.

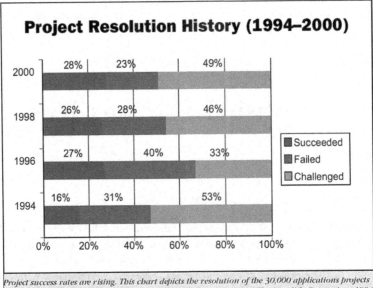

Project success rates are rising. This chart depicts the resolution of the 30,000 applications projects in large, medium, and small cross-industry U.S. companies tested by The Standish Group since 1994.

Figure I.1   Project resolution history (source: standishgroup.com).

Project Duration, Team Size Affect Project Success

Project Size	People	Time (mos.)	Success Rate
Less than $750K	6	6	55%
$750K to $1.5M	12	9	33%
$1.5M to $3M	25	12	25%
$3M to $6M	40	18	15%
$6M to $10M	+250	+24	8%
Over $10M	+500	+36	0%

The smaller the team and shorter the duration of the project, the greater the likelihood of success. Obviously, this does not suggest that compressing the schedule and reducing the resources of a large project will make it successful. Nor should it be construed that large projects with large teams cannot be successful. The Standish Group believes any project can be successful if all the key criteria are met.

Figure I.2   Success by project size (source: standishgroup.com).

Furthermore, many applications build in features that are either never used, rarely used, or only sometimes used (as shown in Figure I.3); this results in more expensive software and wasted efforts.

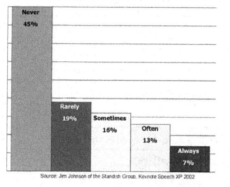

Feature Usage Within Deployed Applications

Source: Jim Johnson of the Standish Group. Keynote Speech XP 2002

Figure I.3   Feature usage within deployed applications.

The Future: Agile Methods

According to the Standish Group, the top 10 factors for a project's success are shown in Figure I.4.

Note

Most of the stats provided in this document are taken from the Standish Group International, Inc. Although these are taken from one source, they match what I have experienced over my 20 years in Information Technology (IT).

Many of the problems outlined earlier in this document can be solved using newer, truly iterative style methodologies.

In 2001, 17 methodologists came together to unify their methodologies under one umbrella. They jointly defined the term *Agile* (agilemanifesto.org, agilealliance.com). The remarkable thing about this event was that these 17 methodologists agreed on a common set of principles (see story at martinfowler.com/articles/agileStory.html).

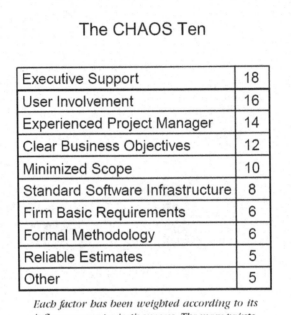

Figure I.4   The CHAOS Ten project success factor (source: standishgroup.com).

Some of the underlying values of the various Agile methods are the following:

- Be customer focused—In short, satisfy the customer. Develop only what is requested, nothing more, nothing less.

- Embrace change—In today's fast-paced world, change is bound to happen. Users should be able to change the system (they are paying for it). So it is better to accept this fact and embrace it.

- Iterative development—Develop working software in small chunks (for example, two-month major release with two-week iterations resulting in production-ready code). Favor building software in increments with continuous enhancement (via refactoring) versus big requirements and design up front (BRUF/BDUF).

- Motivated people—Build projects around a motivated staff; give them the environment and space they need to get the job done.

- Communication—This is the key to success, and accordingly, users, developers, testers, and other stakeholders must communicate well. Also, favor face-to-face communications (versus emails, for example).

- Measure of progress—Use working software (code, database) as a measure of progress versus documentation and project plans.

- Sustainable development—Project stakeholders (users, developers, testers, and so on) must be able to maintain a constant pace of software development (see iterative development above).

- Simplistic elegance—Favor high-impact business features versus overengineered or cool technical solutions.

- Continued efficiency—Capture lessons learned, good design, best practices, templates, checklists, glossary, and the like.

My Perspective

In my opinion, which is based on the Agile values previously mentioned combined with 20 years of experience in IT, some current issues with software development include big requirements, big design, and terminology. These are discussed next.

BRUF and BDUF

In the Agile community, big requirements up front and big design up front are often referred to by their acronyms, BRUF and BDUF, respectively.

The idea of getting all the requirements done up front (waterfall method) and locked down is insane and an archaic style of developing software. Some release level requirements should be done up front. The remaining (more detailed) requirements can be obtained at the beginning of an iteration in the form of acceptance tests (which are incidentally coded into unit tests).

Similar to BRUF, trying to get all the architecture and design done up front is unreasonable because you will invariably discover better ways of developing the system at hand after developers begin coding. Some architecture/design in Cycle 0 (Jim Highsmith) is a good idea, but it should be kept to a minimum, requiring minutes to hours of discussion depending on the complexity of the system (but certainly not many days or weeks). Furthermore, keeping BRUF and BDUF documents up-to-date throughout the software life cycle is a task many organizations attempt but invariably fail to keep current.

Terminology

This is a personal pet peeve of mine because I find this to be an issue that many technical people are ashamed to admit is an issue. When you have acronyms galore, redundant terms (store, persist), or ambiguous terms (pessimistic locking, immutability), it not only causes problems among the technical staff, but also is an ineffective way of communicating with the users.

Join the Community?

In the coming months, I will be building a global virtual community composed of people from various parts of the world—this process has already begun. Our objective will be to research better modeling and unique visual process techniques to address some of the problems discussed in this appendix.

If you are interested in joining this virtual community, contact me via visualpatterns.com.

Index

D

H

handler mapping in Spring Web MVC Framework, 133, 141

help system (Eclipse), 201-203

Hibernate, 15, 49, 276

advantages of, 90

associations, 106-107

CLASSPATH files, 104

configuration files, 92-93

connection pooling, 97

Criteria interface, 105

data types, 98

database records

deleting, 104

as objects, 97

databases supported, 90

developing Timesheet table (Time Expression sample application), 100-103

dialect class, 97

EJB 3.0 and, 81, 91

exception handling, 106

HibernateUtil.java helper class, 99-100

installing, 95-96

interceptors, 246

locking objects, 107-108

logging, 223

mapping files

naming conventions, 91

sample program setup, 93

native SQL queries, 245

object states, 98

online discussion forums, 278

running test suites with Ant, 104-105

sample program setup, 91-95

Session object, 97

SessionFactory object, 97

Spring Framework and, 252

declarative transaction management, 253, 255-256

unit testing, 256

Spring-Hibernate integration

files for, 291

refactored sample application (Time Expression), 294-295

Transaction object, 97

transactions, 99

unique object identifier, 98-99

Hibernate plug-in (Eclipse), 195-196

Hibernate Query Language (HQL), 98

HibernateDaoSupport, 255

HibernateUtil.java helper class, 99-100

hiding files, 138, 210

horizontal mapping, 83

hot deploying WAR files, 135

Hotswap, JDT debugging, 227

HQL (Hibernate Query Language), 98

HSQLDB, 15

bundling in WAR file, 89

creating database, 87-88

Data plug-ins (Eclipse), 192-193

Database Manager, 88

persistent and in-memory modes, 89

SqlTool, 88

starting server, 87-88

I

IBM, SWT (Standard Widget Toolkit), 267

<id> element (Hibernate), 98-99

IDE (Integrated Development Environment), SDK versus, 163

ideal days in user stories, 37

in-memory mode (HSQLDB), 89

in-memory objects, persistent objects versus, 84

injection. *See* **dependency injection pattern**

installing

Eclipse, 170-173

Hibernate, 95-96

servlet containers, 134-135

Q–R